Empathy, Emotion and Education

"This seminal work brings new meanings and a depth of understanding to familiar terms and everyday language illustrating the crucial difference between a-ffective and e-ffective teaching, exploring baby morality and the deeply embedded childhood need for fairness and reciprocity. The scope and originality of this work reflects half a lifetime of research into classroom life and pupil voice. A must-read for teachers, parents and those who 'care' for children, in both meanings of that word."
—Emeritus Professor John MacBeath, *University of Cambridge, UK*

"This fascinating book provides the reader with deep insight into the development of children and young people. The vital importance of empathy within the individual and the social context is explored. This evidence-informed study will support teachers seeking to engage with the voice of the child in creating an environment for teaching and learning where limits are not set. I recommend this highly."
—Professor Dame Alison Peacock, *Chief Executive of the Chartered College of Teaching, UK*

"This book makes a compelling case for empathy being at the core of human social life. Demetriou is an expert on the development of empathy from infancy through childhood and its importance for children's education. Across the chapters of her book, she weaves together different strands of theory and research on empathy, showing how the ability to feel for and take on the perspective of other people contributes to life in families, peer groups and classrooms. Her synthesis of the literature on empathy will be of interest to psychologists, education researchers, teachers and others who work with children and their families."
—Professor Dale Hay, *Cardiff University Centre for Human Developmental Science, UK*

Helen Demetriou

Empathy, Emotion and Education

palgrave
macmillan

Helen Demetriou
Faculty of Education
University of Cambridge
Cambridge, UK

ISBN 978-1-137-54843-6   ISBN 978-1-137-54844-3   (eBook)
https://doi.org/10.1057/978-1-137-54844-3

Library of Congress Control Number: 2017964551

Cover illustration: Nenov / Getty Images

Printed on acid-free paper

This Palgrave Macmillan imprint is published by Springer Nature
The registered company is Macmillan Publishers Ltd.
The registered company address is: The Campus, 4 Crinan Street, London, N1 9XW, United Kingdom

Dedicated to Professor Jean Rudduck (1937–2007)

We have two ears and one mouth so that we can listen twice as much as we speak.
(Epictetus, Greek philosopher, circa 50 AD)

Acknowledgements

There are two main inspirations for this work. Professor Dale Hay was my PhD supervisor, and despite being a long time ago now, her work and approach have continued to inspire me and paved the way for an enduring interest in the topic of empathy. Special mention extends to Professor Jean Rudduck, who introduced me to education research and its applications. From psychology to education, both women shared a passion and enthusiasm for what they knew were the endless possibilities and capabilities of children. It has been a privilege also to know and/or work with Michael Rutter, Robert Goodman, Simon Baron-Cohen, Judy Dunn and Robert Plomin in the fields of developmental psychology and psychiatry; and within education, those with whom I have worked and collaborated include Elaine Wilson, Julia Flutter, Alison Cook-Sather, John MacBeath, Kate Myers, Chris Doddington, John Gray, Beverly Hopper, Paul Goalen, Mark Winterbottom, Dave Pedder, Michael Fielding, Eve Bearne, Pam Burnard, Jan Vermunt, and in fond memory of Barry Jones and Donald McIntyre. Special thanks go to the parents, teachers and children who made all my research possible over the years and to my students, both undergraduates and postgraduates, whose academic enquiry and enthusiasm infuse my teaching. On a more personal level, I would like to thank my husband for his constant encouragement and support for this book and also our children for being an inspiration in their own right.

Contents

1

Introduction: Empathy—The Building Block of Social Life

In the grounds of Homerton College, Cambridge, next to the Faculty of Education building where I work, stands a sculpture of a child by Betty Rea (1959) entitled *Stretching Figure*. It has been described as "…expressing the Diverse emotions, activities, and grace of youth" (Whiteley, 2004). Such qualities are explored in this book and specifically children's capacity for empathy, emotion and engagement in education and life itself. Not so long ago, children were considered incapable of all these things. Not only do we now know that they are proficient in these activities, but their aptitude has in its wake informed and helped adults to understand not only the children, but in turn the adults themselves, both as parents and as teachers.

Children are at forefront of this book. We begin our lives as babies and it is therefore important to be able to understand why, when and how we start thinking. In particular, the focus for the book is why, when and how children exhibit empathy and emotion and the role that we as adults have in shaping this emotion for their development but also for their education. It is apparent that babies arrive already equipped with a social and emotional awareness of others, but it is also apparent that this awareness is malleable and affected by the people around them. In other words,

© The Author(s) 2018
H. Demetriou, *Empathy, Emotion and Education*,
https://doi.org/10.1057/978-1-137-54844-3_1

people's responses to the growing infant matter, and have the potential to make or break that growing individual. So, from parenting to pedagogy, let's set the scene: the people: *babies, children, parents and teachers*; the places: *home and school*; and the themes: *empathy, emotion and education.*

The *who*, the *where* and the *how*: bringing all these aspects together, this book is a confluence and culmination of work focusing on a special concept of empathy that bestows affinity with, identification to, and a reflection for others. This is the story of one concept and its power on the lives of others in a variety of situations: one concept and its influence on a range of people and contexts. As Alfred Adler wrote: "Empathy is seeing with the eyes of another, listening with the ears of another, and feeling with the heart of another". When we as parents and teachers listen and respond appropriately to children, they respond appropriately back and thrive as people and as learners. Moreover, just as children learn from parents and teachers, so parents and teachers can learn from children. It is about us listening as parents and insisting that schools should listen too. From babies to children to parents to teachers, we all have empathy and the capacity to use it from an early age, and for the better. It may sound obvious and simple to most people, but often it is the most obvious and simple tasks that get overlooked. And as well as being simple and obvious, it is effective and essential. This book is a journey from empathy to emotion and from emotion to education and back to empathy again. It advocates the recognition and use of a synthesis of emotion and cognition among children, parents and teachers and sets out to prove that through a combination of thoughts and feelings working in synchrony, where there are secure attachments with parents and teachers, where adults listen to the voices of children, the outcome is engaged and empowered individuals—both children and adults—who value their teaching and learning and indeed themselves.

People respond in a variety of ways to the experiences they encounter. Some immerse themselves in the situations they experience, others attempt to do so, whilst others don't seem to be able to do so at all. This reflects the degree of empathy that each one of us possesses. Of course, even within the same individual, the amount of empathy can be context-dependent, depending on how far we can or want to identify with the situation in hand. Such a range of empathic responding and mixed emotions might take a variety of forms ranging from an extreme reaction, as in the case when one of my children was very young and I found myself responding excessively to a situation whilst walking in the garden as my son began to pluck newly sprung daffodils. In an attempt to stop him doing this, I urged him not to pick any more, saying that the daffodils would be "sad and cry", my son retorted that they couldn't cry because they didn't have eyes. How sensible! And bodes well to my son's logical nature but also questioningly to my over-empathising, anthropomorphising side. A less extreme example is where the onlooker is trying their best to empathise, such as in the words I heard on the radio the other day, spoken by a man trying to make sense of a contentious issue: "I can't imagine what it's like, but it must be *awful*…". And from this to the complete and utter lack of empathic ability, such as that shown by psychopaths, hardened terrorists, or people who haven't been exposed to empathy themselves.

From daffodils to displays devoid of empathy, such responses range from over-emotional to completely lacking in emotion. Most of us have something in between—a healthy balance of empathy, which we have most probably acquired throughout our lives from babies via our social interactions. In order to empathise effectively, we typically will have experienced the situation ourselves and are able to understand and/or feel what that person is going through and also give an appropriate response to it. Examples of this are apparent when a child witnesses another child's anguish on losing their toy and approaches the distressed child offering their own toy in order to help. Effective empathy therefore is not only an asset in helping to understand and feel along with the other, but can also result in appropriate and constructive responses. Like DNA, which is the building block of life, empathy is the building block of social life; and like DNA, a form of empathy is present at birth. But unlike the building block of life that is DNA, the building block of social life that is empathy is further affected by life's experiences and amasses throughout one's lifetime, or at least has the potential to do so. This social phenomenon is acquired contagiously through social interaction with parents, siblings and peers; and it has profound uses in establishing relationships throughout life, so that we can understand each other on a level playing field and know where the other is 'coming from'.

A Fusion of Psychology and Education

I have been fortunate to work in the fields of both psychology and education, and in more recent years I have taught the disciplines together focusing on the field of psychology and how its various theories inform and relate to education. My research in developmental psychology goes back to my PhD when I researched the construct of empathy. Despite since researching a variety of topics within education, I have come to realise that within these topics and in education generally, empathy was never far away. This bird's-eye view has enabled me to connect the concept of empathy across the two disciplines of psychology and education. Specifically, this vantage point has allowed me to link the ability of children to empathise across the two domains of psychology and education, and this book will incorporate my own research with selections of work from the literature. So, the idea for this book emerged when after years of researching and teaching in psychology and education, despite working within different disciplines and with different agendas, a serendipitous common thread with interlinked themes was identified. Themes were identified that are not only interlinked but informed each other, within and across the two disciplines. The book therefore represents a convergence of my work, past and present, firstly in the field of developmental psychology and then in education, and an attempt to unite the disciplines of psychology and education in a common goal of effectively connecting and learning through an inter-disciplinary perspective.

This book has been inspired predominantly from my research over the last 25 years. I have researched empathy in a variety of forms, as well as other constructs of emotion and moral development, beginning at the department of Child and Adolescent Psychiatry at the Institute of Psychiatry of the University of London, through my PhD thesis looking at children's capacity to engage with their peers in distress. Subsequently again at the Institute of Psychiatry but this time in the centre of Social, Genetic and Developmental Research, I researched topics that included children's relationships in association with their social and moral development. And then through my research at the Faculty of Education of the University of Cambridge, I focused on pupils' and teachers' abilities to engage in teaching and learning and thus improve the quality of learning.

It has been an empathy journey that has come full circle, firstly by looking at toddlers' and young children's abilities to empathise with their peers and then turning to the school context and engaging with pupils in order to empower them and enhance their empathy and awareness for a variety of issues that affect their teaching and learning. The journey has taken me from the arena of developmental psychology to research in education. Despite conducting research into education on a variety of topics and for a number of funding bodies such as the Qualifications and Curriculum Authority (QCA), Department for Education (DfE), Office for Standards in Education (Ofsted), as well as my own personally applied for research grants, my original psychologically based research re-emerged. A relatively recent epiphany revealed that quite unintentionally and despite working in different places with different agendas, most of what I have researched is not unrelated. Indeed much of the research has covered similar ground and consolidated the other. My early research investigated children's capacity to empathise through their reactions to their peers' distress across early and middle childhood. Subsequent research focusing on children's friendships, their awareness of fairness and then pupil voice research where pupils were consulted about their teaching and learning, all emerged with a remarkable insightfulness on the part of pupils both at primary and secondary school to empathise with their own and others' situations. The diverse focus of my research has been complemented by the varied methodological techniques: both qualitative and quantitative, from case studies to small data sets to large data sets; inductive exploratory versus deductive hypothesis-driven; and using observation, interviews, specific tasks and questionnaires as a means of data collection. Although varied, much of my more recent research corroborates and reinforces my early research, bringing clarity and piecing together bits of the puzzle that is children's capacity for empathy and its uses for education.

Within the context of education, it is of course important to know your subject matter as a teacher. But the thesis of this book also advocates the importance of knowing *who* is being taught, so that both the *what* and *who* are taught go hand in hand. Coming from both developmental psychology and education perspectives, this book pools research that emphasises the importance of acknowledging and incorporating the social and emotional aspects of teaching. As a consequence, this book will be of interest to a broad audience, namely, parents, educators, researchers, psychologists, new teachers and policy makers. The book aims to provide the audience with a rounded view of the children they parent, teach, research, and the benefits of conceptualising the child/pupil/student/learner as a social and emotional being, as well as a learning being. Indeed, Palmer (1998) spoke of the separation of the head from the heart as contributing to an educational system filled with broken paradoxes that result in "…minds that do not know how to feel and hearts that do not know how to think" (p. 68). But, as the next section shows, youngsters have not always been afforded with a particularly sophisticated social and emotional prowess. So I will recount briefly how babies and toddlers have been perceived historically and how that has changed relatively recently and over a relatively short space of time.

"Nobody Puts Baby in a Corner"!

Up until the recent past, the faculties of babies and children were regarded as limited. They have been placed 'in a corner' and ignored, as per the draconian notion of 'seen and not heard'. Influential psychologists such as the behaviourist John B. Watson who wrote *Psychological Care of Infant and Child* in 1928 recommended strict schedules and warned against excessive affection. Another psychologist around the late 1920s, G. Stanley Hall, concurred with Watson regarding the parent-child relationship, warning against sentimentality and emotional connection and promoting physical punishments. Both men viewed children as being malleable, but Watson went a step further, believing in the Pavlovian tradition, much like the salivating dogs, that children could be manipulated and moulded entirely. The main thesis of this book is that this perception and treatment was to the detriment of both children and adults. Even as relatively recently as the 1950s, the science of developmental psychology has come a long way. My children would say that that was a long time ago, positively prehistoric. But in the whole scheme of things, it is the recent past, and a past that held babies and infants in a very different light to the one we know today. Researchers were now beginning to understand more about the capabilities of babies and young children, and as such came revelations and revolutions in parenting and teaching.

From the 1950s, researchers were discovering new and hitherto unknown bona fide features of babies and infants. Such skills included their sensitivity to others and their influence in relationships, and moreover that parents and the love they provide do matter for children's ensuing development. Two ground-breaking books that emerged postwar contributed to this cornerstone in history. As we were discovering babies' capabilities, Dr Benjamin Spock's (1946) book *The Common Sense Book of Baby and Child Care* prescribed a more child-centred approach to children's upbringing. Despite attracting considerable criticism for many of his recommendations, especially in the early editions, Spock's book appealed to parents as it pioneered a child-focused concept involving parent-child interaction that was hitherto unfamiliar. The book's popularity led to it being a staple among books in many a household, including my own as I was growing up. Many editions of the book have since been produced, improved and updated to make them relevant to the present day, but its core concept of engaging with the child has endured.

By 1973, a book emerged entitled *The Competent Infant* by Stone, Smith and Murphy, which eradicated notions of the previously regarded passive babies as a mere bunch of reflexes whose insensibilities made them oblivious to faces, colour and pretty much everything in their vicinity. Such revolutionary thinking went against the grain of the previous schools of thought that endorsed withholding affection from their children, especially by fathers, and not attempting to understand their children. Seeing a gap in the market, Spock encouraged parents to attend to their babies' and children's psychological as well as physical needs. In so doing, Spock reflected the work of psychologist B.F. Skinner who believed in positive reinforcement to encourage desirable behaviour. Rather than classical conditioning as espoused by Watson and Pavlov, in which responses become conditioned by environmental factors, Skinner believed responses could be moulded through so-called operant conditioning. Even as recently as 1964, the human infant at birth and soon after was described crudely as brainless: 'decorticated'. The books by Spock and Stone et al. were therefore revolutionary in showing that babies are sensitive to others, take heed of and value and nature of relationships, and moreover that parents and love matters. The headline was that babies were now to be perceived as real people with feelings and emotions. Such books also sparked arguments about the effect of the environment on the developing infant in relation to their genetic make-up. This was an important discussion as it alluded to the impact of the environment and whether nurturing could make a difference.

The nature versus nurture debate is overarching, all-encompassing, and continues to this day, constantly seeking to discover the origins and reasons behind our behaviour. Over the years, researchers, scientists and philosophers in the areas of psychology and education have envisioned the developing, learning child in different ways. From an empty vessel to a blank slate, the philosophy of empiricism as advocated by John Locke whose vision of the child was a blank slate or *tabula rasa,* meant that the quality of parenting would have a significant effect. The psychology of behaviourism, as promoted by John Watson and B.F. Skinner surmised that babies are born impartial but with an inborn capacity to learn from experience and require social and emotional experiences to shape their development, an essential ingredient without which they cannot develop socially, emotionally or intellectually. By contrast, some philosophers such as Jean Jacques Rousseau took a nativist stance believing in an innate capacity of children that would ensure their development regardless of social and emotional intervention. Around the same time as these psychological developments were revolutionising our thinking about children's abilities and the effects of caregivers' interactions with them, the field of education was valuing the use of emotion in teaching. John Dewey (1933) wrote of the necessity to address students' emotions in education: "…There is no education when ideas and knowledge are not translated into emotion, interest, and volition" (p. 189). Combining nature and nurture, others such as Maria Montessori believed that both play a part in development, and along with others such as Jean Piaget, they maintained such a constructivist approach. All these views were visionary and are still debated today, and their perspectives have prevailed and stood the test of time, as they are still being taught at all levels and applied and incorporated to lesser and greater degrees, depending on allegiances, in both research and practice. What this book aims to show is that there is a balance between the two opposing views, taking the stance of an already equipped baby's brain, which has the potential to be moulded through social interaction to form a social, emotional and thinking individual. More recently, the field of education has acknowledged the importance of emotional intelligence and recognised a focus beyond that of the acquisition of content knowledge thereby providing a greater and more wholesome understanding of teaching and learning.

Empathy has the potential to generate altruistic or helpful responses. John Pounds is an example of a person whose empathy and subsequent help for disadvantaged children came about as a result of an unfortunate accident. Born in Portsmouth in 1766, he created the so-called 'Ragged Schools'; but he might not have done so, were it not for an incident whilst working at the dockyard as a teenager in which he became physically incapacitated. Pounds decided thenceforth to make his living as a shoemaker and would gather poor and homeless children and teach them reading, writing and arithmetic. He is now considered a pioneer in Portsmouth and beyond. Perhaps, through his impairment, Pounds was able to empathise with the children he taught, who were also disadvantaged through poverty and homelessness.

Aims of This Book

From emotion to education, the vital connecting factor is empathy: it is the glue that links the two, and provides the force that enables the two to function. This book will follow the historical, developmental and educational trajectories of empathy and examine its origins, development and use for psychology and education. In so doing, it will chart how and when it begins and is affected by others, and its uses for children, and also for adults as parents and teachers. This source of emotion and cognition, being able to feel and know, plays a vital part in the development of children's lives—but as we will see, also in the lives of the adults with whom they interact, in order that the potential for social, emotional and cognitive development is fully realised. I will chart my work involving empathy that has spanned a quarter of a century in different shapes and forms, across disciplines with different destinations, and moreover transcended itself as a concept that is not just fascinating in its own right but has a valuable function for both everyday life and the field of education. This book aims to bridge the divide between the origins of empathy and its use in education. To what extent can young children empathise? How can we as parents and educators use empathy to enhance the quality of life? And what use has empathy for education? Drawing on my own research and that of others in the fields of developmental psychology and education, my aim is to communicate how we can use our knowledge of children's empathic abilities to help them, and us, in their educational endeavour.

This book will plot the literature on the origins and evolution of the concept of empathy, the word itself, the variety of definitions afforded to it and the philosophy that surrounds it. Debated and researched in a variety of guises over the centuries, its implications and applications will be discussed, but in particular, the focus is on the historical, developmental, psychological and educational perspectives of empathy and how these are interrelated. A developmental perspective emphasises the social nature of children from a very early age and thereby advocates the importance of conceptualising the child as an emotional as well as a cognitive being. When does empathy emerge and how does it develop? Is it present from birth or rather something that develops with age, experience and socialisation? How has this multifaceted construct been measured over the years and what ultimately constitutes empathy? Do some of us have a greater propensity to empathise than others? Moreover, why is empathy useful? Are there implications for other prosocial behaviours, such as morality, that enhance social life, and when do such behaviours manifest? The focus will be on children's abilities to empathise, how this is affected by their caregivers, and to what extent empathy can be used in education. We will begin by seeing how babies have been propelled to the forefront of research and attention having virtually been ignored or dismissed as having limited abilities. Then we'll see how they are able to understand, know and feel others' emotions. In particular the book will address the benefits of promoting and nurturing empathy with research that has examined children's ability to empathise and not least at school. From the child who was once thought to be incapable of such a task, to the child who we now know can indeed empathise and experience emotion and from a very young age, to the child in the classroom, who when given the opportunity, can use these skills to enhance teaching and learning with an overwhelming degree of success. Empathy's capacity to elicit a variety of responses, some more positive than others, will be explored, which will include some of my research of children's reactions to their peers in distress. There is then a focus on the nature/nurture debate outlining the biological basis for empathy and the significance of attachments and their impact on empathy. Attachment is then revisited and brought together with empathy within the realm of education, and specifically through giving pupils a voice about their own education and affording them the role of researcher. I will describe some of my own research that elicited pupils' views on the subject of friendships and fairness in school, and advocate the effectiveness of using pupil voice in teaching but also within my research with newly qualified teachers. This book brings together the importance of listening to a child by parents and by teachers. The mere act of listening has the power to engage children and increases in turn their capacity to empathise. From attention to attachment, the book also highlights the crucial attachments throughout the lifespan from those formed during childhood to those in the classroom. And what are the factors that enhance empathy and in turn promote student engagement? Similarities and responsibilities lead to enhanced understanding and commitment and it is our responsibility to encourage such behaviours and traits. From the perspective-taking of the infant to the critical thinking of the pupil or student (and note that the words 'pupil' and 'student' will be used interchangeably throughout this book), the two constructs have the same underlying premise, and these abilities in children are a far cry from the previously perceived child with limited abilities and whose place was confined to a corner. I will address research and theories and in particular, the role that empathy commands in pupil voice research investigating children's teaching and learning, and its power of enhancing the educational experience.

Ultimately I wish to communicate the idea that it is not the teacher teaching anymore, but rather the learner learning, and also coming back to the idea of viewing the learner as an emotional and social being as well as a cognitive recipient and purveyor of facts, where e-ffective teaching incorporates an a-ffective content. Children are already equipped socially and morally, and the premise of the book is that teachers should use this to their advantage. It is a case of capitalising on the social and emotional sides of teaching to communicate most effectively with students in order to achieve a rounded, fulfilling, enjoyable and productive teaching and learning experience and environment for all involved. The research of other authors in the field of pupil voice will be cited, many of whom I have collaborated with. An influx of recent research has highlighted the positive and powerful outcomes of consulting pupils and students for their teaching and learning, listening to pupil voice and thereby affording learners ownership of their learning. The findings have been disseminated widely and the potential for schools in consulting pupils has escalated ever since. Moreover, government education policy in England has acknowledged the significance of pupil involvement for citizenship education and personalised learning. This book focuses on the effectiveness of pupil voice in not only maximising the potential of pupils and students, but also the consequences for helping teachers in turn. Individual learning involves mind, body and emotions and is embedded in social and physical situations and practice. Emotions play a crucial role in communication and engagement between people, they act as a catalyst for expression and learning, and there is an inherent interplay between them and their cognition counterpart. The field of education has extolled the virtues of emotionality through its ability to consolidate cognitive scaffolding of concepts and teaching strategies. The book is therefore a reconciliation of cognition and emotion and a recommendation to be psychologically, emotionally, empathically and educationally aware.

My circuitous voyage has circumnavigated the fields of psychology and education with a bird's-eye view of empathy. This work, which bridges the two disciplines of psychology and education, is a fusion of the disciplines via the concept of empathy: from its childhood origins, to its uses in teaching and learning. As my own early research showed, empathy is present early on and its fruition is aided by attentive teachers, whose own empathy for their pupils fortifies and energises teaching and learning. My aim therefore is to connect that capacity for early childhood empathy that I identified from my days as a developmental psychologist, to the empathy that is present among school age children, and to make parents and professionals alike aware of it presence, uses and effectiveness when engaging with children. The premise of the book is that teaching and learning are not always instant and automatically attainable, but often require patience before results are achieved. The book emphasises the social and emotional side of teaching that can help realise these aims. Overall, the aim is for complementarity and for dualism but also holism to come across, where parent and child, teacher and learner work as a team, supporting and enhancing the other, allowing for the voice of the child to be heard and leading to empowerment and democracy. And overarchingly, the aim is to address the juxtaposing but at the same time complementary concepts of affect and cognition, two sides of the same coin, a paradox, contradiction in terms, technically opposites. But opposites attract and they form the bedrock of empathy: its emotional and intellectual attributes working in synchrony to produce balanced beings from early childhood and as the vital ingredients for parenting and teaching. This is the story of empathy in childhood and teaching: a concept with a split personality comprising emotion and cognition, opposing, but at the same time, complementary forces. Without one or other, empathy breaks down, or is at the least incomplete. The concept of childhood has evolved from the previously perceived passive inert being to a being that is not only responsive but also instrumental in their own and others' lives and learning. Let's begin by examining empathy through some well-known figures in history who have embraced, embodied and propelled it into the limelight.

References

Dewey, J. (1933). *How we think: A restatement of the relation of reflective thinking to the educative process*. Boston: Houghton Mifflin.

Palmer, P. J. (1998). *The courage to teach: Exploring the inner landscape of a teacher's life*. New York: Wiley.

Rea, B. (1959). *Stretching figure* (Bronze resin). Original held in Herbert Art Gallery and Museum, Coventry, UK.

Spock, B. (1946). *The common sense book of baby and child care*. New York: Duell, Sloan and Pearce.

Stone, J. L., Smith, H. T., & Murphy, L. B. (Eds.). (1973). *The competent infant: Research and commentary*. New York: Basic Books.

Watson, J. B. (1928). *Psychological care of infant and child*. New York: Norton.

Whiteley, G. (2004). Rea, Betty Marion (1904–1965). *Oxford dictionary of national biography*. Oxford, UK: Oxford University Press.

2

The Empathy Factor: Its Transcending Power

A few well-known people from history have felt the need to experience the lives of others less fortunate than themselves. From St Francis of Assisi to George Orwell to Mahatma Gandhi—names from religion to literature to politics have become the personification of empathy. Through their writings and political rhetoric, such people went through a meteoric rise highlighting and experiencing the lives of neglected and marginalised communities from different walks of life to their own, and in so doing encapsulated Euripides's statement from around 400 BC: "When a good man is hurt all who would be called good must suffer with him".

An early empathy experiment was conducted in 1206 by Giovanni Bernardone who was the 23 year old son of a wealthy merchant. Travelling on a pilgrimage to Saint Peter's Basilica in Rome, he was struck by the contrast between the opulence of the bejewelled mosaics and majestic columns inside, and the poverty of the beggars sitting outside. He persuaded one of the vagrants to exchange clothes with him and experienced the rest of the day in rags. This was a pivotal moment in his life and he went on to establish a religious order living in poverty and working for the poor and the sick. Subsequently, he became known as Francis of Assisi, later to be canonised.

© The Author(s) 2018
H. Demetriou, *Empathy, Emotion and Education*,
https://doi.org/10.1057/978-1-137-54844-3_2

A riches to rags story was also experienced by the author George Orwell. Whilst working as a colonial police officer in Burma (modern day Myanmar) he witnessed the brutality of colonialism. This appalled him to such a degree that when he returned to Britain he decided to take on the role of everyday working people in order to understand their lifestyles first hand. In his book, *The Road to Wigan Pier* (1937) he talked about this: "I felt that I had got to escape not merely from imperialism but from every form of man's dominion over other man. … I wanted to submerge myself, to get right down among the oppressed; to be one of them and on their side against the tyrants" (p. 129). He had achieved this by disguising himself as a vagabond and living amongst the beggars on the streets of East London, as described in *Down and Out in Paris and London* (1933).

Another person who submerged himself in empathy was Mahatma Gandhi and who was inspired by Henry David Thoreau's (1910) words: "Could a greater miracle take place than for us to look through each other's eye for an instant?" Gandhi's ethos of empathy emerged in 1915 on his return to India from South Africa when he decided that in the run up to his campaign for Indian independence from British rule he should understand first hand what life was really like for the poorest people in his country. Substituting his barrister's garments for a *dhoti* or loincloth, he experienced a very different life from his own. Stepping into the shoes of peasant farmers, he undertook work assigned to the Untouchable caste. He claimed: "Three quarters of the miseries and misunderstandings in the world would finish if people were to put on the shoes of their adversaries and understood their points of view" (Gandhi, 1924, p. 271). Gandhi's empathic instinct enabled him to traverse religious boundaries. He was horrified by the violence exhibited between Hindus and Muslims, and opposed the creation of a separate Muslim state. When Gandhi was asked if he was a Hindu, he claimed using powerfully empathic words: "I am a Muslim! And a Hindu, and a Christian and a Jew – and so are all of you".

Religion, literature and politics continue to resonate with empathic echoes. Currently and a century after Gandhi, there seems to be a continued awareness of the concept of empathy from politics to social media to visitor attractions. Barack Obama (2006) warned about society's empathy deficit: "We are in great need of people being able to stand in somebody else's shoes and see the world through their eyes … empathy is a quality of character that can change the world". In technology and social media, 'Facebook' has introduced the 'dislike' button because in the words of Facebook's creator Mark Zuckerberg: "what people really want is the ability to express empathy" (Ferner, 2015). And the first ever empathy museum opened its doors in 2015, the curator of which has claimed that empathy is: "the imaginative act of stepping into another person's shoes and being able to look at the world from their perspective – is a radical tool for social change and should be a guiding light for the art of living" (Krznaric, 2007, p. 8). Has society become stuck in an empathy rut and had to place it in the spotlight because there is indeed an 'empathy deficit' that needs to be addressed through politics, social media and museum guides? Have we really got to that stage in life where people have to spell out the word 'empathy' in order to make it seen and known?

Empathy is a construct that, despite having only relatively recently acquired its name, has nevertheless fascinated philosophers, theorists and researchers alike. It is a small word with a vast meaning and ability to augment. As a society we function through empathy. It has the potential to establish unity, enable congruity, achieve harmony, solidify society, invigorate community and enhance humanity. Indeed, as de Waal (2005) has claimed: "Empathy is the one weapon in the human repertoire able to rid us of the curse of xenophobia" (p. 54). Through its powers of emotion and cognition, it educates and sustains social life, has the capacity to transcend cultures so that we are able to 'read from the same page' and ultimately motivates prosocial and moral behaviour. Empathy ranges in strength, enabling a commonality between people who may not even have met. It can appear in a weak form through a mere recognition and self-affirming process when for example waving in camaraderie to another Land Rover driver; to an otherwise timid mother befriending and being uncharacteristically animated with another mother at school because they share the experience of having children in the same class; to tolerating the incessant cries of a baby in a public place having experienced one's own baby doing the same many years previously. And then there is the case of the woman I read about in the news who gave shelter to some people fleeing from a war-torn country of a different culture from her own, remembering the fear she experienced as a child when she herself was a refugee. This latter example reflects the capacity of empathy to break through barriers of language, continents, religion and transcend culture, through appreciating others' plights and placing itself on the frontline. Empathy entails appreciation, passion and courage. Perhaps, when empathy is not exhibited by a person, they are lacking a form of 'bravery'. As Maya Angelou claimed: "I think we all have empathy. We may not have enough courage to display it" (Murphy, 2013).

As well as outsmarting cultural divisions, empathy can also break down the barriers of age, and it is evident that it is alive and present in even the youngest of infants. Our task as adults is to keep it going throughout the lifespan, as it enables our earliest relationships with siblings and peers (and indeed is enabled by those people) and helps to pave the way for a successful lifestyle from preschool through to school and beyond. This book aims to show how this emotional construct, through its capacity to achieve a common denominator between people and thereby power to engage, can and should combine with our places of school and work to empower and enrich our environment. Firstly, let us look at some definitions of this elusive construct and references to it across history, from art to literature to philosophy to science, among other spheres of life.

Empathy in Art and Literature: Feeling with the Heart

Although the actual word 'empathy' was not coined until the early 1900s, the concept and power of the empathic process pervades the literature up until that point and of course beyond to the present day. On a recent visit to the Valley of the Kings in Egypt, I learnt that the ancient Egyptians valued the heart over the brain. For them it was the font of all knowledge, wisdom, emotions and even memory and personality, and as such was retained in the mummified body. The emotional, affective side of empathy is particularly prevalent in the arts, which are built on its very foundations, and artists have sourced empathy's involuntary nature of feeling emotions to convey a concept or desire through making it their own. James Baldwin (1963) explained the power of empathy in literature: "You think your pain and your heartbreak are unprecedented in the history of the world, but then you read. It was Dostoyevsky and Dickens who taught me that the things that tormented me most were the very things that connected me with all the people who were alive, or who ever had been alive. Only if we face these open wounds in ourselves can we understand them in other people" (p. 89). And Edith Sitwell believed: "Poetry ennobles the heart and the eyes, and unveils the meaning of all things upon which the heart and the eyes dwell. It discovers the secret rays of the universe, and restores to us forgotten paradise" (Knight, 2006, p. 100).

From the eighth century BC, empathy is elicited in the words of the ancient Greek poet Homer (1725), author of the *Iliad* and *Odyssey* written around the seventh and eighth centuries BC, and quoted as saying: "Yet, taught by time, my heart has learned to glow for others' good, and melt at others' woe" (Book XVIII, line 269). Jumping forward to the Bible, there are echoes of empathic verse in Romans 12:15: "Rejoice with them that do rejoice, and weep with them that weep". Another leap forward to the sixteenth century, Shakespeare's use of the word 'fellowship' was his way of conveying empathy. In *Love's Labour's Lost* (1598) Duke Ferdinand describes men who have succumbed to love as sharing a "sweet fellowship in shame" (Act 4 Scene 3); and Juliet of *Romeo and Juliet* (1597) waxes lyrical about the sharing of emotions: "sour woe delights in fellowship" (Act 3 Scene 2). Other key Shakespearian characters have been dumbfounded by others' lack of responsiveness to their situation and urged them to share their experiences, as when in *King Lear* (1608), the protagonist discovers that his daughter Cordelia is dead, he is beside himself with grief and exclaims to all around: "O, you are men of stones" (Act 5 Scene 3), thereby accusing everyone around him of depravity and hardheartedness. They were far from wearing their 'heart on their sleeve', and in fact the expression itself originates from Shakespeare's *Othello* (1622, Act 1 Scene 1)—referring to an open display of emotions.

In eighteenth-century literature, the empathic process was recognised by English poets as being indispensable, and by the nineteenth century empathy was delivered through poetry. In a response to Shakespeare, Samuel T. Coleridge (1802) analysed the challenges of empathy when exclaiming: "It is easy to cloathe Imaginary Beings with our own Thoughts & Feelings; but to send ourselves out of ourselves, to think ourselves in to the Thoughts & Feelings of Beings in circumstances wholly and strangely different from our own" The romantic poet Percy Bysshe Shelley (1821) in his 'A Defence of Poetry' claimed that: "The imagination is enlarged by a sympathy with pains and passions so mighty, that they distend in their conception the capacity of that by which they are conceived" (p. 285); and: "The great secret of morals is love; or a going out of our nature, and an identification of ourselves with the beautiful which exists in thought, action, or person, not our own. A man, to be greatly good, must imagine intensely and comprehensively; he must put himself in the place of another and of many others; the pains and pleasure of his species must become his own. The great instrument of moral good is the imagination" (p. 112). From playwrights to poets and also musicians, as with Wolfgang Amadeus Mozart (1781), whose frustrations with the greed and politics of others led to his attempts to communicate the language and passion of his music. He exclaimed in eighteenth-century Vienna: "it is the heart that ennobles man"; and "… the music is not in the notes but in the silence between them".

Powerful images of empathy permeate Emily Brontë's novel *Wuthering Heights* (1847). Heathcliff's seeming loss of empathy from a sensitive, inno-cent victim to a self-obsessed, tyrannical individual leads to the collapse of his relationship with Cathy. In the meantime, Cathy exudes the ultimate empathy for Heathcliff by declaring "I *am* Heathcliff". Her identification with him resonates with Freud's theory (1930/1961) when "at the height of being in love the boundary between ego and object threatens to melt away … a man declares that 'I' and 'you' are one" (p. 66). A unity has been achieved also by great artists, not least Vincent van Gogh who, writing to his brother Theo in 1882 claimed: "I want to do drawings which touch some people". Evidence of this is in *The Potato Eaters*, which showed an intense identification with the peasant class, as well as a love for humanity that he desired but never achieved. Around the same time, Oscar Wilde used empathy in his short story 'The Selfish Giant' (1888). Despite driving the children away from his garden, on realising his selfishness and the chil-dren's sadness, the giant eventually relinquishes and allows them to play there: the children at last can play to their hearts' content, spring and sum-mer enter the garden, when previously there was only winter, and the giant himself reaps the benefits as his previously selfish behaviour makes way for empathy and new found happiness.

In *Jude the Obscure* (1895) by Thomas Hardy, the young Jude Fawley is overwhelmed by a shared feeling of rejection and compassion for the hungry birds: "at length his heart grew sympathetic with the birds' thwarted desire. They seemed, like himself, to be living in a world which did not want them. ... A magic thread of fellow-feeling united his own life to theirs. Puny and sorry as their lives were, they much resembled his own". Hardy's powerful connection of fellow-feeling transcends species, overriding the differences between boy and birds. Empathy also emerges in the poetry of the First World War such as in the poem 'Insensibility' by Wilfred Owen (1917): "But cursed are dullards whom no cannon stuns, that they should be as stones. ... By choice they made themselves immune To pity and whatever moans in man" (p. 191). In addition, the fiction of Sir Arthur Conan Doyle addresses empathy when the very meticulous and obsessive nature of Holmes leads him to crack the crimes when he expresses the ability to put himself in another's shoes: "You know my methods in such cases, Watson. I put myself in the man's place, and having first gauged his intelligence, I try to imagine how I should myself have proceeded under the same circumstances" (1950, pp. 112–13).

A phenomenological perspective of empathy has been attempted by pioneers the world over. It has transcended obstacles for the blind, deaf and dumb. Helen Keller (1903) claimed that "the best and most beautiful things in the world cannot be seen or even touched – they must be felt with the heart". Indeed, Picasso spoke of painting from "the perspective of a blind man and painting through feeling rather than through seeing". Inspired by a proverb that dates back to the Cherokee tribe of Native Americans, which said: "Don't judge a man until you have walked a mile in his shoes", in *To Kill a Mockingbird* (1960), Harper Lee's character Atticus Finch says: "If you can learn a simple trick, Scout, you'll get along a lot better with all kinds of folks. You never really understand a person until you consider things from his point of view, until you climb inside of his skin and walk around in it" (p. 36). In 1984, Milan Kundera encapsulated empathy in his book *The Unbearable Lightness of Being*: "There is nothing heavier than compassion. Not even one's own pain weighs so heavy as the pain one feels with someone, for someone, a pain intensified by the imagination and prolonged by a hundred echoes" (p. 18). Of course, artists and writers have been inspired through identifying themselves in others. A biography about

Alfred Hitchcock (Ackroyd, 2015) revealed that as a young man he read the works of Edgar Allan Poe and claimed "I felt an immense pity for him … because in spite of his talent, he had always been unhappy" (p. 13). The 'pity' felt by Hitchcock seems to have been more than just feeling sorry for Poe, but rather an identification with him. Both the director and the writer shared phobias, habits and sensitivities that affected their lives and infused their work, arguably enhancing the fantasy and detail in the terror of their creations.

The citings above portray an empathy that reflects thought and feeling for another's situation. Often these responses are not judgmental, and as pointed out by Alaa Al Aswany (2015), literature is not a tool of judgement but instead of human understanding. Whereas typically an unfaithful spouse is judged as being undesirable, two classic novels are purposefully not judgmental. Citing *Madame Bovary* (1857) and *Anna Karenina* (1878), Aswany explains the importance of the authors' intentions, so that rather than judging or condemning the wives' behaviours, attempting instead to rationalise the reasons and understand the motives behind the unfaithful behaviour. Moreover, Aswany argues that such literature would never be appreciated by fanatics, as fanaticism is purely judgmental, black and white with no shades of grey, and seeing others as good or bad. His views on literature are that it should reflect the spectrum of human potential and teach us how to feel other people's suffering: "When you read a good novel, you forget about the nationality of the character. You forget about his or her religion. You forget about his skin colour or her skin colour. You only understand the human. You understand that this is a human being, the same way we are. And so reading great novels absolutely can remake us as much better human beings". Possibly one of the most powerful empathy-eliciting literary works is *Uncle Tom's Cabin* (1852) by Harriet Beecher Stowe, which raised awareness about the cruelty of slavery and reformed public policy. Linked with this is some interesting research that has uncovered the power of engaging with literary fiction on the reader's emotional skills of empathy, mentalising and theory of mind by Kidd and Castano (2013, 2016) who claimed that the more subtle stories and characters of literary fiction, rather than those of popular fiction, are particularly powerful in enhancing readers' abilities to understand others' mental states.

Empathy in Philosophy and Science: From a Concept with No Name to the *Most Essential Quality*

Empathy has emerged through history from a concept with no name to being regarded as an indispensable part of life, as claimed by Roger Ebert when he said: "I believe empathy is the most essential quality of civilisation" (2011). Theories can be traced historically to the ideas of early aesthetic, philosophical, sociological, psychological, developmental and clinical writers and together have brought empathy to the fore and to the familiar concept we know today. The core dimension of empathy underlies evolutionary, neuroscience and functionalist perspectives which stress the importance for survival of being able to read others' emotions, to understand their motives and intentions and to be positively invested in interpersonal relationships (Bretherton, Fritz, Zahn-Waxler, & Ridgeway, 1986). Eastern philosophy extends the diction to citing each person as one and the same. Signs of such intricate interpersonal relationships could be said to have originated around two million years ago in our predecessor, homo erectus, who lived as a hunter-gather and who showed signs of a social life equipped with social skills similar to that of his modern human counterpart. Evolutionary developments resulted in an increase in brain size and in particular the presence of the Broca's area of the brain which introduced language, all of which enabled homo erectus to hunt in organised groups, use complex tools and care for less mobile peers.

In the eighteenth century, the philosopher, historian and economist David Hume (1738) pioneered the link between empathy and moral action. Using terms such as 'sympathy' and 'fellow-feeling', he suggested that both children and adults have an intrinsic ability to empathise with one another due to shared life experiences: "the minds of men are mirrors to one another" (T2.2.5). He also attributed empathy with cognitive characteristics believing that the basis of empathy is imagination and that similarity among people is conducive to imagining oneself in another's place, thereby converting others' feelings into mental images that evoke feelings in oneself. Moreover, in his *A Treatise of Human Nature* (1738), Hume extended his thoughts of empathy to within the scope of animals: "'Tis evident, that sympathy, or the communication of passions, takes place among animals, no less than among men" (T2.2.12.6). Adding his own moral and cognitive dimensions to the debate, the Scottish philosopher Adam Smith (1759) likened sympathy to a social glue. He highlighted the importance of cognition in empathy with the argument that when a person responds to expressive cues alone, the empathic response is insufficient and imperfect and creates in the observer "a curiosity to inquire into the other's situation", so that "… by the imagination we place ourselves in [the other's] situation, we conceive ourselves enduring all the same torments" (p. 258). Indeed Smith's portrayal of empathy claims that moral relationships are based on emotional attitudes between people and as such our capacity to empathise with a whole spectrum of others' feelings lays down the foundation for our development as morally sensitive human beings.

With echoes of Hume a hundred years before him but now with a naturalist perspective, Charles Darwin propounded the functions of emotions and in particular sympathy in his book *The Expression of the Emotions in Man and Animals* (1872) through his detailed observations of a variety of animal species, saying "the social instincts lead an animal to take pleasure in the society of its fellows, to feel a certain amount of sympathy with them, and to perform various services for them" (p. 74). Commenting on sympathy, in 'The Descent of Man' (1871), Darwin said "which, as we shall see, forms an essential part of the social instinct, and is indeed its foundation-stone" (p. 471). Because the word 'empathy' had not yet been coined, the word 'sympathy' was being used as its forerunner, and soon after a German philosopher and historian named Friedrich Theodor Vischer used the term 'Einfühlen' meaning 'feel into'. His son, Robert Vischer, a German art historian and philosopher, is noted in 1873 as the first person to use the word Einfühlung to explain how we 'feel into' and project our feelings into works of art. Soon after, the new word for empathy was applied from a psychological perspective by Wilhelm Wundt, pioneer of experimental psychology, who defined the empathic process when relating to a work of art as the onlooker imitating and imaginatively projecting oneself into the object. However, the first detailed analysis of empathy in psychology was made by the German psychologist Theodor Lipps, who was a student of Wundt and who applied the word 'Einfühlung' in 1897 in a psychological context, assigning it the meaning of 'feeling into another'. Lipps used the term to refer to interpersonal knowledge and employed the concept in the branch of philosophy concerned with the reflection of life in art known as aesthetics. He depicted this doctrine as an 'inner participation' in foreign experiences, as an awareness of another's experience from within during an aesthetic appreciation, and as a 'self-activation', believing that people are able to acquire an energy that enables them to empathise. Lipps (1903) communicated the projective process of empathy through the example of watching a performance "when I observe a circus performer on a hanging wire, I feel I am inside him". By accentuating its objectivity and 'demanding' character and by indicating also how it is akin to memory and expectation, Lipps's major contribution was to approach the debate from a psychological, non-metaphysical perspective, and to use a phenomenological method to document his ideas. He claimed that: "Empathy is the fact here established, that the object is myself and by the very same token this self of mine is the object. Empathy is the fact that the antithesis between myself and the object disappears, or rather does not yet exist" (p. 291).

The word 'empathy' made its debut in 1909, declared by the English psychologist Edward Titchener, who constructed it from the Greek roots of *empatheia*, which implies intimating passion and appreciation of another's feelings, and explains the process of humanising objects and reading or feeling ourselves into them. He claimed: "Not only do I see gravity and modesty and pride and courtesy and stateliness, but I feel or act them in the mind's muscle. This is, I suppose, a simple case of empathy, if we may coin that term as a rendering of Einfühlung" (p. 21). From 1909, the adjective 'empathic' became part of the vernacular.

Continuing with the psychological theme, Sigmund Freud took empathy through a psychoanalytic journey. He admired the writings of Lipps and highlighted the importance of preserving a 'sympathetic understanding' during the therapeutic process in 'On Beginning the Treatment' (1913). Moreover, Freud (1921) claimed that empathy was a prerequisite for the consideration of another person's mental life. He spoke of the difficulty in apprehending the conscious workings of another's mind thereby establishing the emotional understanding of empathy as an essential element in all intensive psychotherapy. He knew that, whereas consciousness made us aware only of ourselves, identification could be extended by the

ego to others, and viewed the ability to empathise as the result of prolonged refinement of instinctual impulses. He stressed the significance of
empathy by stating that "… a path leads from identification by way of
imitation to empathy, that is, to the comprehension of the mechanism by
means of which we are enabled to take up any attitude at all towards
another mental life" (p. 50). Thenceforth, the psychoanalytic literature
became replete with references to empathy, to which it was commonly
referred as a manifestly complex ego state. Jung (1921) proposed a hypothesis of empathy based on the processes of projection and introjection.
Whilst the former process encompasses the first 'active' conscious and
intentional phase, the latter brings the object into intimate relation with
the subject. The therapeutic situation was thought to provide an excellent
example of a process in which empathic feelings are fostered and convey
the understanding of and responsiveness to the client's perspective. Heinz
Kohut's (1957) 'self psychology' emphasised the multiple roles of empathy
as 'vicarious introspection' during the infant's development and for the
analyst's therapeutic technique and considered empathy as a form of internal scientific enquiry through "the mode by which one gathers psychological data about other people and, when they say what they think or feel,
imagines their inner experience even though it is not open to direct observation" (p. 450). Kohut envisaged empathy as the function by which we
attempt to perceive and understand what is happening in other people
through the process of introspection, and in so doing concurred with
Hume. The move within psychoanalysis to a combination of thinking and
feeling with the client was further emphasised by Deutsch and Madle
(1975): "empathy was no longer viewed as purely a perceptual awareness of
an individual's affect or sharing of feeling, but rather as an ability to understand a person's emotional reactions in consort with the context" (p. 270).
   With the advent of the twentieth century came the discipline of phe-
nomenology. Phenomenologists employed a perceptual theme to the process of empathy that involved acquiring an internal sense of an object or
event. Edith Stein (1917) analysed the phenomenological structure of
empathy. She viewed empathy as a 'reproduction' of another's experience,
when for example, one sees the sadness in another's face. She acknowledged that, although one is not undergoing the other's experience, one is
able to 'project' oneself into the place of the other so that "I am at the

subject of the [other's experience] in the original subject's place" (p. 10). She continued "empathy ... is the experience of foreign consciousness in general. ... This is how man grasps the psychic life of his fellow man" (1964, p. 11).

In 1924, the verb 'empathise' was coined and from this point forward the word was analysed for its properties and functions. For example, Wolfgang Köhler who co-founded the school of Gestalt psychology in 1910 argued that empathy was more cognitive rather than 'feeling into', as previously defined by Lipps, Titchener and Vischer. Henceforth the cognitive dimension of empathy was incorporated into the discussion. This cognitive (rather than emotional) consideration of empathy was also favoured by George Herbert Mead (1934) in his philosophical stance of perspective-taking when understanding how people view the world.

Within the discipline of developmental psychology, Jean Piaget (1932) employed the cognitive dimension of empathy as perspective-taking in his studies of child development. The development of empathy was con-ceptualised as a discontinuous process that proceeds through a series of hierarchical stages that follow from general cognitive development. In this view, empathy is manifested in children as a conscious awareness that others have feelings that are different from one's own. This culminates in adolescence in what Piaget described as true relativistic thinking, which involves the ability to put oneself in the other's place and to see the world through another's eyes. The arena of developmental psychology has employed a variety of different techniques to measure children's empathic development, such as observations, interviews, picture-stories and experi-ments (Feshbach & Roe, 1968; Hoffman, 1976; Murphy, 1937) with psychologists favouring cognitive, affective or indeed both dimensions of empathy.

By the 1950s, empathy had acquired a more cognitive meaning in clinical discussions also, when it referred to understanding accurately and dispassionately the client's point of view. In 1975, clinical psycholo-gist Carl Rogers took a therapeutic stance to empathy affording it as "one of the most potent factors in bringing about change and learning" (p. 3) through "frequently checking with him/her as to the accuracy of your sensing, and being guided by the response you receive, so that ... to be with another in this way means that for the time being you lay aside the views and values you hold for yourself in order to enter another's world without prejudice" (p. 4). In an effort to assess Roger's (1957) vision of therapeutic empathy, Truax and Carkhuff (1967) viewed empathy as a cognitive rather than an emotional process, with the result that therapeutic sensitivity to the feelings and needs of the client does not entail the therapist's sharing of the client's emotional experience. Moreover, Wispé (1986) envisioned empathy as "the attempt by one self-aware self to comprehend non-judgmentally the positive and negative experiences of another self" (p. 318).

The biological underpinnings of empathy have been a focus for research as have its biologically based disposition for altruistic behaviour, as championed by Giacomo Rizzolatti in the 1990s who discovered mirror neurons involved in empathy (see Rizzolatti & Craighero, 2004). These so-called mirror neurons also complement the thoughts of Hume 300 years previously who espoused that the minds of men are mirrors to one another. Other findings have shown animals such as elephants, apes, dogs, dolphins, chickens and voles to share the emotional states of others, as for example, found by primatologist and ethnologist Frans de Waal and colleagues (1979, 2009, 2016) and which confirms Hume's and Darwin's earlier suppositions about the potential of animals to empathise.

The colourful concept of empathy has therefore evolved dramatically, been embraced by a number of different disciplines from the arts to the sciences, and emerges into emotional and cognitive guises. The present day champions words such as 'mindfulness', 'mentalisation' and 'critical thinking', all arguably encompassing elements of empathy. Its rise and recognition have prompted scientists and artists alike to question what gives us the energy to empathise as well as enquiring about its properties that empower and accelerate positive behaviours, such as being helpful. Overall, empathy is deemed to be an asset, going hand in hand with morality (Kalliopuska, 1992) and better physical and mental health, lowering for example levels of stress, anxiety, hopelessness and depression. The perplexing phenomenon of empathy has sparked debates not only about its conceptualisation and application, but also about the fundamental principles on which it is based. Moreover, various definitions of empathy have been propounded.

Present Day Definitions and Debates About Empathy

The power and complexity of the empathic process has been described by Carl Rogers (1980) as: "a complex, demanding, strong yet subtle and gentle way of being" (p. 143). But what does it mean to be truly empathic? What does it take to be able to empathise with another person? Is it possible for me to empathise with another person if I haven't experienced or felt similar feelings to that other person? Is true empathy only possible and genuine when the onlooker has experienced all the same issues and feelings as the person they are observing? Can we only really empathise therefore when we have experienced the same success or undergone the same torment as another person? So, can I truly empathise with someone who has experienced loss when I haven't myself, and what kind of empathy or response am I able to give? Or is it still possible to understand what another person is going through even though we do not feel the emotions that they are necessarily feeling; conversely, can we feel the emotions and experiences of others without necessarily understanding them? In an attempt to capture the concept of empathy, myriad contemporary dictionary definitions include the ability to feel, share, imagine, project, identify, understand or experience another's perspective through their feelings, thoughts and actions, such as: "the ability to understand and share the feelings of another" (Oxford English Dictionary, 2016). Definitions fluctuate between an empathy where there is an understanding of the other person's perspective, to an empathy where there are similar feelings experienced, and in some cases where extremes of these feelings can lead to emotional overload. In contrast to sympathy, which reflects a more general emotional attitude from outside the object of perception and feeling *for* someone, akin to sentimentalisation and potential sanctimony, empathy goes beyond this, it is a feeling *with* the person, and has the ability to truly understand what another being is going through but also to harness a deep-seated emotional appreciation of another's situation. The other end of the scale from empathy are personality traits that render a person incapable of empathising with others, such as the sociopath, and those who have the cognitive capacity to step into the mind of others but make no emotional bond, such as the psychopath.

The endless variety of definitions of empathy generally reflect aspects of human understanding of an emotional nature, which emphasise that empathy is associated with feeling *with* the other and is a catalyst for helpful behaviour. Most researchers agree that empathy and such synonyms as *fellow feeling, social awareness, sympathy, insight, concordance* and *reciprocation* refer to the response of one person to the affective state of another (Mood, Johnson, & Shantz, 1978), thereby affording empathy as one of the basic human attributes supportive of social life. Throughout its history, the word 'empathy' has been employed in a variety of contexts and in fact, the unnamed empathic process was written about long before the term was used. For example, the native American Indian phrase "You have to walk a mile in another man's moccasins" was their way of illustrating the means by which empathy is achieved, reflecting the necessity for experience and endurance in another person's life before one can truly appreciate the situation of that other person. The thesis of this book is that the empathy possessed by young children, and as will be demonstrated, is apparent at very early ages, is an invaluable tool for their education, but also for us as educators. A recent visit to the Freud museum in Vienna alerted me to Freud's (1930) claim that: "It is not easy to deal scientifically with feelings" (p. 65), and as we will see, both children and adults sometimes struggle to grasp others' feelings, 'scientifically' or otherwise. Appreciating children's empathic capacity and putting it to use ourselves in turn, can help to accelerate and ameliorate teaching and learning. I will give a developmental trajectory into the child's empathic journey. But before focusing specifically on empathy, I will look at what is arguably its polar opposite—egocentrism.

References

Ackroyd, P. (2015). *Alfred Hitchcock*. London: Vintage Press.
Aswany, A. A. (2015, August 18). How literature inspires empathy. *The Atlantic*.
Baldwin, J. (1963). Doom and glory of knowing who you are by Jane Howard. *LIFE Magazine, 54*(21), 89.
Bretherton, I., Fritz, J., Zahn-Waxler, C., & Ridgeway, D. (1986). Learning to talk about emotions: A functionalist perspective. *Child Development, 57,* 529–548.

Brontë, E. (1847). *Wuthering heights*. London: Thomas Cautley Newby.
Coleridge, S. T. (1802). Letter to William Sotheby, July 13th. In E. L. Griggs (Ed.), *Collected letters of Samuel Taylor Coleridge* (Vol. II). Oxford, UK: Oxford University Press, 1956.
Darwin, C. (1871). *The descent of man*. London: John Murray.
Darwin, C. (1872). *The expression of the emotions in man and animals*. London: John Murray.
de Waal, F. B. M. (2005, October 8). The empathic ape. *New Scientist*, 52–54.
de Waal F. B. M. (2016). To each animal its own cognition. *The Scientist*, 30.
de Waal, F. B. M., & van Roosmalen, A. (1979). Reconciliation and consolation among chimpanzees. *Behavioural Ecology and Sociobiology*, 5, 55–66.
Deutsch, F., & Madle, R. A. (1975). Empathy: Historic and current conceptualisations, measurement, and a cognitive theoretical perspective. *Human Development*, 18, 267–287.
Doyle, A. C. (1950). The Musgrave Ritual. In *The memoirs of Sherlock Holmes*. London: Penguin Books Ltd.
Ebert, R. (2011). *Roger Ebert's movie yearbook 2011* (p. 1500). Andrews McMeel Publishing, 14 December 2010.
Ferner, M. (2015, September 15). Mark Zuckerberg: Facebook is working on a 'dislike button'. *The Huffington Post*.
Feshbach, N. D., & Roe, K. (1968). Empathy in six- and seven-year-olds. *Child Development*, 39, 133–145.
Flaubert, G. (1857). *Madame Bovary*. Paris: Michel Lévy Frères.
Freud, S. (1913). *On beginning the treatment*. London: The Hogarth Press.
Freud, S. (1921). Group psychology and the analysis of the ego. In *Complete psychological works* (Vol. 18). London: Hogarth Press.
Freud, S. (1930). *Civilisation and its discontents*. Internationaler Psychoanalytischer Vienna: Verlag Wien.
Gandhi, M. (1924). *Collected works*, 27, p. 271.
Hardy, T. (1895). *Jude the obscure*. London: Osgood, McIlvaine & Co.
Hoffman, M. L. (1976). Empathy, role-taking, guilt and development of altruistic motives. In T. Lickona (Ed.), *Moral development and behaviour: Current theory and research*. New York: Holt, Rinehart & Winston.
Homer. (1725). *The Odyssey of Homer (Alexander Pope)*. Poetic Interpretation.
Hume, D. (1738). *A treatise of human nature*. London: Gutenberg.
Jung, C. G. (1921/1954). Psychological types. In *The collected works of C. G. Jung* (Vol. 6). London: Routledge & Kegan Paul.
Kalliopuska, M. (1992). *Empathy – The way to humanity*. Edinburgh, Scotland: The Pentland Press Ltd.

Keller, H. (1903). The story of my life. New York: Cosimo Classics.

Kidd, D. C., & Castano, E. (2013). Reading literary fiction improves theory of mind. *Science, 342*(6156), 377–380.

Kidd, D. C., & Castano, E. (2016). Different stories: How levels of familiarity with literary and genre fiction relate to mentalising. *Psychology of Aesthetics, Creativity, and the Arts, 11*, 474–486.

Knight, B. (2006). *Wild women and books: Bibliophiles, bluestockings & prolific pens*. New York: Conari Press.

Kohut, H. (1957). Introspection, empathy, and psychoanalysis. *Journal of the American Psychoanalytic Association, 7*, 459–483.

Krznaric, R. (2007). *Empathy and the art of living*. Oxford, UK: Blackbird Press.

Kundera, M. (1984). *The unbearable lightness of being*. London: Faber and Faber.

Lee, H. (1960). *To kill a mockingbird*. London: Minerva Paperback.

Lipps, T. (1903). *Empathy, inner imitation, and sense-feelings*. In Rader (Ed.), *Aesthetics* (pp. 291–304). Translated from Einfühlung, inner Nachahmung, und Organ-empfindungen. *Archiv fur die gesamte Psychologie, 2*, 185–204, by Rader and M. Schertel.

Mead, G. H. (1934). In C. M. Morris (Ed.), *Mind, self, and society*. Chicago: University of Chicago Press.

Mood, D. W., Johnson, J. E., & Shantz, C. U. (1978). Social comprehension and affect matching in young children. *Merrill-Palmer Quarterly, 24*, 63–66.

Mozart, W. A. (1781, June 20). Letter from Mozart to his father Leopold.

Murphy, L. B. (1937). *Social behaviour and child personality: An exploratory study of some roots of sympathy*. New York: Columbia University Press.

Murphy, K. (2013, April 20). A chat with Maya Angelou. *The New York Times*.

Obama, B. H. (2006, June). *Commencement address*. Speech presented at the Northwestern University Commencement, Evanston, IL.

Orwell, G. (1933). *Down and out in Paris and London*. London: Victor Gollancz Ltd.

Orwell, G. (1937). *The road to Wigan Pier*. London: Victor Gollancz Ltd.

Owen, W. (1917). Insensibility. In J. Silkin (Ed.), *The Penguin Book of first world war poetry* (2nd Edn. 1981). London.

Oxford English Dictionary. (2016). Oxford, UK: Oxford University Press.

Piaget, J. (1932). *The moral judgement of the child*. London: Routledge & Kegan Paul.

Pokorny, J., & de Waal, F. B. M. (2009). Face recognition in capuchin monkeys (*Cebus apella*). *Journal of Comparative Psychology, 123*, 151–160.

Rizzolatti, G., & Craighero, L. (2004). The mirror-neuron system. *Annual Review of Neuroscience, 27*, 169–192.

Rogers, C. R. (1957). The necessity and sufficient conditions of therapeutic personality change. *Journal of Consulting Psychology, 21*, 95–103.
Rogers, C. R. (1980). *A way of being*. Boston/New York: Houghton Mifflin Company.
Shakespeare, W. (1597). *Romeo and Juliet*.
Shakespeare, W. (1598). *Love's labour's lost*.
Shakespeare, W. (1608). *King Lear*.
Shakespeare, W. (1622). *Othello*.
Shelley, P. B. (1821). A defence of poetry. In M. Shelley (Ed.), *Essays, letters from abroad, translations and fragments*. In two volumes. London: Edward Moxon, 1840.
Smith, A. (1759). *The theory of moral sentiments*. Edinburgh: Andrew Millar.
Stein, E. (1917/1964). *On the problem of empathy* (trans: Stein, W.). The Hague, The Netherlands: Martinus Nijhoff (Originally published by Halle).
Stowe, H. B. (1852). *Uncle Tom's cabin*. Boston: John P Jewett & Co.
The Holy Bible: King James Version. Romans 12:15. Harper Collins.
Thoreau, H. D. (1910). *Walden*. London: Dent.
Titchener, E. B. (1909). *Lectures on the experimental psychology of the thought-processes*. New York: Macmillan.
Tolstoy, L. (1878). *Anna Karenina*. Moscow: The Russian Messenger.
Truax, C. B., & Carkhuff, R. (1967). *Towards effective counselling and psychotherapy training and practice*. Chicago: Aldine.
van Gogh, V. (1882, July 21). Letter from Vincent van Gogh to Theo van Gogh. *The Hague*.
van Gogh, V. (1885). *The potato eaters*. Amsterdam: van Gogh Museum.
Vischer, R. (1873). *On the optical sense of form: A contribution to aesthetics*. US: Mallgrave and Ikonomou.
Wilde, O. (1888). The selfish giant. In *The happy prince and other tales*. London/Edinburgh: Ballantyne Press.
Wispé, L. (1986). The distinction between sympathy and empathy: To call forth a concept, a word is needed. *Journal of Personality and Social Psychology, 50*, 314–321.

3

Emerging Empathy: A Developmental Perspective

Reclining in her baby bouncer chair, my daughter at a very young age would, quite contentedly and seemingly knowingly, observe the world going by. Her vigilance would lead people to comment on her 'social' skills of observation as if she knew exactly what was happening all around her. Years later and now as a teenager, my daughter is as sociable as ever and her friendships all-consuming. Educational pioneers such as Maria Montessori (1912) claimed: "Little children, from the moment they are weaned, are making their way toward independence" (p. 118), and identified birth to 3 years of age as a time when "the fundamental features of development which characterise the human potential are established through an unconscious absorbent mind" (1948, p. 90). This is a far cry from the 'decorticated' infant of the 1950s who was henceforth credited with psychological as well as physical needs and abilities. But how 'social' are children at these young ages? The evidence suggests the presence of not only a social but also a moral understanding of others at very young ages. But before looking at children's early understanding of emotions, let's look at what some have labelled as egocentric behaviour.

© The Author(s) 2018
H. Demetriou, *Empathy, Emotion and Education*,
https://doi.org/10.1057/978-1-137-54844-3_3

Early Confusion Between Self and Other: The Case of Egocentrism

Early writers depicted empathy as emerging once egocentrism has been relinquished, thereby enabling the child to differentiate between the self and others. For example, Baldwin (1897) wrote of three stages of growth. He named the first of these perspective-taking, which involves the differentiation between people and objects; the second subjective stage involves actions in the form of imitation when the child assimilates other experiences; and the final ejective stage occurs when the child becomes aware of other people. Furthermore, Hoffman's (1975) theory of empathy, although predominantly focusing on an affective, emotional basis, acknowledges the changes in empathy that are likely to occur with the emergence of new cognitive structures. Resultant "non-egocentric thought …implies the ability to anticipate what someone else might think or feel precisely when those thoughts and feelings are different from one's own" (Chandler & Greenspan, 1972, p. 105).

By psychoanalytic standards, the essential component of empathy which is thought to be lacking in the infant is the capacity to separate self from non-self. Spitz (1965) theorised that children are psychologically undifferentiated during the first 3 months of life and are unable to differentiate between their inner and outer worlds due to an inability to distinguish between id and ego. Also, Mahler (1968) suggested that it is due to the infant's incomplete separation-individuation and limitation in cognitive functions such as memory, thought, comprehension and conceptualisation that the empathic process is curtailed. In these terms, empathy consists of more than an immediate affective response; it requires significant ego development so that the capacity for empathy increases with age and experience. Psychoanalytic and neoanalytic theories portray the emergence of empathy in the context of the emotional intimacy shared by mother and infant (Burlingham, 1967; Freud, 1953), with some theorists going as far as suggesting that empathy is rooted in the umbilical unity between the infant and mother (Ferreira, 1961). Owing to the infant's dependence on the mother and the early symbiotic relationship between them, the child is viewed as being highly sensitive to variations in maternal affect and moods, with the result that a deep, mutual empathy results between mother and child. It is in the second year that the child's capacity for empathy increases in sophistication and scope with the growth of object relations and self-other differentiation.

Developmental psychologist Jean Piaget (1951) gave a classic example of deferred imitation of a temper tantrum by his 16-month-old daughter Jacqueline. Such observations of the development of imitation in infants and very young children led him to conclude that children reproduced the observed behaviour of others through a developmental progression of mechanisms ranging from what he called sensory-motor processes to representational thought. It was from his observations of young children's spontaneous language, their behaviour in collective games, and their responses to cognitive tasks, that Piaget concluded that social sensitivity is analogous to cognition in that it proceeds in a series of hierarchical stages. In order to assess the child's ability to take account of another's point of view in the literal sense, Jean Piaget and his colleague Bärbel Inhelder (1956) devised the 'Three Mountains' task which consisted of a model of three mountains and required 4- to 12-year-old children to select a picture which represented the viewpoint of a doll observing a mountain scene from different angles. Accuracy on these trials was found to be low up until the age of 9 years, and children below the age of 7 years tended to describe their own view of the landscape rather than the view as seen by the doll. This led Piaget (1966) to conclude that children younger than 7 years of age are consumed with extreme egocentricity and unable to differentiate the self from the non-self, so the child between 18 months and 7 years of age is predominantly egocentric, demanding, dependent, socially inept and "…unconsciously centred upon himself", and "experiences the greatest difficulty in entering into anyone else's point of view" (p. 216).

Piaget charted aspects of cognitive development into a stage-wise theory, including the cognitive dimension of empathy in his investigations. However, although Piaget made a case for the cognitive process of perspective-taking during childhood, it is important to note that he himself did not describe these processes as empathy per se. The closest Piaget came to describing empathy was through his assertion that forms of egocentrism were present during all cognitive stages of development and that perspective-taking skills were minimal until the emergence of concrete operational thought from around 7 years of age. He wrote of the child that "...his thought is isolated, and while he believes himself to be sharing the point of view of the world at large he is really still shut up in his own point of view. The social bond itself, by which the child is held...implies an unconscious intellectual egocentrism which is further promoted by the spontaneous egocentrism peculiar to all primitive mentality" (1932, p. 26). Furthermore, Piaget (1950) stated that the child between the ages of 18 months and 7 years of age "...cannot yet distinguish his point of view from that of others...[so that]...both on the social and on the physical plane, he is egocentric through ignorance of his own subjectivity" (p. 160).

At the level of cognitive operations, empathy depends on 'decentering', a term used by Piaget to describe the ability to take an objective view towards oneself through reflection. Specifically, Piaget suggested that the assimilation-accommodation cycle facilitates the transformation from infancy to maturity through changes in cognitive organisation, and that it is this differentiated route which marks the developmental progress from imitative precursors to maturely structured empathy. Until then, these egocentrically minded children are only capable of considering and appreciating their own point of view. By middle childhood from around 6 to 12 years of age, Piaget (1932) described children's social interactions as being essential to the development of mature relativistic moral thought. During this time he hypothesised that there was a decline in egocentrism and heightened sensitivity to the experience of others. A primary catalyst for these changes was thought to be the increased reciprocity and egalitarianism, which characterises peers' social interactions as more extensive, intense, and influential than those of the earlier years. Consequently, the child's increasing ability to co-ordinate social perspectives was thought to lead to an increased ability to be empathic. In particular, a major change occurs at 9 and 10 years with children's ability to co-ordinate their own point of view with the perspective of others, referred to as role-taking or perspective-taking. Piaget claimed that the first true conservation of feelings occurs at this time, thereby enabling the child to develop enduring sentiments for people, to become responsive to the needs of others, responsible for their own actions, and to develop meaningful friendships with peers.

The Piagetian tradition which depicted 6- or 7-year-old children as being egocentric without the capacity to distinguish between their own and others' views of social situations was widely accepted until researchers argued that previous failures to find evidence for role-taking in very young children were due to the complexity of the tasks Piaget used to measure that ability. This was illustrated by Hughes (1975) using a design with a greater degree of familiarity to the child. The task required a child to place a doll so that it is hidden from one and then from two policemen within two walls that intersected in the shape of a cross. Of the 3.5 to 5-year-olds who were given the task, 90% of their responses were correct, thereby implying that children are able to appreciate another's viewpoint much earlier than was previously thought when the context of the task is more familiar to the child. One attempt to challenge Piaget's notion of egocentrism introduced the concept of empathy into the literature on perspective-taking. Using experiments that were constructed with the aim to avoid problems caused by any lack of verbal ability in young children, Borke (1971) assessed the preschooler's understanding of the relations between situations and emotions using situation-based emotion-judgement tasks. Children were asked to indicate how a child in a given story felt by selecting a happy, sad, fearful, or angry face to complete the picture accompanying each story. Borke's results indicated that, through their depiction of situational information to infer a protagonist's emotion, children as young as 3 years of age were able to identify other people's feelings. She concluded that these results demonstrated an awareness on the part of very young children that others have feelings, and that these feelings are related to the situations in which the individuals find themselves. She chose to call this awareness 'empathy'. Refining methodological approaches to the research has confirmed that children younger than those identified by Piaget are able to interpret accurately others' facial emotions. Therefore, by minimising task demands and engaging the child in realistic and recognisable situations, children are given a greater opportunity to demonstrate their ability to consider another person's perspective—one of the traits of empathy.

Accentuating the Positive: Baby Morality and Social Skills

What is striking about the studies that follow is the extent to which children at very early ages understand and use social and emotional cues—for themselves but also for the needs of others. Studies have shown that infants distinguish and are biased towards others based on certain physical characteristics, behaviours and degree of familiarity. Perhaps even more impressive is that infants have been shown to be particularly sophisticated in the impressions they form of individuals based on how those individuals interact with others, seemingly distinguishing those who behave prosocially versus antisocially, and thereby displaying an understanding of helpful behaviour, or at least a bias towards it. Research has also uncovered infants' social competence and moral awareness. For example, an inherent social nature seems to be apparent even at very young ages when infants exhibit a preference for specific individuals. A social smile is apparent from 8 weeks when infants typically smile at a happy face and also differentiate between degrees of attractiveness, preferring to gaze at physically attractive faces and positive emotional expressions (Grossmann, Striano, & Friederici, 2007). Typically, 12-month-olds associate helping actions with attractive faces compared with associations of hindering actions with unattractive faces (Principe & Langlois, 2012); and children of this age expect consistency, so that a character who has previously approached another and helped, should do so again. Also, a developmental pattern reveals that the individuals that young infants choose to look at correspond with the individuals that older infants are likely to interact positively with, thereby providing evidence that older children's actual behaviours originate in infants' visual preferences (Langlois, Roggman, & Rieser-Danner, 1990).

When infants are observers of social behaviour, they are typically accurate judges of others' actions. Using computer-animated figures, Premack and Premack (1997) found that infants recognise and categorise actions that are prosocial, such as helpful and nurturing, versus those that are antisocial in nature, such as aggressive and hindering. At 6 and 10 months of age, infants are successful in socially evaluating the motivations of actors involved in positively and negatively motivated acts in that they show a preference for those who are helpful towards others in achieving their goals, compared with others who purposely hinder and who they tend to avoid (Wynn & Bloom, 2014). Such studies have revealed that 3-month-old infants are able to distinguish between the cooperative and uncooperative behaviours of puppet characters and give preferential treatment to the ones that display helpful behaviour. Such baby morality goes against the grain of the teachings of Freud, Piaget and Kohlberg and shows children to be morally sensitive at ages younger than previously thought. This preference for helpers over hinderers reflects an early moral mechanism but also arguably through being able to project their thoughts, an early empathy with the characters concerned. The presence of this seemingly innate moral-empathic quality in humans, can, if not exercised, dissipate and dissolve. The almost instinctive social preferences and appreciation of positive emotions are apparent in experiments that have measured a particular kind of understanding known as 'social referencing'. Such experiments have shown that infants seek affective cues from adults when in doubt in order to appraise a predicament, and during which infants become capable of attributing a meaning to an emotional expression. The so-called 'visual cliff' construction is a table with a transparent surface, half of which is covered and the other half exposed. The apparatus was originally constructed to investigate depth perception in a variety of species including humans (Gibson & Walk, 1960; Walk, 1966). James Sorce subsequently used the apparatus to gauge the effects of maternal emotional signalling towards their 1-year-old babies. A baby was placed on the covered or 'shallow' side and encouraged to crawl across to the side where the mother or caregiver was standing and where there appears to be a sheer drop, the point at which babies become unsure and are fickle about crossing. The age at which social referencing occurs, as shown by infants' abilities to regulate their willingness to risk visual cliffs in response to facial and vocal emotional expressions from mothers (Sorce & Emde, 1981), coincides with the age at which infants become adept at noting and following a caregiver's direction of gaze.

As a consequence of social referencing, infants detect the intentional object or target of a caregiver's emotional state, so that, if the caregiver expresses emotions such as fear or happiness when the infant approaches a particular object or location, the infant will modify its response to that target. For example, in a laboratory procedure conducted by Hirshberg (1990) when 12-month-olds were given happy, fearful and conflicting emotional signals by a parent with reference to five unusual toys, infants showed more positive and less negative affect and greater toy proximity with happy compared to fearful signals. Moreover, when conflicting emotions were expressed, infants did not select a signal but responded instead to both signals and thereby experienced conflict and confusion; and they showed greater negative and less positive affect and toy exploration with conflicting signals compared with separate episodes comprising happy and fearful signals. This result reflects claims that the early development of emotional empathy in children provides emotional and cognitive support for the subsequent internalisation of moral values and controls (Hoffman & Saltzstein, 1967). Although findings from social referencing studies imply that infants read and rely on a caregiver's emotion as an appraisal of a specific target, there is evidence to the contrary as described by Jenkins, Franco, Dolins and Sewell (1995). They studied children between 18 and 24 months of age who observed two people engaging in emotional displays of sadness and found that toddlers did not look towards their mothers when there were negative emotional exchanges. By the second year however, children display higher-order, self-conscious moral emotions that reflect their capacity to take on the perspective of another. Furthermore, they begin to develop an elementary behavioural control, which is essential to execute a desirable act.

Such research indicates that babies are able to understand and use others' emotions as signposts, which in turn provide them with security in times of uncertainty and ambiguity. The next sections will move on from a mere understanding of emotions for personal needs, to the taking on of those emotions in another person in some form of empathy, be it in a capacity where the child understands what that person is going through, or else, a more emotional form of empathy, where the child actually feels the emotion that another person is experiencing. It is important to realise at the outset that a variety of accounts have described the young child as having difficulty separating or distinguishing themselves from another person and confusing others' emotions with their own, thereby dismissing the fact that the young child can be empathic at all. However, what is clear from many of these conclusions is that they were based often on assessments or experiments that were not particularly 'child-friendly' or age-appropriate. When such considerations were taken into account, children have been found to exhibit clear forms of empathy and at younger ages than previously imagined.

Empathy's Capacity for Feeling, Understanding and Action

Empathy is a conflicting demand of intellect and evocation of feeling, a dynamic duo of cognition and emotion. Indeed, "Empathy is about standing in someone else's shoes, feeling with his or her heart, seeing with his or her eyes…it makes the world a better place" (Pink, 2008). Thus far we have looked at the degree to which young children can understand other people's emotions for their own benefit and also the extent to which they can appreciate the other person's viewpoint. We now examine the extent to which children are able to empathise with other people. Not merely understanding their emotion for self-fulfilling purposes or to understand the point of view of another, but to really understand and feel what others are experiencing. Such empathy takes two forms: one is a cognitive form of empathy otherwise known as perspective-taking, and the other is an affective form of empathy also known as vicarious emotion. Of striking coincidence is the almost identical distinction made between the dual nature empathy by Adam Smith (1759) and Herbert Spencer (1870) a century apart from each other.

Researchers have claimed that "Empathy is admittedly an elusive concept, difficult to define, and even more difficult to measure" (Feshbach, 1989, p. 101). It follows therefore that "…the difficulties evident in the conceptualisation of empathy are reflected in the methodological problems entailed in its assessment" (Feshbach, 1978, p. 10). With its concomitant cognitive and affective dimensions, and the subsequent array of definitions, the number of guises that are known as empathy make it difficult to specify one definition by which it can be measured. Indeed, conclusions from research on age and sex differences in empathy are inconsistent partly because empathy has been defined in a variety of ways. For example, the term 'empathy' has been used to refer to qualities including knowing what the other person is feeling (Dymond, 1949), feeling what another person is feeling (Eisenberg et al., 1989; Feshbach, 1975; Feshbach & Roe, 1968; Mehrabian & Epstein, 1972) and responding compassionately to another's distress (Batson, 1987). Despite being dynamically interdependent on one another, empathy's emotional and cognitive components can be researched and experienced separately. Theorists such as Freud (1958) and Piaget (1932) advocated that young children's egocentricity and lack of cognitive maturity inhibited empathy. That said, studies have shown that very young children are actually capable of responding with an empathic prowess previously unthought-of. Differences between the two types of empathy were noted by Murphy (1937) who claimed that "…the primitive sympathy of the baby who cries at the cry of another, and even the 4-year-old's overt responses to the distressed person are two different things" (p. 301). A clue to the triggers but also to the nature of these two forms of empathy lies in the longitudinal study by Bedford, Pickles, Sharp, Wright, and Hill (2015) whose toddlers at 5 months who exhibited a preference for human faces compared to a red ball were also those children at two and half years who displayed less callous and unemotional behaviours, as well as greater empathy through distress for another's distress, and overall better understanding of emotions.

The literature has generally regarded young infants' reactions to be limited and unhelpful to the distressed other in that they are not able to fully differentiate themselves from others and to have only the most basic emotion regulation capabilities. Rather than seemingly being able to detach themselves and show a 'constructive' type of empathy, young infants tend to become entrenched with the other's situation, confusing it with their own and in their confusion, employing strategies to assuage their own situation instead. However, during the second year, along with the differentiation of self-other and development of perspective-taking and emotion regulation, there is a shift from self-concern to an ability to project towards the other (Demetriou & Hay, 2004; Hay, Castle, Davies, Demetriou, & Stimson, 1999; Knafo, Zahn-Waxler, Van Hulle, Robinson, & Rhee, 2008). Research often uses the medium of distress to elicit empathy and identify what role distress plays in the ecology of toddlerhood, and measure the extent to which very young children address the distress of their companions. During infancy, feelings of personal distress in response to others' negative emotions have been assigned as the forerunners of empathic concern (Hoffman, 1975; Zahn-Waxler & Radke-Yarrow, 1990). The following passages describe research strategies that have attempted to depict empathy's development through its two distinct components of perspective-taking and vicarious emotion.

The Role of Cognition: The Developmental Course of Empathy as Perspective-Taking

Also described as *person perception, recognition of affect in others, social cognition,* and *role-taking,* this purely social cognitive conception of empathy has inspired considerable research. These terms all refer to a cognitive phenomenon with a research focus on the 'intellectual' processes of accurate perception of another's perspective (Dymond, 1949). Others have described perspective-taking as the "tendency to spontaneously adopt the psychological point of view of others" (Davis, 1983b, p. 114). This involves the ability to take on the perspective of another person and equips one with an awareness of another's thoughts, feelings, intentions and self-evaluations. However, it does not require an emotional response. An early formulation of empathy in predominantly cognitive terms appeared in the writings of George Herbert Mead (1934), whose theory supported the acquisition of social empathy through role-taking and imitation leading to "the capacity to take the role of the other and to adopt alternative perspectives vis-à-vis oneself" (p. 27). Many of the elements of Mead's exposition found experimental expression in Dymond's (1949) pioneering efforts to develop an objective measure of empathy. She viewed the empathic process as "…the imaginative transposing of oneself into the thinking, feeling, and acting of another and so structuring the world as he does" (p. 127). Moreover, Kohut (1971) defined empathy as "…a mode of cognition which is specifically attuned to the perception of complex psychological configurations" (p. 300), and he regarded introspection and empathy to be prerequisites of psychoanalytic observation. In an attempt to conceptualise the cognitive capacity of empathy, Redmond (1995) constructed a theoretical framework and measured the social judgement process through which an individual attempts to understand, respond to, or make sense of the thoughts, feelings, or perspective of another. He called this process *social or affective decentering* and described it as a means by which a person seeks to determine the effects of a given situation on another by taking the other's cognitive and emotional perspective. Overall, the ability to role-take has been regarded as the accurate assimilation and appreciation of another person's feelings (Goldstein & Michaels, 1985). For others, models such as the 'interpersonal inference model' developed by Flavell (1974) reflect an individual's awareness of another, their motivation to role-take, after which they make inferences, and conclude with some action towards the other.

Many studies of empathy during the childhood years have emphasised its cognitive dimension in the form of perspective-taking. Indeed, it has been noted that: "The 'cognitive' child was an acknowledged favourite of study by developmental psychologists in the 1950s and early 1960s, a time during which there was little advance in knowledge concerning the child's affective and social attributes" (Yarrow & Waxler, 1976, p. 118). Darwin (1872) claimed that facial expressions function to facilitate communication, the decoding of which hold important implications for social and emotional development. Thus, one of the initial steps in the development of social understanding is the ability to understand facial expression. A seemingly biological predisposition of the young child which functions to communicate mutuality and shared understanding with another person is the early awareness of facial signals through the newborn's interest in tongue protrusions and facial and vocal expressions of emotions and by the imitation of others' emotions (Meltzoff, 2007). Some have claimed (Atkinson, 2007) that infants' imitations of facial emotional expressions could be reflecting an internalisation of the other person's emotional experience. So the smile of the infant in response to another person's smile may have the effect of making the infant feel happy as a result of the smiling and in so doing experiences the shared happy emotions which over time become more spontaneously emotional. As well as developing the emotional side of empathy, such imitation has the power to enhance the cognitive side of empathy and develop theory of mind skills through engaging with and internalising others' experiences.

Newborns have been shown to discriminate and react in a variety of ways to different emotional expressions in face-to-face interactions (Haviland & Lelwica, 1987; Rigato, Menon, Johnson, & Farroni, 2011). Infants also develop an understanding of emotional signals in voices as well as faces. For example, studies of the effect of maternal vocalisation have shown infants to be selectively responsive to signals, so that at 5 months of age, expressions of positive affect are displayed in response to expressions of approval, and negative affect is detected in response to expressions of prohibition. With the emergence of joy, fear and anger, the child at 9 months is equipped with elation and anxiety, whilst the addition of angry moods marks the end of the first year. Further salient evidence of this kind is reflected in findings of the suppression of smiling by babies when they are confronted by a film of their mother's animated face rather than a live monitor. Also, newborns' preferences to faces over distractors (Frank, Vul, & Johnson, 2009) imply an innate mechanism sensitive to certain kinds of sensory input which gives rise to differential behaviours towards social and non-social objects.

A prerequisite to understanding others' emotions is an understanding of one's own social behaviour, and mirror image reaction experiments have shown that much self-exploratory behaviour takes place between 6 to 13 months of age. But this narcissistic attention does not render the child unconscious of others, as a study has shown that an interest in others' behaviours is apparent among 1-year-olds who looked longer at a peer through a one-way window than at their own image in the mirror (Cantor, Hay, Acker, & Pinkham, 1981). Studies have also shown that from 8 months, infants' responses to their mothers' and peers' distress reflect evidence of perspective-taking through attempts to label or understand the distress and ranging from simple verbal statements or enquiries to more complex inferences, which they called 'hypothesis-testing' (Davidov, Zahn-Waxler, Roth-Hanania, & Knafo, 2013; Roth-Hanania, Davidov, & Zahn-Waxler, 2011; Zahn-Waxler, Radke-Yarrow, Wagner, & Chapman, 1992). Also, an effect of age in the attainment of toddlers' cognitive abilities to empathise was identified by Zahn-Waxler, Robinson, and Emde (1992), who found increases between 14 and 20 months of age in hypothesis-testing, defined as exploration or attempts to comprehend distress, with corresponding significant decreases in unresponsiveness/indifference as children grew older.

During the second year of life and with the dawning of representational thought and the use of symbols, children are able to deduce the perspectives and feelings of others. Consequently, self-recognition and self-other differentiation develop, during which time the child's emotion language describes internal states. The second year is characterised by marked developmental changes, including the beginning of mutual interactions between peers. A study showed that 18- to 25-month-old toddlers exhibited perspective-taking with another's distress, even in the absence of obvious distress signals (Vaish, Carpenter, & Tomasello, 2009). From a theoretical standpoint, empathy could be viewed as a form of imitative behaviour or identification. On observing 2- to 5-year-olds' responses to another's distress, Bridges (1931) claimed that social development manifests itself from the imitation of another child's actions and words as, compared to the more sophisticated interventions of the older children, the younger ones were more likely to stare or perhaps cry in 'sympathetic imitation'. In the second and third years of life, the role of imitation for early socialisation has shown that whereas older children are more competent at imitation of conventional social behaviours such as mannerisms and expressive behaviours, younger children display imitation of affective and non-instrumental behaviours (Kuczynski et al., 2015).

With increasing cognitive development, children's comprehension of the feelings and thoughts of others ameliorates, and by 2 to 3 years of age, the first signs that children comprehend others' distress emerges. Indeed, by 3 years of age, children can understand the links between situations and the emotional reactions they provoke. Moreover, researchers have found that children are able to understand the concept of experiencing more than one emotion simultaneously (Harter & Buddin, 1987). During their preschool years, children of 2 to 3 years of age have been found to become increasingly adept at identifying emotion expressions and situations, whilst also becoming able to verbalise coherently and fluently about the causes of their own and others' emotions. Also, by this age, children use language to communicate not only about current emotions, but also about past and future emotions. In fact, during their third year, children become increasingly likely to talk about inner states and to ask questions about the cause and consequences of emotions, beliefs and desires. Such inner states appear increasingly in their narratives (Dunn, 1988) and in their excuses and justifications in conflict with others, so that they interweave their understanding of other people in their personal interactions in ways that markedly affect the quality of their relationships (Eisenberg, Spinrad, & Morris, 2014).

Children also talk about circumstances in the immediate environment that give rise to emotion and reveal that they understand the important feature of emotion through their recognition of it as a state that depends on the individual's appraisal of the intentional target. For example, studies confirm that 2- and 3-year-olds appreciate that individual emotional reactions to an outcome will diverge depending on the desires or preferences that those individuals bring to that outcome. Others have shown that preschoolers can identify positive and negative emotions, displaying both non-egocentric and inferential abilities to understand others' feelings (Denham, 1986; Widen & Russell, 2010). Moreover, Wellman, Harris, Banerjee, and Sinclair (1995) demonstrated that, when 2- to 4-year-olds explain how an emotion has arisen, they refer to the intentional object of the emotion. A landmark in the naturalistic investigation of children's reactions to their peers' distress was a study devised by Lois Murphy (1937). This focused on 55 2- to 4-year-old nursery school children's sympathetic responses to their peers' distress and achieved this through a mixed method approach of 432 hours of observation, teacher ratings, experiments and parent reports. Using objective diary records of responses to distress as they occurred in the playground, Murphy noted the types of distress that initiated sympathetic responses and the subsequent responses to the different distress situations. In particular, the most common stimuli for sympathetic reactions to distress were physical causes such as an accident, or emotional distress such as the snatching of a toy. Responses to distress were classified as either 'social and sympathetic' or 'egocentric and unsympathetic'. Among the former category, although the emphasis rests mainly on children's direct interventions towards the alleviation of distress, an 'emotional identification type' of sympathy was noted which incorporated children's questions about the distress such as "Why is he crying?", arguably a forerunner to perspective-taking in the child's attempt to understand the distress. A description of such a behaviour was given by Murphy on 19th January 1934: "Wallis had been playing with Holden near a low slide; then they played with a ball. Wallis threw the ball to Daniel, then into the air. Daniel fell and cried. Wallis to L. B. M. (Murphy): 'Look, look, he's crying; see, he's crying'" (1937, p. 101).

In an attempt to examine children's understanding of others' impromptu emotional reactions, Fabes, Eisenberg, Nyman and Michealieu (1991) interviewed 62 3- to 5-year-olds. The accuracy of children's appraisals varied with age and the type and intensity of emotion. Children identified positive emotions most accurately although they struggled to identify the underlying causes of those positive emotions. Picture-story measures involve structured situations that provide opportunities for children to react to a story character's emotions. Generally, a positive relation is apparent with age and picture-story indices among children of 4 to 7 years of age. Moreover, when children are given perspective-taking tasks of a perceptual and conceptual nature, such as those presented by Zahn-Waxler, Radke-Yarrow, and Brady-Smith (1977) to 102 3- to 7-year-olds, results typically indicated significant age effects on performance. However, other studies (Marcus et al., 1985) have instead revealed either a stable trend or a decrease in empathy with age. Either way, 4 years of age has been shown to be significant for a specific type of perspective-taking known as 'theory of mind'.

Theory of Mind: A Special Case of Perspective-Taking

The cognitive, perspective-taking dimension of empathy is also sometimes referred to as 'theory of mind' (Premack & Woodruff, 1978) which is the ability to understand the mental states of others. It is central to socialisation as it allows individuals to comprehend the intentions, beliefs, desires and motivations of others in order to accurately imagine another's experience when it differs from one's own. It is an important skill to foster in education as it contributes to empathising with others, understanding and predicting people's actions and making moral judgments. Based on the assumption that children need some understanding of others' mental states in order to understand their emotional reactions, attempts have been made to link perspective-taking with research that has aimed to tap children's understanding of others' minds (Astington, Harris, & Olson, 1988). A developmental landmark has been identified at the ages of 4 to 5 years when children typically become capable of taking another's perspective as measured by false-belief tasks, which is a frequently used indicator of theory of mind development (Wellman, Cross, & Watson, 2001). The tasks typically involve showing children a scenario involving two characters. One of the characters is shown placing an item in a given location and leaves the room; the second character arrives subsequently and takes the item to a new location. The child is then shown the first character re-entering the room and asked where they will look for the item. The child equipped with a theory of mind should respond with the original location rather than the actual location, thereby indicating a capacity to view the situation from the other person's perspective. The development of a theory of mind facilitates the perspective-taking ability of empathy so that one's own experiences are superseded by another person's experience. The early emotional empathy that caused confusion in the child, not only about the experiences the other person was going through, is now accompanied by the cognitive empathy that enables an appreciation of the other person's perspective. Such perspectives also provide a greater platform for the child to attempt to help. So whereas the previous emotional empathy may have made the child sit up and take note, the additional presence of the cognitive component now alerts the need for assistance.

The Role of Affect: The Developmental Course of Empathy as Vicarious Emotion

The conceptualisation of empathy with emotional facets emphasises a vicarious affective emotional response to the perceived emotional experiences of others based on the apprehension and experiencing of another's emotional state or condition (Stotland, 1969). Consequently, empathy has been variously defined as "feeling any vicarious emotion, feeling the same emotion that another person is feeling, or feeling a vicarious emotion that is congruent with but not necessarily identical to the emotion of the other". This view was taken by Watson (1938) in a paper on the nature of insight in which he said that accurate insight entailed sharing the feeling of the person who is being observed. William James claimed that "the most immutable barrier in nature is between one man's thoughts and another's" and in his 1884 article 'What is an Emotion?' favoured a behavioural approach. In a similar way to Charles Darwin (1872) and William James (1884) before him, Lipps (1903) viewed empathy as an isomorphic 'motor mimicry' response during which the observation of another's affect leads to automatic imitation with slight changes in posture and facial expression, resulting in inner kinaesthetic cues that contribute to the experiencing of another's affect.

Affect, like the adjective *affective*, refers to the experience of feeling or emotion. Piaget (1981) noted: "The term, affectivity includes feelings, properly so-called, as well as the various drives or tendencies including 'higher tendencies' such as the will" (p. 2). The experimental psychology of the nineteenth century began with investigations of perception and during the middle of the century was still almost exclusively concerned with cognitive processes. At this time, it seldom occurred to the investigator to consider the influence of the social experience of participants or even the social influence exerted by the experimenter or people in contact with them. By the middle of the century however, social theorists had promoted the demand for a discussion of the influence of individuals upon one another. Since the 1960s, empathy has been assigned this more emotional meaning, and by the late 1970s, the concept was defined even more narrowly to refer to one specific set of congruent emotions, namely those feelings that are more other-focused than self-focused. In the realm of psychoanalysis Kohut (1977) claimed that "the idea itself of an inner life of man, and thus of a psychology of complex mental states, is unthinkable, without our ability to know via vicarious introspection – my definition of empathy" (p. 306). This affective component provides a bridge between the feelings of one person with those of another, and is consistent with the other's emotional state or condition. In an attempt to explain the origins of the vicarious emotional response, Hoffman (1987) suggested that vicarious arousal might occur through the association of another's distress cues with similar personal experiences.

Emotional empathy is the vicarious experiencing of another's emotional state that children may experience in some form as early as infancy and toddlerhood. During his observations of early forms of what could be termed empathy, Darwin (1872) found that infants respond to emotions in others almost from birth. He explained these as being inborn species-specific patterns and claimed that "…when we witness any deep emotion, our sympathy is so strongly excited, that close observation is forgotten or rendered almost impossible…" (p. 358). As a result of his observations of a 6-month-old infant, Darwin (1872) wrote "…an innate feeling must have told him that the pretend crying of his nurse expressed grief; and this, through the instinct of sympathy, excited grief in him…[so that the infant]… instantly assumed a melancholy expression" (p. 358). Subsequently, John Watson continued this mode of investigation through his attempts to define the emotional make-up of the newborn and to demonstrate conditioned emotional responses in infants (Watson & Rayner, 1920).

Reflexive crying in newborns could be said to be precursors to empathic responding. The first weeks of a child's life are characterised by an affective form of empathy when babies cry as a result of an awareness of another baby's distress (Darwin, 1877; Sagi & Hoffman, 1976). Simner (1971) found that when 2-day-old babies were exposed to other babies' cries versus computer simulations of babies' cries, they would only cry with spontaneous anxiety in response to the authentic cries rather than a variety of stimuli, including silence, white noise, simulated cries, non-human cry sounds and their own cries, thereby arguably conveying the existence of an inborn empathy mechanism. This reflexive or reactive crying, matching of negative emotion, and displaying of distress reactions of an infant as a primitive empathic response is debatable as the crying might merely reflect either emotional contagion or personal distress, thereby hinting at a biological disposition for responding empathically to others' negative emotions in the form of distress. Further evidence of early vicarious emotion at 6 months of age has been shown in an investigation by Hay, Nash, and Pedersen (1981). They observed pairs of infants in a playroom with toys in the presence of their mothers, and examined interactive episodes that began when an infant touched the peer or a toy held by the peer. Observations revealed that infants of this age match their peers' overtures on being touched, and this was especially likely to occur in the absence of toys when contact episodes were more frequent. In a laboratory experiment, 9-month-old infants watched their mothers express facial and vocal sadness during a 2-minute emotion-induction period after which mothers continued to express sadness whilst their infants played with four sets of toys. Infant emotion expressions were analysed using the Max (Izard, 1979) and Affex (Izard, Hembree, Dougherty, & Spizziri, 1983) coding systems. Moreover, infant behaviour during play was coded with a system developed by Belsky and Most (1981), and the amount of time that infants looked at their mothers was also measured. Results showed that infants displayed more sadness, anger, less play and gaze aversion during the sadness condition, compared with conditions in which mothers expressed happiness.

A series of cross-sectional home-observational studies were conducted in which mothers were trained to observe and record their children's responses to naturally occurring expressions of emotion. Despite orienting and exhibiting personal distress, few of these 10-month-olds acted constructively to relieve another's distress (Zahn-Waxler, Radke-Yarrow & King, 1979). Responses of 8- to 20-month-olds to naturally occurring and simulated expressions of anger, affection and distress reveal that by around 1 year of age, children are not only aware of others' emotions, but they are also likely to experience an emotional reaction to them (Cummings, Zahn-Waxler, & Radke-Yarrow, 1981; Roth-Hanania, Davidov, & Zahn-Waxler, 2011). Moreover, the study by Zahn-Waxler et al. (1992) in which monozygotic and dizygotic twin pairs of 14 and 20 months of age were filmed in home and laboratory settings for their reactions to simulations of distress found that empathic responding in the form of vicarious affect increased with age.

Defined by Feshbach and Roe as a vicarious affective response, empathy was investigated using their Feshbach Affective Situation Test of Empathy (FASTE: Feshbach & Roe, 1968). This is a picture-story measure which consists of four pairs of narrated slide sequences showing children in situations designed to elicit happiness, sadness, anger and fear.

Of the 5- to 8-year-old children who were asked about their feelings, and whose responses were rated on the degree to which they matched the affect of the child featured in a slide sequence, the older children were more able to share the feelings and emotions of story characters. Other investigations have attempted to assess the degree of 5- to 13-year-old children's concordant emotions in response to observed emotions of stimulus vignettes from documentaries (Strayer, 1993). Having viewed films, the children were interviewed about them so that the degree of affect match could be ascertained. Only slight increases with age were evident in concordant emotion and the protagonist's emotional intensity correlated with children's emotional intensity and affect match. As well as recording children's self-reported emotions, some investigators rate children's facial expressions and gestures whilst they observe films of the enactment of others in affect-laden situations. Alternatively, reactions are assessed whilst children respond to picture-story measures of empathy. For example, lifelike distress situation experiments by Zahn-Waxler, Friedman, and Cummings (1983) examined the facial and gestural responses of 4- to 11-year-olds when confronted with a person in distress with the result that an increase in facial and gestural reactions was found with age. Similar results have been shown of a positive relation between age and reports of fear in response to viewing a film of a fearful other. However, film depiction experiments by Solomon (1985) have found decreases in facial reactions from 5 to 11 years, and in studies of 4- to 5-year-olds and 7- to 8-year-olds by Kuchenbecker (1977), no age-related changes in facial expression were extrapolated.

Questionnaire measures have also been widely used with school-aged children. Among these, although more than one type of empathic reaction in terms of sympathetic concern, role-taking, and general emotionality is assessed, the emphasis generally rests on the vicarious aspect of empathy. Examples of these are the Bryant (1982) modified version of the Mehrabian and Epstein (1972) scale which measures the trait (rather than state) of empathy, the Davis (1983b) scale of sympathetic concern and the empathy subscale on the Junior Eysenck Personality Questionnaire, which also measures impulsiveness and enterprising nature (Eysenck, Easting, & Pearson, 1984). These measures have generally revealed age-related increases in scores of empathy in the early school years. However, as with other measures, results are not clear-cut. For example, whereas S. Eysenck et al.'s (1984) questionnaire has generated no coherent age differences in empathy between the ages of 8 and 15 years, Kalliopuska (1980) found an age-related increase in scores on the Mehrabian and Epstein (1972) questionnaire among 9- to 11-year-old Finnish children, but decreases in scores from 11 to 12 years.

Self-report techniques of temporary affect in experimental contexts that have operationalised empathy as the report of emotional arousal consistent with another's state have found that children in their middle childhood and adolescent years express more sadness than those in the preschool years (Strayer, 1985). And using the medium of television, the emotional responses in the form of self-reports of emotion and facial expressions of 8- to 11-year-olds to the social content were examined when the children were shown factual and fictional television programmes that depicted family conflict (Huston et al., 1995). Children overwhelmingly displayed vicarious emotion on viewing the programmes, thus reflecting the emotions of the people they watched. In an experiment by Chisholm and Strayer (1995) which examined 9- to 11-year-old girls' emotional and empathic responses to emotional stimuli using both verbal and nonverbal measures, facial expressions were filmed unobtrusively whilst they viewed six stimulus vignettes individually during which they were required to press a button to indicate awareness of emotional arousal whilst viewing the stimuli. Expressive responses at button presses were micro-analytically analysed using Affex (Izard et al., 1983) and post-viewing interviews assessed children's reported emotions and the empathy between children's reported emotion for themselves and the stimulus characters. Findings showed links between children's reported and facially displayed emotions as well as links between their verbal and facial empathy scores. Additional evidence that suggests an increase in emotional reactions with age has emerged with the employment of physiological measures such as electromyography (EMG) which monitor vicarious responding through muscle arousal and temperature levels. Also, vicarious affect via heart rate patterns has been measured in response to others' emotions (Fink, Heathers, & de Rosnay, 2015; Tully, Donohue, & Garcia, 2014).

Other Classifications of Emotional Empathy: *Sympathy, Personal Distress* and *Emotional Contagion*

There is often confusion between the constructs of empathy and sympathy, but in fact, they are different processes with different implications and consequences. Lipps's choice of the term *Einfühlung* contrasts with the term *Mitfühlung* (feeling along with others) and thereby distinguishes the processes of empathy and sympathy. Greenson (1960) differentiated between sympathy and empathy, highlighting the condolence, agreement and pity necessary for sympathy whilst articulating empathy as a special mode of perceiving he termed 'emotional knowing', which is a consequence of experiencing another's feelings. Other attempts to distinguish between the two constructs have been proposed by Wispé (1986) when she claimed that: "In empathy, the empathiser reaches out for the other person. In sympathy, the sympathiser is moved by the other person. In empathy, we substitute ourselves for the others. In sympathy we substitute others for ourselves. To know what it would be like if I were the other person is empathy. To know what it would be like to be that other person is sympathy" (p. 318). Through its definition as an other-oriented emotional reaction to others' emotional circumstances which leads to the accurate appraisal of another's emotional condition, sympathy has been regarded as a form of social competence (Eisenberg, 1986), and has moreover been empirically related to prosocial behaviour (Eisenberg & Fabes, 1991).

Alternatively, personal distress is the individual's vicarious experience of emotion that may be experienced as self-concern. Because the focus of the emotion is on the self rather than on the other, this type of response is unlikely to generate concern for another or to promote helpful behaviour. Moreover, if someone feels that they do not have the capacity to cope with another's experience of suffering, their defensive response to avoid exposure to that suffering results in an internalising personal distress reaction. In this respect, personal distress is a self-focused, aversive reaction to the vicarious experience of another's emotion that may manifest itself as discomfort or anxiety (Eisenberg, Eggum, & Di Giunta, 2010). The general rule of thumb is that the greater the distress of the victim, the greater the empathic distress displayed by the observer. Such overwhelming levels of empathy occur voluntarily when the observer's empathic distress becomes so painful and intolerable and results in intense feelings of personal distress, which, as Hoffman (1978, 2000) proposed may prohibit the person's capacity for empathy. Emotional contagion on the other hand, is a response that refers to the vicarious experience of an affect that matches the emotion of another, feeling in the same way to another person, and sometimes referred to as affective resonance (de Waal, 2008). It is measured by techniques in which empathy is operationalised as the degree of match between an individual's response and the emotion of another. The importance of the affective dimension of empathy is evident in McDougall's (1908) description of a 'primitive passive sympathy' of emotional contagion that sometimes takes place in group situations, and also in Sullivan's (1953) description of the emotional communication between infant and mother. For both McDougall and Sullivan, the empathic reaction is an undifferentiated, fairly automatic, essentially unlearned emotional reaction.

Synthesising Affect and Cognition: The Coming Together of Feeling and Understanding

Bringing the affective and cognitive elements of empathy together produces an "…ability to experience and understand what others feel without confusion between oneself and others" (Decety & Lamm, 2006, p. 1146). Starting with perspective-taking as enabling the noticing and appraising another's experience and leading to empathic concern or personal distress that are the consequences of that noticing and appraising and where empathic concern is an "…other-oriented emotional response elicited by and congruent with the perceived welfare of a person in need" (Batson & Ahmad, 2009, p. 6). From the psychoanalytic viewpoint, empathy has been perceived as an affective consequence of the mechanism of identification by Fenichel (1946) who stated that it "…consists of two acts: (a) an identification with the other person, and (b) an awareness of one's own feelings after the identification, and in this way an awareness of the object's feelings" (p. 511). Others have recommended the use of empathy as a psychoanalytic technique due to its capacity to provide 'immediate comprehension' and '… insider knowledge that is almost first-hand'. Others' observations emphasise a distancing from the object whilst, at the same time, maintaining the quality of sameness of affect assumed by the individual. Therefore, whilst empathy leads to feeling 'one with the object', 'individuality and perspective' is also maintained. Furthermore, the transient identification through empathy of one's own personality into that of another in order to achieve a better understanding leads to a temporary sense of oneness with the object, followed by a sense of segregation in order to appreciate that one has felt not only *with* the patient but *about* him.

Benjamin Bloom et al.'s (1956) taxonomy of affect describes how individuals' affective reactions form the foundations for cognitive shifts, and also vice versa, so that affective reactions can be initiated by cognitive thoughts. Over the years, theorists and researchers have argued over how, when, where and why the two main components of empathy work. Some have seen them as entities that work independently, whilst others have debated the order of events. Does perspective-taking come first in order to understand another's situation and then followed by an emotional empathy with an appropriate response? Or does the onlooker respond emotionally at the outset and use these emotions to help them take the perspective of the other? Theorists such as Piaget considered affect and intellect to be opposite sides of the same coin, and have favoured the cognitive component. Similarly, indexes of empathy have tended to centre on one or other of the empathic dimensions, an example of which is the Mehrabian and Epstein (1972) questionnaire which measures emotional empathy. However, an increasing band of interest regards affect and cognition as interacting in most phases of the empathic process. So that, whereas cognition *acts*, affect *energises*; so that the understanding of another's feelings may be motivated by our own affective responses to them. The changing face of empathy has led to the production of multidimensional instruments, such as the Interpersonal Reactivity Index by Davis (1983b), which includes four subscales designed to measure empathy fantasy, perspective-taking, empathic concern and personal distress. This scale has since been adapted for children aged 8 to 9 years, resulting in a 'Feeling and

Thinking' 12-item measure (Garton & Gringart, 2005). Indexes such as this were inspired by two developmental theorists in particular, who incorporated these action and energising alternatives into models in order to explain the multifaceted nature of the empathic response. These theorists were Martin Hoffman and Norma Feshbach, and the year was 1975.

Martin Hoffman's empathic process is predominantly affective in nature, however, he also incorporated a cognitive component in his developmental model of empathy (Hoffman, 1975). The model begins with a subjective experience of vicarious affective response to others as in the newborn *reactive cry* which reflects a "…combination of mimicry and conditioning, with each getting an assist from imitation" (Hoffman, 2000, p. 65). The young infant's failure to differentiate self from other is regarded by Hoffman as a primitive form of *egocentric* empathy when the 1- to 2-year-old confuses the distress of a peer with that of their own and in whom the distress of others provokes similar feelings of distress. In Hoffman's view, this vicarious affective reaction to another's distress is bound up with Piagetian egocentrism so that the child is of futile assistance to the peer as the distress manifests in the previously non-distressed child. Moreover, these children provide assistance with a view to alleviating their own distress so that their attempts to help may consist of offering comfort in a form that the child would personally seek. For example, an infant might offer their own toy to a distressed adult. This genuine confusion about who exactly is in distress led to the oxymoronic coining of the term *egocentric empathic distress*. Early in the second year, the development of a sense of self prompts the child to attempt to help the distressed other, but with their perspective in mind, such as bringing another crying child to *their* mother instead of the child's own mother. The desire to help is there—the downside is that it is from the child's own point of view. A milestone that occurs late in the second year "…has all the basic elements of mature empathy and continues to grow and develop throughout life" (Hoffman, 2000, p. 72). At this point, children begin to display a distinction between others' inner states and those of their own. Corrective feedback features here and indeed into adulthood, when for example, one's egocentric efforts to relieve another's distress fall short and instead lead to behaviour that succeeds in taking the other's perspective into account. Thereafter, by late childhood to early adolescence, empathic distress becomes more refined, extended and is able to transcend one's immediate experience. Hoffman's developmental model of empathy thereby encompasses cognitive, affective and motivational components. Empathic behaviour is primarily affective but subsequently incorporates a cognitive competence thereby heralding a change from early affective vicarious responding to cognitive perspective-taking.

Visualising the emergence of empathy somewhat differently, Norma Feshbach took the cognitive mechanism as a starting point. Her 1975 amalgamation of the two components represents empathy as an emotional response that incorporates cognitive skills such as the ability to label another's emotional state. This is illustrated in her model of empathy which contains three components of empathy, two of which are cognitive and one of which is affective. The first component, at the most primitive cognitive level, is the ability to discriminate and label affective states of others. The second cognitive component involves the ability to assume the perspective and role of another person. The third component is emotional responsiveness when the child is able to experience the positive or negative emotion that is being witnessed in order to share that emotion. Moreover, Feshbach promoted her argument for integration when she went on to say that "…when empathy is defined solely in cognitive terms, it appears to have little theoretical utility beyond that contributed by the cognitive functions themselves; that is, empathy becomes a concept without surplus meaning or special theoretical properties" (1978, p. 7). Despite differences in their developmental models of empathy, Hoffman and Feshbach concurred that, as well as containing both cognitive and affective components, the empathic process leads to action. Sometimes however, the differing developmental trajectories for these two forms of empathy may lead to social dysfunction and atypical empathy development.

When Empathy Doesn't Emerge: Empathy Imbalances from Autism to Psychopathy

Conditions have been identified where the capacity for empathy is limited: where the energy and/or the identification for an emotion in another person is lacking and curtails or prohibits any form of helpful behaviour;

but also where the type of empathy varies according to the specific condition and thereby lends itself to the nature of condition. Two such conditions that will be described in which aspects of empathy are limited and even absent include autism and psychopathy.

The aforementioned cognitive empathic perspective-taking known as 'theory of mind' is acquired by most of us at a specific age; but when it isn't, gives a clue to the internal workings of the empathic system. Theory of mind development has both social and educational implications, as its development is key for both the proficiency of social skills and also critical thinking. Whereas a typically developing child will acquire a theory of mind by the age of about 4 years, children on the autistic spectrum for whom social situations can be bewildering and overwhelming find the aforementioned tasks challenging and indeed fail to acquire theory of mind even past the age of 4 years (Baron-Cohen, Leslie, & Frith, 1985). But of course, and worthy of note from the person after whom the high-functioning autistic condition of Asperger syndrome was named: "Not everything that steps out of line, and thus 'abnormal', must necessarily be 'inferior'" (Hans Asperger, 1938). However, when empathy is brought into the equation, studies have shown that infants of 20 months with autism are less likely to respond and show concern for others in distress and exhibit impairments in tasks that require social gaze compared to their typically developing counterparts (Charman, Swettenham, Baron-Cohen, Cox, Baird, & Drew, 1998). The acquisition of theory of mind brings with it social and emotional awareness, critical thinking skills, and skills that involve perspective-taking, rational and objective judgements (Lecce, Caputi, & Pagnin, 2014). But when high-functioning children with autism are tested on empathy-related tasks that involve discriminating the affective states of others, perspective-taking and emotional response, they perform less well than their typically developing peers. The specific dimension of empathy that is lacking appears to be the cognitive rather than the emotional component, as found in research with adults with Asperger's. Such findings are consistent with theory of mind understanding in autism. The individual as a consequence exhibits difficulty in *understanding* and appreciating the ideas, feelings, or behaviours of others. Through the use of a photo-based measure called the Multifaceted Empathy Test (MET), Dziobek et al. (2008) assessed the different components of empathy in a group of 17 individuals with Asperger syndrome and 18 well-matched controls. Results showed that although individuals with Asperger's were impaired in cognitive empathy, they did not differ from controls in emotional empathy. Furthermore, rather than lacking empathy, Markram and Markram (2010) claim that despite often having a social naivety, people with autism spectrum disorders such as Asperger's often feel others' emotions too intensely to the degree that they are unable to cope with them. It seems that the emotional empathy that they possess gives way to overwhelming feelings that hamper any kind of caring or helpful behaviour as the individual will typically withdraw from the situation.

Autism spectrum disorders can be identified in infancy through deficiencies in social interaction and reciprocal communication, as well as limited and specific interests, behaviours that involve repetition and thought processes that are rule-based. And in fact, empathy deficits are one of the criteria used for diagnosing the disorder using the Diagnostic and Statistical Manual of Mental Disorders (DSM-5, 2013). Such characteristics are particularly prevalent in the autistic male brain and suggests that autism may be a variant of normal male intelligence, with an overreliance on, and extreme preference for, predictable, systematic situations not always typical in the social world (Baron-Cohen, 2002). This theory is supported by the predominance of males to females diagnosed with autism spectrum disorders (Jacquemont et al., 2014) as well as sex differences among typically developing individuals favouring females to males in social areas such as mindreading and empathy. Investigations into the neural underpinnings of empathy deficits in individuals with autism spectrum disorders have revealed dysfunction in various regions of the brain important for empathy. Some findings have shown mirror neuron system dysfunction in people with autism spectrum disorders (Dapretto et al., 2006; Oberman & Ramachandran, 2007) and its salience to the perspective-taking side of empathy. There is also evidence that individuals with autism spectrum disorders show amygdala dysfunction, which has been linked with the emotional experience of empathy (Ashwin, Baron-Cohen, Wheelwright, O'Riordan, & Bullmore,

2007; Baron-Cohen, 2004; Blair, 2008). Other research among individuals with autism has revealed the condition of alexithymia, present among half of people with autism and where there is gaze avoidance towards areas of the face that display emotion as characterised by an impairment of emotional processing (Bird & Cook, 2013). Predominantly however, research points to a cognitive basis for empathy dysfunction in such individuals, which may give a clue to procedures for improving the ability to empathise in individuals with autism spectrum disorders.

From a lack of understanding of another's situation through the perspective-taking side of empathy, we now turn to conditions of psychopathy that lack instead the vicarious emotion of people devoid of feeling, recounted eloquently by Reisel (2013) "…as though they knew the words but not the music of empathy". Psychopathy is typically characterised by a lack of empathy and guilt, as well as the presence of antisocial behaviours (Baron-Cohen, 2011). However, whereas autism spectrum disorders typically involve deficits in cognitive empathy, individuals with psychopathy are characterised by deficits in emotional empathy. So that, where studies have failed to find theory of mind impairments in individuals with psychopathy (Dolan & Fullam, 2004), by contrast, psychopathically diagnosed individual's physiological responses to distress cues are milder and fewer, with deficits in their ability to recognise facial affect such as fear (Blair et al., 2004; Hastings, Tangney, & Stuewig, 2007). A study by Mullins-Nelson, Salekin, and Leistico (2006), for example, found emotional deficits in psychopathy and correlations with perspective-taking and antisocial behaviour in a community sample using the Psychopathic Personality Inventory Short Form to assess psychopathy along with psychological measures to test empathy that included the Interpersonal Reactivity Index, the Diagnostic Analysis of Nonverbal Accuracy, and the Test of Self-Conscious Affect. Neuroscientific research with psychopathic individuals has shown dysfunction in empathy-related brain areas, particularly those of the limbic and paralimbic system and specifically the amygdala (Shirtcliff et al., 2009). As a consequence of such limited empathy, and despite understanding others' perspectives, such individuals display a lack of emotion and concern for the feelings, needs, or suffering of others as well as an absence of remorse after harming or mistreating another. The role of the amygdala in emotional processing and empathic reactions is evident when it lights up in experiments as subjects are viewing different emotions. The typical psychopath will be more than able to label the emotion but will not display a physiological or emotional response. The psychopathic personality also gives a clue to the motivation for prosocial behaviour, in that although the cognitive component of empathy is in place, the missing emotional element hampers the person's ability to feel along with the other's situation and thereby inhibiting prosocial behaviour. Emotional empathy therefore seems to play an important part in at least abating antisocial behaviour; so in its absence, cognitive empathy alone tips the balance towards behaviours that can be threatening and consequently and ironically turns the whole concept of empathy on its head. Atkins and Parker (2012) contended that a person might take the perspective of another and fully understand that the other is suffering, but fail to respond appropriately if they appraise the person as irrelevant to their agenda or themselves in some way. This personalised, internalised, self-serving response reflects a cold, distant perspective-taking of understanding the other without really caring about them. Moreover, if an appraisal is made that the other is deserving of their suffering, then other emotions such as anger or disgust may creep in.

Such examples of autism and psychopathy provide us with a glimpse of only two conditions that lack particular components of empathy. Their conditions are indicative of fully functioning empathy as a multidimensional construct comprising the cognitive and emotional, where the presence of both components is necessary in promoting healthy balanced social functioning. When one or the other is missing, be it the cognitive or the emotional, there is an empathic disparity, imbalance or void. Other conditions that exhibit imbalances and deficiencies of empathy are disorders with antisocial, schizoid and narcissistic characteristics, and William's syndrome, just some examples the characteristics of which, rather than leading to altruistic behaviours or self-serving egoistic reactions, instead can result in a complete absence of empathy, and in some cases with serious repercussions. However, even in the presence of 'complete' empathy, resulting behaviours can be either egoistic or altruistic or both, and these will now be described in turn.

Feeling and Identifying with an Emotion—But also Acting on It

The powerful force of empathy and its consequences for action has been researched widely "…empathy is the art of stepping imaginatively into the shoes of another person, understanding their feelings and perspectives, and using that understanding to guide your actions" (Krznaric, 2015). But are those actions necessarily positive and does the mechanism behind empathy always drive us to perform in a helpful manner? Empathy is a force that can spark a range of behaviours from malevolence to benevolence, not least inflicting pain on a perpetrator causing distress towards another person and prioritising punishing the perpetrator over helping the victim (Buffone & Poulin, 2014). Here we look at the egoistic as well as the altruistic motives behind empathy. Given that our ability to interact with others affects our daily lives, the importance of understanding interpersonal relations through the socialisation of empathy is beyond question. Empathy is an important competence in our social world, a motivator of prosocial behaviour that develops throughout the first year of life, and typically, children with a greater awareness of both positive and negative emotions are more socially skilled (Saliquist, Eisenberg, Spinrad, Eggum, & Gaertner, 2009). The enhancement of social life is thought to be made possible through the mediating role of empathy (Iannotti, 1985; Segal, 2011). But does an empathic connection or thought always lead to a positive and helpful reaction? Or can an empathic reaction actually lead to an unproductive response, as when the onlooker has taken on an affective vicarious empathic reaction and instead internalises the thoughts of the other resulting in personal distress?

The constant and copious experiences of empathy over the centuries have prompted researchers to consider the motivation behind it. Some researchers have suggested that witnessing another person in need can lead to the two qualitatively distinct emotional responses of empathy as feeling with the other and personal distress as feeling for oneself (Batson, Eklund, Chermok, Hoyt, & Ortiz, 2007). McDougall (1908) made a distinction between the 'tender emotion' of empathy and the 'sympathetic pain' of personal distress, contending that the former led to concern for the welfare of others compared with the latter which led to concern for one's own welfare. Similarly, Batson (1987) defined empathy as an emotional response elicited by and congruent with the perceived welfare of another, whereas he defined personal distress as a self-concerned reaction to the vicarious experiencing of another's emotion. Moreover, researchers have suggested that these distinct emotional responses can lead to two qualitatively different kinds of motivation to help. Whilst empathy results in a genuinely altruistic motivation to help and desire to reduce the distress of the person in need, personal distress evokes an egoistic desire to reduce one's own distress which leads to self-focused, aversive, personal distress reactions so that helpful behaviour is curtailed. Batson proposed that an observer is likely to react in one of two primary ways to someone's plight, either through helping and thereby reducing the need, or alternatively by fleeing from the situation completely. Typically, the altruistically oriented observer will attempt to assuage the other's suffering, whereas the egoistically motivated onlooker will select the scenario that results in the least personal impact. Then again, some evidence indicates that feeling empathy for a person in need is the main motivator for helping (Mehrabian & Epstein, 1972), regardless of whether it is motivated by altruism with the goal of reducing the other's distress (Hoffman, 1975, 1984) or by egoism with the goal of benefiting oneself (Cialdini, Kenrick, & Baumann, 1982).

Overall, empathy is thought to be an important precursor to and motivator for prosocial or helping behaviour. For decades, the role of empathy in the development of prosocial behaviour has interested psychologists (Feshbach, 1978; Hoffman, 1976; Murphy, 1937). In particular, interest has escalated in the cognitive and affective processes that are related to prosocial and moral behaviour, and social competence (Davis, 1983a). Empirical research has confirmed that the vicarious experiencing of another's misery motivates one to alleviate the other's distress, and supports the belief that empathy facilitates the emergence of prosocial behaviour (Batson, 1987). In fact, with the upsurge of interest in factors that motivate helping behaviour, the study of vicarious affect in response to another's suffering has emerged as an important research area in its own right. Within the context of witnessing another person in distress for example, the observer can internalise the distress which in turns triggers a helping response that reflects the type of help that the observer would appreciate had they been in the distressing situation. Overall, the literature shows positive correlations between empathy and prosocial behaviour (de Waal, 2008; Knafo et al., 2008). It could be that empathy motivates selfless altruistic behaviour; or altruistic behaviour is motivated by a desire to reduce the resulting negative arousal through viewing another's distress. The argument that an empathic orientation prompts individuals to feel enhanced sadness, who are then motivated to act through their own egoistic forces has been researched widely (Sarlo, Lotto, Rumiati, & Palomba, 2014). Explanations for such egoistic alternatives are that an observer's heightened empathy for a sufferer brings with it the subjectively unpleasant feeling of increased personal sadness in the observer and that it is the egoistic desire to relieve that sadness, rather than the selfless desire to relieve the sufferer, that motivates helping.

Setting aside the motivation behind empathic reactions, studies have shown that infants as young as 8 months are able, in the presence of naturalistic peer distress, to display sophisticated responses, such as gaze, socially preferentially directed behaviours, looking at the peer and mothers of their peers. Moreover, infant responses to peer distress led to a cessation of the distress episode as much as one third of the time. Such results provide evidence of an early empathic concern coupled with prosocial behaviour (Liddle, Bradley, & McGrath, 2015). Empathy-related responding to distress is evident among 10-month-olds who are able to recognise distress and know how to help (Spinrad & Stifter, 2006). Where 14-month-old children make purposeful attempts to comfort their siblings, by 18 months, most children recognise their sibling's distress and are capable of either trying to alleviate or even aggravate it. In keeping with Hoffman's (1975) ideas, the early childhood years have been shown to play host to vicarious emotional reactions to distress incidents. For example, the study conducted by Zahn-Waxler et al. (1992) focused on the development of prosocial and reparative behaviours through children's responses to distress during the second year of life. Expressions of concern, defined as emotional arousal that appeared to reflect sympathetic concern for the victim and which was manifested in facial or vocal expressions or gestures, emerged between the ages of 1 and 2 years and increased in frequency and variety over this time period. By 2 years of age, infants have been shown to display tension and frustration during doll-breaking and juice-spilling incidents (Cole, Barrett, & Zahn-Waxler, 1992).

The development of empathy-related behaviours from 2 to 3 years of age has been examined through extensive longitudinal studies. One such study by Zahn-Waxler et al. (1992) examined the nature of 14- to 36-month-old children's responses to the simulated distress of a stranger versus a parent and in home and laboratory conditions. A variety of empathically oriented responding was measured among the toddlers, including concern when showing sadness and apologising to actual attempts and displays of helpful behaviour. Findings revealed that such responses increased across the second year of life between 14 and 24 months of age, with nearly all toddlers engaging in some helping behaviour in response to real and simulated distress by 2 years of age. Moreover, the quality of the prosocial behaviour became more sophisticated over the second year of life, in that whereas the youngest infants' responses reflected mainly physical actions, by 18 to 20 months, toddlers had a repertoire of helping behaviours where they were able to comfort verbally, give advice, share their possessions and use distraction tactics. Other studies have shown that children between 18 and 24 months of age who observed two people engaging in emotional displays of sadness were noted for their vocalisations, constructive play, looks towards their mothers, gaze towards their experimenters and proximity to their mothers (Jenkins et al., 1995). Children stopped their current activities and attended to the interchange as well as curtailing their explorations, vocalisations and play. However, none of the children became distressed during the displays of emotion and when mothers were asked about their children's reactions, none reported witnessing significant distress in their infants. There were similar findings by Svetlova, Nichols, and Brownell (2010) who explored the changing nature of prosocial behaviour across toddlerhood at 18 and 30 months. Opportunities to help an adult were observed across three contexts: instrumental, empathic and altruistic. The instrumental tasks were most easily achieved by even the youngest toddlers, whilst the youngest children found empathic helping difficult; and altruistic helping, which involved sacrificing an object, was the most challenging for children at both ages. Also, increasingly sophisticated responses have been shown with age from 18 to 30 months to peers' negative emotions, as have the variety of reasons for failing to help depending on age and the task itself (Nichols, Svetlova, & Brownell, 2014; Waugh & Brownell, 2017).

Among the social and sympathetic responses to distress shown by 2- to 4-year-olds in Murphy's (1937) study, children's vicarious emotions were noted under the heading of 'projected anxiety type' of sympathy, which reflected 'anxious' or 'disorganised' behaviour. However, such behaviours were few and far between compared with the extremes of both helpful and aggressive reactions, and leading Murphy to conclude that typically, preschool-aged children do not try to help distressed classmates very often, though most do on occasion. In a study by Caplan and Hay (1989) of 3- to 5-year-old children in two preschool classrooms over the course of 30 hours of observation, 85% of the children responded prosocially to distress on at least one occasion, but only 11% of all episodes of distress evoked a prosocial response. When interviewed about a filmed incident of distress involving a classmate, the children showed that they are well aware of how a hurt classmate might be helped, but stated that it was the responsibility of adults to tend to children's needs. When researching the motivation behind prosocial behaviour among 3- to 6-year-olds, other studies have revealed that empathic concern triumphed over personal distress (Williams, O'Driscoll, & Moore, 2014).

Enigmatic Empathy: The Paradox That Is the Coexistence of Altruism and Egoism

There can be a paradoxical fine line when responding empathically. But what determines whether perspective-taking is followed by personal distress and avoidance, rather than empathic concern and compassion? The degree of emotional separation of self-other differentiation seems to play a part. Carl Rogers's use of empathic approaches to psychotherapy advocated viewing "…the client's private world as if it were your own, but without ever losing the 'as if' quality" (1992, p. 829). Through retaining the 'as if', adverse reactions such as personal distress in the form of secondary traumatic stress or 'compassion fatigue' can be avoided (Badger, Royse, &

Craig, 2008). Evidence has since revealed that emotional separation is negatively associated with burnout and compassion fatigue (Thomas & Otis, 2010) and warns of the risks involved for practitioners. Empathy appears to be motivated by feeling a sense of connection between self and other. However, an excessive identification with another can lead to personal distress and avoidance rather than empathic concern.

This fine line leads to the possibility that altruistic and egoistic motivations are, in fact, not mutually exclusive, but instead coexist. Hoffman (1981), for example, treated these two emotional reactions as one, speaking of 'empathic pain' or 'empathic distress', and, in doing so, minimised the differences between egoistic and altruistic motivation. He suggested that: "Empathy may be uniquely well suited for bridging the gap between egoism and altruism, since it has the property of transforming another person's misfortune into one's own feeling of distress. Empathy thus has elements of both egoism and altruism" (p. 133). Moreover, Hoffman (1975) claimed that: "A type of moral encounter of increasing interest to psychology is that in which an individual witnesses another person in distress. Whether or not the individual attempts to help is presumably the net result of altruistic and egoistic forces" (p. 607). However, when pressed to decide on one or other motive, he argued that "…the arousal condition, aim of the ensuing action, and basis of gratification in the actor are all dependent on someone else's welfare" (p. 617), therefore designating sympathetic distress as an altruistic motive compared with a more direct self-interested, egoistic motive. Furthermore, Davis (1983a) regarded the importance of distinguishing between empathically experienced emotions that lead to an excess of personal distress rather than concern for the other as being "…the rule, rather than the exception", and felt that "…actual feelings of empathic concern and personal distress co-occur to a great degree" (p. 183). Therefore, the question of the existence of a basis for the claim that distress and empathy are experienced as qualitatively distinct emotions still remains, as does their motivational properties of egoism and altruism respectively. The research suggests that the extent to which toddlers respond to distressed peers is a function of developmental level. However, adults' responses to distress are affected by the social context (Latané & Darley, 1970), so very early reactions to distressed companions may be similarly sensitive to context.

References

Ashwin, C., Baron-Cohen, S., Wheelwright, S., O'Riordan, M., & Bullmore, E. T. (2007). Differential activation of the amygdala and the 'social brain' during fearful face-processing in Asperger syndrome. *Neuropsychologia, 45*, 2–14.

Asperger, H. (1938). Das psychisch abnorme Kind [The psychically abnormal child]. *Wiener klinische Wochenschrift* (in German), *51*, 1314–1317.

Astington, J. W., Harris, P. L., & Olson, D. R. (Eds.). (1988). *Developing theories of mind*. New York: Cambridge University Press.

Atkins, P. W. B., & Parker, S. K. (2012). Understanding individual compassion in organizations: The role of appraisals and psychological flexibility. *Academy of Management Review, 37*, 524–546.

Atkinson, A. P. (2007). Face processing and empathy. In T. F. D. Farrow & P. W. R. Woodruff (Eds.), *Empathy in mental illness* (pp. 360–386). New York: Cambridge University Press.

Badger, K., Royse, D., & Craig, C. (2008). Hospital social workers and indirect trauma exposure: An exploratory study of contributing factors. *Health and Social Work, 33*, 63–71.

Baldwin, J. M. (1897). *Social and ethical interpretations in mental development*. New York: Macmillan.

Baron-Cohen, S. (2002). The extreme male brain theory of autism. *Trends in Cognitive Sciences, 6*, 248–254.

Baron-Cohen, S. (2004). The cognitive neuroscience of autism. *Journal of Neurology, Neurosurgery and Psychiatry, 75*, 945–948.

Baron-Cohen, S. (2011). The evolution and diagnosis of empathy. *The Evolutionary Review, 2*, 55–57.

Baron-Cohen, S., Leslie, A. M., & Frith, U. (1985). Does the autistic child have a 'theory of mind? *Cognition, 21*, 37–46.

Batson, D. C. (1987). Prosocial motivation: Is it ever truly altruistic? In L. Berkowitz (Ed.), *Advances in experimental social psychology*. New York: Academic.

Batson, D. C., & Ahmad, N. Y. (2009). Using empathy to improve intergroup attitudes and relations. *Social Issues and Policy Review, 3*, 141.

Batson, C. D., Eklund, J. H., Chermok, V. L., Hoyt, J. L., & Ortiz, B. G. (2007). An additional antecedent of empathic concern: Valuing the welfare of the person in need. *Journal of Personality and Social Psychology, 93*, 65–74.

Bedford, R., Pickles, A., Sharp, H., Wright, N., & Hill, J. (2015). Reduced face preference in infancy developmental precursor to callous-unemotional traits? *Biological Psychiatry, 78*, 144–150.

Belsky, J., & Most, R. K. (1981). From exploration to play: A cross-sectional study of infant free play behaviour. *Developmental Psychology, 17*, 630–639.

Bird, G., & Cook, R. (2013). Mixed emotions: The contribution of alexithymia to the emotional symptoms of autism. *Translational Psychiatry, 3*, 285.

Blair, R. J. (2008). Fine cuts of empathy and the amygdala: Dissociable deficits in psychopathy and autism. *Quarterly Journal of Experimental Psychology, 61*, 157–170.

Blair, R. J., Mitchell, D., Peschardt, K., Colledge, E., Leonard, R., Shine, J., et al. (2004). Reduced sensitivity to others' fearful expressions in psychopathic individuals. *Personality and Individual Differences, 37*, 1111–1122.

Bloom, B. S., Engelhart, M. D., Furst, E. J., Hill, W. H., & Krathwohl, D. R. (1956). *Taxonomy of educational objectives: The classification of educational goals*. Handbook I: Cognitive domain. New York: David McKay Company.

Borke, H. (1971). Interpersonal perception of young children: Egocentrism or empathy? *Developmental Psychology, 5*, 263–269.

Bridges, K. M. B. (1931). *The social and emotional development of the preschool child*. London: Routledge & Kegan Paul.

Bryant, B. K. (1982). An index of empathy for children and adolescents. *Child Development, 53*, 413–425.

Buffone, A. E. K., & Poulin, M. J. (2014). Empathy, target distress, and neurohormone genes interact to predict aggression for others – Even without provocation. *Personality and Social Psychology Bulletin, 11*, 1406–1422.

Burlingham, D. (1967). Empathy between infant and mother. *Journal of the American Psychoanalytic Association, 15*, 764–780.

Cantor, D., Hay, D. F., Acker, D., & Pinkham, L. (1981). *A new method for exploring and measuring the development of self*. Poster presented at the International Society for the Study of Behavioural Development, Toronto, ON.

Caplan, M. Z., & Hay, D. F. (1989). Preschoolers' responses to peers' distress and beliefs about bystander intervention. *Journal of Child Psychology and Psychiatry, 30*, 231–242.

Chandler, M. J., & Greenspan, S. (1972). Ersatz egocentrism: A reply to H. Borke. *Developmental Psychology, 7*, 104–106.

Charman, T., Swettenham, J., Baron-Cohen, S., Cox, A., Baird, G., & Drew, A. (1998). An experimental investigation of social-cognitive abilities in infants with autism: Clinical implications. *Infant Mental Health Journal, 19*, 260–275.

Chisholm, K., & Strayer, J. (1995). Verbal and facial measures of children's emotion and empathy. *Journal of Experimental Child Psychology, 59*, 299–316.

Cialdini, R. B., Kenrick, D. T., & Baumann, D. J. (1982). Effects of mood on prosocial behaviour in children and adults. In N. Eisenberg (Ed.), *The development of prosocial behaviour* (pp. 339–359). New York: Academic.

Cole, P. M., Barrett, K. C., & Zahn-Waxler, C. (1992). Emotion displays in two-year-olds during mishaps. *Child Development, 63*, 314–324.

Cummings, E. M., Zahn-Waxler, C., & Radke-Yarrow, M. (1981). Young children's responses to expressions of anger and affection by others in the family. *Child Development, 52*, 1274–1282.

Dapretto, M., Davies, M. S., Pfeifer, J. H., Scott, A. A., Sigman, M., Bookheimer, S. Y., et al. (2006). Understanding emotions in others: Mirror neuron dysfunction in children with autism spectrum disorders. *Nature Neuroscience, 9*, 28–30.

Darwin, C. (1872). *The expression of the emotions in man and animals*. London: John Murray.

Darwin, C. (1877). A biographical sketch of an infant. *Mind, 2*, 285–294.

Davidov, M., Zahn-Waxler, C., Roth-Hanania, R., & Knafo, A. (2013). Concern for others in the first year of life: Theory, evidence and avenues for research. *Child Development Perspectives, 7*, 126–131.

Davis, M. H. (1983a). The effects of dispositional empathy on emotional reactions and helping: A multidimensional approach. *Journal of Personality, 51*, 167–184.

Davis, M. H. (1983b). Measuring individual differences in empathy: Evidence for a multidimensional approach. *Journal of Personality and Social Psychology, 44*, 113–126.

Decety, J., & Lamm, C. (2006). Human empathy through the lens of social neuroscience. *Scientific World Journal, 6*, 1146–1163.

Demetriou, H., & Hay, D. (2004). Toddlers' reactions to the distress of familiar peers: The importance of context. *Infancy, 6*, 299–318.

Denham, S. A. (1986). Social cognition, prosocial behaviour, and emotion in preschoolers: Contextual validation. *Child Development, 57*, 194–201.

de Waal, F. B. M. (2008). Putting the altruism back into altruism: The evolution of empathy. *Annual Review of Psychology, 59*, 279–300.

Dolan, M., & Fullam, R. (2004). Theory of mind and mentalising ability in antisocial personality disorders with and without psychopathy. *Psychological Medicine, 34*, 1093–1102.

DSM-5. (2013). *Diagnostic and statistical manual of mental disorders: American Psychiatric Association* (5th ed.). Arlington, VA: American Psychiatric Publishing.

Dunn, J. F. (1988). Sibling influences on childhood development. *Journal of Child Psychology and Psychiatry and Allied Disciplines, 29*, 119–127.

Dymond, R. F. (1949). A scale for the measurement of empathic ability. *Journal of Consulting Psychology, 13*, 127–133.

Dziobek, I., Rogers, K., Fleck, S., Bahnemann, M., Heekeren, H. R., Wolf, O. T., et al. (2008). Dissociation of cognitive and emotional empathy in adults with Asperger syndrome using the multifaceted empathy test (MET). *Journal of Autism and Developmental Disorders, 38*, 464–473.

Eisenberg, N. (1986). *Altruistic emotion, cognition, and behaviour.* Hillsdale, NJ: Erlbaum.

Eisenberg, N., Eggum, N. D., & Di Giunta, L. (2010). Empathy-related responding: Associations with prosocial behaviour, aggression, and intergroup relations. *Social Issues and Policy Review, 4*, 143–180.

Eisenberg, N., & Fabes, R. A. (1991). Prosocial behaviour and empathy: A multimethod, developmental perspective. In P. Clark (Ed.), *Review of personality and social psychology* (Vol. 12). Newbury Park, CA: Sage.

Eisenberg, N., Fabes, R. A., Miller, P. A., Fultz, J., et al. (1989). Relation of sympathy and personal distress to prosocial behaviour: A multimethod study. *Journal of Personality and Social Psychology, 57*, 55–66.

Eisenberg, N., Spinrad, T. L., & Morris, A. (2014). Empathy-related responding in children. In M. Killen & J. G. Smetana (Eds.), *Handbook of moral development* (2nd ed., pp. 184–207). New York: Psychology Press.

Eysenck, S. B. G., Easting, G., & Pearson, P. R. (1984). Age norms for impulsiveness, venturesomeness, and empathy in children. *Personality and Individual Differences, 5*, 315–321.

Fabes, R. A., Eisenberg, N., Nyman, M., & Michealieu, Q. (1991). Young children's appraisals of others' spontaneous emotional reactions. *Developmental Psychology, 27*, 858–866.

Fenichel, O. (1946). *The psychoanalytic theory of neurosis.* London: Routledge & Kegan Paul Ltd.

Ferreira, A. J. (1961). Empathy and the bridge function of the ego. *Journal of the American Psychoanalytic Association, 9*, 91–105.

Feshbach, N. D. (1978). Studies of empathic behaviour in children. In B. A. Maher (Ed.), *Progress in experimental personality research* (Vol. 8). New York: Academic.

Feshbach, N. D. (1975). Empathy in children: Some theoretical and empirical considerations. *The Counselling Psychologist, 5*, 25–30.

Feshbach, N. D. (1989). Empathy training and prosocial behaviour. In J. Groebel & R. A. Hinde (Eds.), *Aggression and war: Their biological and social bases.* New York: Cambridge University Press.

Feshbach, N. D., & Roe, K. (1968). Empathy in six and seven year olds. *Child Development, 39*, 133–145.

Fink, E., Heathers, J. A. J., & de Rosnay, M. (2015). Young children's affective responses to another's distress: Dynamic and physiological features. *PlosOne, 10*, e0121735. https://doi.org/10.1371/journal.pone.0121735

Flavell, J. H. (1974). The development of inferences about others. In T. Mischel (Ed.), *Understanding other persons*. Totowa, NJ: Rowman and Littlefield.

Frank, M. C., Vul, E., & Johnson, S. P. (2009). Development of infants' attention to faces during the first year. *Cognition, 110*, 160–170.

Freud, A. (1953). Some remarks on infant observation. *The Psychoanalytic Study of the Child, 8*, 9–19.

Freud, A. (1958). Child observation and prediction of development: A memorial lecture in honour of Ernst Kris. *The Psychoanalytic Study of the Child, 13*, 92–116.

Garton, A. F., & Gringart, E. (2005). The development of a scale to measure empathy in 8- and 9- year old children. *Australian Journal of Education and Developmental Psychology, 5*, 17–25.

Gibson, E. J., & Walk, R. D. (1960). The "visual cliff". *Scientific American, 202*, 67–71.

Goldstein, A. P., & Michaels, G. Y. (1985). *Empathy training: A components approach to development, training, and consequences*. Hillsdale, NJ: Erlbaum Associates.

Greenson, R. (1960). Empathy and its vicissitudes. *International Journal of Psychoanalysis, 41*, 418–424.

Grossmann, T., Striano, T., & Friederici, A. D. (2007). Developmental changes in infants' processing of happy and angry facial expressions: A neurobehavioural study. *Brain and Cognition, 64*, 30–41.

Harter, S., & Buddin, B. J. (1987). Children's understanding of the simultaneity of two emotions: A five-stage developmental acquisition sequence. *Developmental Psychology, 23*, 388–399.

Hastings, M. E., Tangney, J. P., & Stuewig, J. (2007). Psychopathy and identification of facial expressions of emotion. *Personality and Individual Differences, 44*, 1474–1483.

Haviland, J. M., & Lelwica, M. (1987). The induced affect response: 10-week-old infants' responses to three emotion expressions. *Developmental Psychology, 23*, 97–104.

Hay, D. F., Castle, J., Davies, L., Demetriou, H., & Stimson, C. A. (1999). Prosocial action in very early childhood: Links with gender and problematic behaviour. *Journal of Child Psychology and Psychiatry and Allied Disciplines, 40*, 905–916.

Hay, D. F., Nash, A., & Pedersen, J. (1981). Responses of six-month-olds to the distress of their peers. *Child Development, 52*, 1071–1075.

Hirshberg, L. M. (1990). When infants look to their parents: II. Twelve-month-olds' response to conflicting parental emotional signals. *Child Development, 61*, 1187–1191.

Hoffman, M. L. (1975). Developmental synthesis of affect and cognition and its implications for altruistic motivation. *Developmental Psychology, 11*, 607–622.

Hoffman, M. L. (1976). Empathy, role-taking, guilt and development of altruistic motives. In T. Lickona (Ed.), *Moral development and behaviour: Current theory and research*. New York: Holt, Rhinehart & Winston.

Hoffman, M. L. (1978). Toward a theory of empathic arousal and development. In M. Lewis & L. Rosenblum (Eds.), *The development of affect*. New York: Plenum Press.

Hoffman, M. L. (1981). Is altruism part of human nature? *Journal of Personality and Social Psychology, 40*, 121–137.

Hoffman, M. L. (1984). Interaction of affect and cognition in empathy. In C. E. Izard, J. Kagan, & R. B. Zajonc (Eds.), *Emotions, cognition, and behaviour*. Cambridge, UK: Cambridge University Press.

Hoffman, M. L. (1987). The contribution of empathy to justice and moral judgement. In N. Eisenberg & J. Strayer (Eds.), *Empathy and its development*. Cambridge: Cambridge University Press.

Hoffman, M. L. (2000). *Empathy and moral development: Implications for caring and justice*. New York: Cambridge University Press.

Hoffman, M. L., & Saltzstein, H. D. (1967). Parent discipline and the child's moral development. *Journal of Personality and Social Psychology, 5*, 45–57.

Hughes, M. (1975). *Egocentrism in preschool children*. Edinburgh University. Unpublished doctoral dissertation. Cited in M. Donaldson (1978).

Huston, A. C., Wright, J. C., Alvarez, M., Truglio, R., et al. (1995). Perceived television reality and children's emotional and cognitive responses to its social content. *Journal of Applied Developmental Psychology, 16*(2), 231–251.

Iannotti, R. J. (1985). Naturalistic and structured assessments of prosocial behaviour in preschool children: The influence of empathy and perspective taking. *Developmental Psychology, 21*, 46–55.

Izard, C. E. (1979). Emotions as motivations: An evolutionary-developmental perspective. In R. A. Dienstbier (Ed.), *Nebraska symposium on motivation* (pp. 163–200). Lincoln, CA: University of Nebraska Press.

Izard, C., Hembree, E. A., Dougherty, L. M., & Spizziri, C. L. (1983). Changes in facial expressions of 2- to 19- month-old infants following acute pain. *Developmental Psychology, 19*, 418–426.

Jacquemont, S., Coe, B. P., Hersch, M., Duyzend, M. H., Krumm, N., Bergmann, S., et al. (2014). A higher mutational burden in females supports a 'female protective model' in neurodevelopmental disorders. *American Journal of Human Genetics, 94*, 415–425.

James, W. (1884). What is an emotion? *Mind, 9*, 188–205.

Jenkins, J. M., Franco, F., Dolins, F., & Sewell, A. (1995). Toddlers' reactions to negative emotion displays: Forming models of relationships. *Infant Behaviour and Development, 18*, 273–281.

Kalliopuska, M. (1980). *Children's helping behaviour: Personality factors and parental influences related to helping behaviour.* Dissertationes Humanarum Litterarum, 24, Helsinki, Finland.

Knafo, A., Zahn-Waxler, C., Van Hulle, C., Robinson, J., & Rhee, S. H. (2008). The developmental origins of a disposition toward empathy: Genetic and environmental contributions. *Emotion, 8*, 737–752.

Kohut, H. (1971). *The analysis of the self: A systematic approach to the psychoanalytic treatment of narcissistic personality disorders.* New York: International Universities Press.

Kohut, H. (1977). *The restoration of the self.* New York: International Universities Press.

Krznaric, R. (2015). *Empathy: Why it matters, and how to get it.* London: Rider Press.

Kuchenbecker, S. L. Y. (1977). *A developmental investigation of children's behavioural, cognitive, and affective responses to empathically stimulating situations.* Doctoral dissertation, University of California, Los Angeles.

Kuczynski, L., Parkin, M. C., & Pitman, R. (2015). Socialisation as dynamic process: A dialectical, transactional perspective. In J. E. Grusec & P. D. Hastings (Eds.), *Handbook of Socialisation: Theory and research.* London: The Guilford Press.

Langlois, J. H., Roggman, L. A., & Rieser-Danner, L. A. (1990). Infants' differential social responses to attractive and unattractive faces. *Developmental Psychology, 26*(1), 153–159.

Latané, B., & Darley, J. M. (1970). *The unresponsive bystander: Why doesn't he help?* New York: Appleton-Century-Crofts.

Lecce, S., Caputi, M., & Pagnin, A. (2014). Long-term effect of theory of mind on school achievement: The role of sensitivity to criticism. *European Journal of Developmental Psychology, 11*, 305–318.

Liddle, M. J., Bradley, B. S., & McGrath, A. (2015). Baby empathy: Infant distress and peer prosocial responses. *Infant Mental Health Journal, 36*, 446–458.

Lipps, T. (1903). *Empathy, inner imitation, and sense-feelings.* In Rader (Ed.), *Aesthetics* (pp. 291–304). Translated from Einfühlung, inner Nachahmung, und Organ-empfindungen. *Archiv fur die gesamte Psychologie, 2,* 185–204, by Rader and M. Schertel.

Mahler, M. S. (1968). *On human symbiosis and the vicissitudes of individuation. Volume 1: Infantile and early contributions.* Madison, CT: International Universities Press.

Marcus, R. F., Roke, E. J., & Bruner, C. (1985). Verbal and nonverbal empathy and prediction of social behaviour of young children. *Perceptual and Motor Skills, 60,* 299–309.

Markram, K., & Markram, H. (2010). The intense world theory – A unifying theory of the neurobiology of autism. *Frontiers in Human Neuroscience, 4,* 224.

Mead, G. H. (1934). In C. M. Morris (Ed.), *Mind, self, and society.* Chicago: University of Chicago Press.

Mehrabian, A., & Epstein, N. A. (1972). A measure of emotional empathy. *Journal of Personality, 40,* 523–543.

Meltzoff, A. (2007). Like me': A foundation for social cognition. *Developmental Science, 10,* 126–134.

McDougall, W. (1908). *An introduction to social psychology.* London: Methuen.

Montessori, M. (1912). *The Montessori method: Scientific pedagogy as applied to child education in the children's houses.* New York: Frederick A Stokes Company.

Montessori, M. (1948). *The discovery of the child.* New York: Ballantine Books.

Mullins-Nelson, J. L., Salekin, R. T., & Leistico, A. M. R. (2006). Psychopathy, empathy, and perspective-taking ability in a community sample: Implications for the successful psychopathy concept. *International Journal of Forensic Mental Health, 5,* 133–149.

Murphy, L. B. (1937). *Social behaviour and child personality: An exploratory study of some roots of sympathy.* New York: Columbia University Press.

Nichols, S. R., Svetlova, M., & Brownell, C. A. (2014). Toddlers' responses to infants' negative emotions. *Infancy, 20,* 70–97.

Oberman, L. M., & Ramachandran, V. S. (2007). The simulating social mind: The role of the mirror neuron system and simulation in the social and communicative deficits of autism spectrum disorders. *Psychological Bulletin, 133,* 310–327.

Piaget, J. (1932). *The moral judgement of the child.* London: Routledge & Kegan Paul.

Piaget, J. (1950). *The psychology of intelligence.* London: Routledge & Kegan Paul.

Piaget, J. (1951). *Play, dreams, and imitation in childhood.* New York: Norton.

Piaget, J. (1966). *The origins of intelligence in children* (trans: Cook, M.). New York: International University Press.

Piaget, J. (1981). *Intelligence and affectivity: Their relation during child development*. Palo Alto, CA: Annual Reviews.

Piaget, J., & Inhelder, B. (1956). The child's conception of space (trans: Langdon, F. J., & Lunzer, E. L.). London: Routledge & Kegan Paul.

Pink, D. H. (2008). *A whole new mind: Why right-brainers will rule the future*. Singapore: Marshall Cavendish.

Premack, D., & Premack, A. J. (1997). Infants attribute value to the goal directed actions of self-propelled objects. *Journal of Cognitive Neuroscience, 9*, 848–856.

Premack, D., & Woodruff, G. (1978). Does the chimpanzee have a 'theory of mind'? *Behavioural and Brain Sciences, 4*, 515–526.

Principe, C. P., & Langlois, J. H. (2012). Shifting the prototype: Experience with faces influences affective and attractiveness preferences. *Social Cognition, 30*, 109–120.

Redmond, M. V. (1995). A multidimensional theory and measure of social decentering. *Journal of Research in Personality, 29*, 35–58.

Reisel, D. (2013). *The neuroscience of restorative justice*. TED Talk.

Rigato, S., Menon, E., Johnson, M. H., & Farroni, T. (2011). The interaction between gaze direction and facial expression in newborns. *European Journal of Developmental Psychology, 8*, 624–636.

Rogers, C. R. (1992). The necessary and sufficient conditions of therapeutic personality change. *Journal of Consulting and Clinical Psychology, 60*, 827–832.

Roth-Hanania, R., Davidov, M., & Zahn-Waxler, C. (2011). Empathy development from 8 to 16 months: Early signs of concern for others. *Infant Behaviour and Development, 34*, 447–458.

Sagi, A., & Hoffman, M. L. (1976). Empathic distress in the newborn. *Developmental Psychology, 12*, 175–176.

Saliquist, J., Eisenberg, N., Spinrad, T. L., Eggum, N. D., & Gaertner, B. M. (2009). Assessment of preschoolers' positive empathy: Concurrent and longitudinal relations with positive emotion, social competence, and sympathy. *The Journal of Positive Psychology, 4*, 223–233.

Sarlo, M., Lotto, L., Rumiati, R., & Palomba, D. (2014). If it makes you feel bad, don't do it! Egoistic rather than altruistic empathy modulates neural and behavioural responses in moral dilemmas. *Physiology & Behaviour, 130*, 127–134.

Segal, E. A. (2011). Social empathy: A model built on empathy, contextual understanding, and social responsibility that promotes social justice. *Journal of Social Service Research, 37,* 266–277.

Shirtcliff, E. A., Vitacco, M. J., Graf, A. R., Gostisha, A. J., Merz, J. L., & Zahn-Waxler, C. (2009). Neurobiology of empathy and callousness: Implications for the development of antisocial behaviour. *Behavioural Sciences and the Law, 27,* 137–171.

Simner, M. L. (1971). Newborn's response to the cry of another infant. *Developmental Psychology, 5,* 135–150.

Smith, A. (1759). *Moral and political philosophy.* New York: Hafner.

Solomon, J. (1985). *The relationship between affective empathy and prosocial behaviour in elementary school children.* Paper presented at the biennial meeting of the Society for Research in Child Development, Toronto, ON.

Spencer, H. (1870). *The principles of psychology* (Vol. 1, 2nd ed.). London: Williams and Norgate.

Spinrad, T. L., & Stifter, C. A. (2006). Toddlers' empathy-related responding to distress: Predictions from negative emotionality and maternal behaviour in infancy. *Infancy, 10,* 97–121.

Stotland, E. (1969). Exploratory studies in empathy. In L. Berkowitz (Ed.), *Advances in experimental social psychology* (Vol. 4, pp. 271–314). New York: Academic.

Strayer, J. (1985). Current research in affective development. Special issue: The feeling child: Affective development reconsidered. *Journal of Children in Contemporary Society, 17,* 37–55.

Strayer, J. (1993). Children's concordant emotions and cognitions in response to observed emotions. *Child Development, 64,* 188–201.

Svetlova, M., Nichols, S. R., & Brownell, C. A. (2010). Toddlers' prosocial behaviour: From instrumental to empathic to altruistic helping. *Child Development, 81,* 1814–1827.

Sorce, J. F., & Emde, R. N. (1981). Mother's presence is not enough: Effect of emotional availability on infant exploration. *Developmental Psychology, 17,* 737–745.

Spitz, R. (1965). *The first year of life.* New York: International Universities Press.

Sullivan, H. S. (1953). *The interpersonal theory of psychiatry.* New York: W.W. Norton.

Thomas, J., & Otis, M. (2010). Intrapsychic correlates of professional quality of life: Mindfulness, empathy, and emotional separation. *Journal of the Society for Social Work and Research, 1,* 83–98.

Tully, E. C., Donohue, M. R., & Garcia, S. E. (2014). Children's empathy responses and their understanding of mother's emotions. *Cognition and Emotion, 29*, 118–129.

Vaish, A., Carpenter, M., & Tomasello, M. (2009). Sympathy through affective perspective-taking and its relation to prosocial behaviour in toddlers. *Developmental Psychology, 45*, 534–543.

Walk, R. (1966). The development of depth perception in animals and human infants. *Monographs of the Society for Research in Child Development, 31*(5), 82–108.

Watson, D. L. (1938). On the role of insight in the study of mankind. *Psychoanalytic Review, 25*, 358–371.

Watson, J. B., & Rayner, R. (1920). Conditioned emotional reactions. *Journal of Experimental Psychology, 3*, 1–14.

Waugh, W. E., & Brownell, C. A. (2017). "Help yourself!" What can toddlers' helping failures tell us about the development of prosocial behaviour? *Infancy, 22*, 665–680.

Wellman, H. M., Cross, D., & Watson, J. (2001). Meta-analysis of theory of mind development: The truth about false belief. *Child Development, 72*, 655–584.

Wellman, H. M., Harris, P., Banerjee, M., & Sinclair, A. (1995). Early understanding of emotion: Evidence from natural language. *Cognition and Emotion, 9*, 117–149.

Widen, S. C., & Russell, J. A. (2010). Differentiation in preschooler's categories of emotion. *Emotion, 10*, 651–661.

Williams, A., O'Driscoll, K., & Moore, C. (2014). The influence of empathic concern on prosocial behaviour in children. *Frontiers in Psychology, 5*, 425.

Wispé, L. (1986). The distinction between sympathy and empathy: To call forth a concept, a word is needed. *Journal of Personality and Social Psychology, 50*, 314–321.

Wynn, K., & Bloom, P. (2014). The moral baby. In M. Killen & J. G. Smetana (Eds.), *Handbook of moral development* (2nd ed., pp. 435–453). New York: Psychology Press.

Yarrow, M. R., & Waxler, C. Z. (1976). Dimensions and correlates of prosocial behaviour in young children. *Child Development, 47*, 118–125.

Zahn-Waxler, C., Friedman, S. L., & Cummings, M. E. (1983). Children's emotions and behaviours in response to infants' cries. *Child Development, 54*, 1522–1528.

Zahn-Waxler, C., & Radke-Yarrow, M. (1990). The origins of empathic concern. *Motivation and Emotion, 14*, 107–130.

Zahn-Waxler, C., Radke-Yarrow, M., & Brady-Smith, J. (1977). Perspective-taking and prosocial behaviour. *Developmental Psychology, 13*, 87–88.

Zahn-Waxler, C., Radke-Yarrow, M., & King, R. A. (1979). Child rearing and children's prosocial initiations towards victims of distress. *Child Development, 50*, 319–330.

Zahn-Waxler, C., Radke-Yarrow, M., Wagner, E., & Chapman, M. (1992). Development of concern for others. *Developmental Psychology, 28*, 126–136.

Zahn-Waxler, C., Robinson, J. L., & Emde, R. N. (1992). The development of empathy in twins. *Developmental Psychology, 28*, 1038–1047.

4

A Study of Empathy in the Early and Middle Childhood Years

Referring to their unpredictable nature, W.C. Fields once said: "Never work with children and animals". However, scientists are discovering that both children and animals have enormous potential and predictability for empathy. In order to assess the capacity for empathy, the context of distress is often used: "Empathy…is switched on by events within their community, such as a youngster in distress" (de Waal, 2005). The two research studies that will be described were conducted as part of my PhD thesis, entitled 'Reactions of girls and boys to the distress of their peers in early and middle childhood' (Demetriou, 1998), which focused on the nature and extent of empathy in early childhood (18–36 months) and middle childhood (7–10 years) and whether context has an effect on children's reactions to distress during these developmental milestones. Distress was targeted using observation techniques and picture-stories respectively in order that children's reactions could be investigated. This approach was similar to Murphy's (1937) observations and Feshbach and Roe's (1968) picture-story procedure, both of which studied a sector of behaviour that is limited in terms of the stimulus of distress. In particular, the present investigation focused on children's empathic, helpful and aggressive reactions. These were assessed according to age, gender, whether the child was

H. Demetriou, *Empathy, Emotion and Education*,
https://doi.org/10.1057/978-1-137-54844-3_4

responding to another child (non-distressed onlooker or distressed peer) of the same sex or the opposite sex, whether the distress had been caused or witnessed by the non-distressed child, and the relation of children's reactions with other aspects of their social functioning as reported by their teachers and parents.

A Contextual Study of Empathy in Early Childhood

I examined reactions to distress during the second and third years of life, when distress occurs fairly often in the course of play with peers using the thesis that such reactions might be precursors to later empathy. The study aimed to show how common an experience it is for young children to either cause or witness a peer's distress, and then to note what, if anything, they do in the face of distress. Unlike many other studies of very young children's peer relations, which often take place in day care centres, nursery schools or laboratory playrooms, this study observed toddlers at home playing with familiar peers. Reactions to peers' distress were recorded for 52 toddlers ('hosts') aged 18–36 months, who were observed playing in their own homes with familiar peers ('guests') during two sessions, 6 months apart. The primary aim of the research was to identify toddlers' reactions to distress with respect to the social context in which the distress occurs. As such, four contextual factors were explored: the host's *personal responsibility* for the guest's distress; the degree of *similarity* between the toddler and the distressed peer; the *relative familiarity* of the peer in terms of the length of their acquaintance; and the toddler's *experience with other children* (notably their peers and siblings).

The presence of a distress episode was detected in the first instance using the vocal signals of cry, scream, shout, sob, weep, choke, fuss, groan, grunt, protest, splutter, whimper and whine as markers for distress onset. Possible sources of distress were *physical discomfort, situation frustration, pretence* and *unknown source*. The coding criteria comprised 18 possible reactions of which one or more could appear in any one episode. These were seeking information (cognitive empathy), vicarious emotion (emotional empathy), assistance, distraction, facial expression, indirect help,

physical comfort, vocal comfort, protection/defence, sharing, aggravation, not in view, ignore, orient, cease ongoing activity, approach, imitation, amusement. The toddlers in this study were not infrequently exposed
to the distress of their familiar peers, either because they themselves made
the peer distressed or because their guests had otherwise become frustrated or uncomfortable. Distress occurred more often during the first
visit and declined thereafter, presumably as a function of the increasing
acquaintance of the pairs of children as well as developmental change.
The absence of significant cohort differences suggested that the decline in
distress was not simply due to increasing maturity and better emotional
regulation on the part of guests, although that no doubt played a part.
Rather, the decline was partly due to changed behaviour on the part of
boys. During the first visit, boys' guests were more likely to become distressed, had longer episodes of distress, and generally spent more time in
a state of distress. These differences as a function of the sex of the host
were no longer evident 6 months later, when the pairs were better
acquainted. Nonetheless, they show that it is important to take into
account the base rates of exposure to distress, and the frequency with
which certain toddlers upset or annoy their peers, when studying empathic
reactions. In this study, there were more boys than girls whose reactions
to distress could be studied because boys were more likely than girls to
have guests who were upset. Thus, the analyses for gender differences in
reactions to distress were constrained by the fact that girls had fewer
opportunities than boys to respond to distressed guests. Overall, hosts
responded more positively to distress they had caused than to distress they
witnessed. Negative reactions were most likely to be shown when hosts
themselves had caused the distress of a guest of the same sex. Hosts were
less likely to respond either positively or negatively if they had known
their guests all their lives. And toddlers who had older siblings were more
likely than other hosts to respond negatively to guests' distress.

Personal Responsibility

Are there differences in children's reactions depending on whether they
themselves have caused the distress to their peer? Do, for example, more

negative reactions occur when children cause rather than witness another's distress, or do perpetrators of distress try to make reparations? In a classic observational study of the origins of sympathy, Murphy (1937) noted that a child's responsibility for another's distress resulted in both helpful and aggressive reactions. Observational studies of family conflict in the home have similarly shown children to be differentially responsive to their own or others' transgressions, which they view with a mingled interest, distress and amusement. How children responded to their siblings' distress depended on whether or not they themselves had caused it. In some cases, the same child responded by showing concern if she or he had not been involved in causing the distress, but laughed at, or exacerbated the distress if she or he had been responsible for it (Dunn & Brown, 1994).

Another study involved mothers of 1.5- to 2.5-year-old children recording their children's reactions to everyday encounters of distress in the form of sorrow, discomfort and pain (Zahn-Waxler, Radke-Yarrow, & King, 1979). Children were more helpful when they were bystanders rather than causes of another's distress. Similar findings emerged in a longitudinal study of 13- to 25-month-olds in which mothers were trained to observe their children's responses to the emotions of others (Zahn-Waxler, Radke-Yarrow, Wagner, & Chapman, 1992). The study demonstrated that, if toddlers had caused physical or psychological harm, they were less likely to show empathic concern, especially as they grew older. Instead, they were more likely to show enjoyment, aggression, personal distress, and less concern for the other, in addition to being less likely to explore the reasons for the distress than when they witnessed distress as bystanders. Boys in particular were more aggressive during incidents of distress that they caused, whilst girls exhibited most affective empathy for episodes of distress they witnessed.

As Hoffman's (1975) theory predicted, nearly half the toddlers did intervene in response to their distressed peers, and the qualitative data showed that clear instances of prosocial responding can be discerned at this early age. However, the nature of the toddlers' reactions to distress did depend on the context in which the distress occurred. The host's personal responsibility for the distress affected the nature of the host's reactions, but not in accordance with earlier findings. At least during the first visit, in contrast to other studies (Dunn & Munn, 1986; Zahn-Waxler, Radke-Yarrow, et al., 1992), hosts were more likely to show prosocial responses to distress they had caused than distress they merely witnessed. However, personal responsibility for the distress also engendered negative reactions. In addition, several hosts showed negative reactions to distress they had caused. For example, a 36-month-old boy guest was playing with a toy at a table. Suddenly, and without an apparent motive, his boy host, grimacing, grabbed his neck and caused the guest to lose his balance and to cry. The host continued to grab his guest, thereby increasing his distress until the intervention of the host's mother, who separated the children. In general, if the toddlers had caused their peers to become distressed, they were more likely to respond actively to the distress they had instigated, either through alleviation or aggravation. Indeed, it was very rare for toddlers to react negatively to distress if they had not been responsible for its occurrence.

Similarity with the Peer

Another contextual factor studied here was the degree of similarity between the toddler and the distressed peer. A comparison was made between children's reactions to peers of the same and the opposite sex. Even before 2 years of age, children demonstrate a preference for interaction with members of their own sex (Legault & Strayer, 1991). Young children direct more social behaviour, of both a positive and a negative nature, to same-sex playmates than to those of the opposite sex (Sippola, Bukowski, & Noll, 1997). However, other findings reveal that 3- to 4-year-olds' social behaviour towards opposite-sex peers increases across this age range (Duveen, Lloyd, & Smith, 1988). Norms governing play with same- and opposite-sex peers become evident in the preschool years and strengthen during the middle childhood years, so that girls play more frequently with other girls, and boys play more frequently with boys (Maccoby, 1988; Rose & Rudolph, 2006). Empathic reactions to same-sex peers, and their precursors, may thus be part of a more general tendency to interact positively with members of one's own sex.

It is unclear, however, whether a tendency to interact differently with same-sex versus opposite-sex peers would be manifested in the context of a peer's distress. Such a pattern might be bound up with differences between overall rates of responding shown by girls and boys. Females are often thought to be more empathic than males, although the extent to which that is true depends on the methods used to assess empathy (Warden & MacKinnon, 2003). It is also unclear when any gender differences in empathic tendencies first appear. Experimental studies of newborns (Sagi & Hoffman, 1976; Simner, 1971) showed that newborn girls cried more often than newborn boys in response to another infant's audio-recorded cry. However, the use of cries of newborn girls in particular may have accounted for the finding that girls cried more often than boys in response to the other's cry. Six-month-old girls and boys tested in same-sex pairs did not differ in the extent to which they cried in response to peers' distress (Hay, Nash, & Pedersen, 1981). Murphy (1937) noted that there was no tendency for nursery school children to react sympathetically or otherwise to 'their own kind'. Indeed, in her sample, boys exhibited more 'active' defence responses to girls than girls gave to boys or girls, or than boys gave to boys.

It thus appears that, if toddlers' responses to distress are not completely random, there might be three alternative patterns of responding to distress, depending on the sex of the focal toddler and the sex of the peer. If similarity is indeed an important contextual factor, both girls and boys might be most likely to pay attention and respond to the distress of a same-sex peer. Alternatively, if girls are generally more empathic than boys, even in the first years of life, very young girls might be more likely to attend to distress and attempt to intervene than boys would be. Finally, to the extent that the two sexes evoke different responses from other people, both girls and boys might be most likely to respond in a particular way to girls as opposed to boys who are distressed. If toddlers caused an opposite-sex peer to become distressed, their reactions were not very positive. At the first visit, the toddlers were more likely to respond negatively to opposite-sex than same-sex peers. This pattern of responding suggests that the phenomenon of gender-segregation in children's formal peer groups (Maccoby, 1988) may be predated by earlier transactions with same- and opposite-sex peers. It would thus appear that differential responding to same- and opposite-sex peers emerges at a time when toddlers' peer relations are primarily organised by parents. It seems likely that children's own emerging preferences and interactive styles contribute to their gender-differentiated responding. At the same time, there was no evidence for overall gender differences in reactions to distress, although the power to test for such differences was limited by the fact that relatively few girls had the opportunity to react to distressed guests.

In my research, somewhat different reactions to distress were shown by hosts who had same-sex as opposed to opposite-sex guests. Similarity between host and guest did not affect prosocial responses. However, during one visit, negative reactions occurred most often when hosts had caused the distress of opposite-sex guests. A majority of hosts with opposite-sex guests responded negatively, as opposed to a minority of hosts with same-sex guests. There was no significant effect of similarity between host and guest at the second visit. The effect of similarity between host and guest was not explained by more general gender differences. There was no evidence for girls being more empathic to distressed peers. The sex of the host did not affect prosocial responses to either caused or witnessed distress, at either time point. At the time of the first visit, boys were more likely than girls to react negatively to distress, but the sexes did not differ in negative reactions by the second visit. There were no significant effects of the guest's sex on the host's reactions.

Familiarity of the Peer

A third dimension of the context in which responses to distress were assessed concerned other characteristics of the peer in addition to gender that might make prosocial responses to the distress more or less probable. One such characteristic is the level of acquaintance between the host and guest. Longitudinal change in responses to distress may reflect the effects of increasing familiarity between the peers, as well as their increasing age. Classic bystander intervention studies have demonstrated the greater readiness of adults to respond to familiar victims, even on the basis of a minimal acquaintance (Latané & Darley, 1970). Similarly, studies of somewhat older children have shown that children are more likely to respond with spontaneous prosocial responses to distress shown by friends as opposed to children with whom they are unacquainted (Farver & Branstetter, 1994). The issue of the degree of the host's familiarity with the guest was addressed here not only by looking at change over time, which is affected by increasing age as well as increasing familiarity, but also by examining whether the toddlers' responses to their guests' distress were affected by their length of acquaintance preceding the first visit.

Longitudinal analyses had indicated no significant change in prosocial responses to distress from the first to the second visit. To supplement the longitudinal analyses, the effect of the host's degree of acquaintance with the guest when the study began was examined with respect to prosocial and negative reactions to the guest's distress. At the first visit, those hosts who had known their guests all their lives were less likely than other toddlers to respond prosocially to their guests' distress. Hosts who had known their guests since birth were also less likely to respond negatively to their guests' distress, but that difference only approached statistical significance. The degree of acquaintance between host and guest did not affect reactions to distress at the second visit. At the first visit, the youngest children (18-month-olds) were significantly less likely to show prosocial behaviour in response to the peer's distress than were the older toddlers. However, fewer children responded to the peer's distress at the second visit, and prosocial responses did not increase over time; indeed, they declined, though the trend over time was not significant. These findings suggest that, as toddlers grow older, they may become more capable of responding to a peer's distress, but, upon increasing acquaintance with particular peers, they may be less likely to choose to do so. This finding was in conflict with the literature that suggests adults and children are more likely to respond positively to familiar people. However, there may be some habituation and extinction processes at work when children regularly spend time with particular peers. For example, in the preschool setting, children who cry frequently are less likely to be responded to positively by their peers (Caplan & Hay, 1989). This is somewhat supported here where the toddlers who had known their guests all their lives were less likely to respond either positively or negatively to guests' distress.

Experience with Other Children

Finally, the social circumstances in which children spend their days might affect their responses to peers. In particular, experiences with other peers and with siblings might affect the likelihood that a toddler will respond to distress. The study examined whether the experiences of being cared for with peers affected the nature of the toddlers' responses to their peers' distress. There are clear links between experiences in day care and the quality of early peer interaction (NICHD Early Child Care Research Network, 2001). To the extent that experience with day care may promote aggression (NICHD Early Child Care Research Network, 2003), toddlers who spend time being cared for with peers may show more aggressive and fewer prosocial responses to a peer's distress. Furthermore, in view of the many links between sibling and peer relationships (Dunn, 1993), we examined whether responses to distress were affected by the experience of having a sibling, and by birth order.

The toddlers' experiences in day care with other peers did not affect their responses to a particular peer's distress. However, experiences with older siblings appeared to have a negative effect, later born children being more likely to respond negatively to a peer's distress. My research asked whether hosts' regular exposure to other children affected their prosocial responses to a familiar peer's distress. Neither prosocial nor negative responses to peers' distress were affected by the experience of being cared for with peers. Nor did the experience of having siblings affect the toddlers' responses to distress. This contrasts with other studies that have shown children without siblings becoming more interested in their peers' distress (Nichols, Svetlova, & Brownell, 2014), although my findings concur with the latter study to the extent that birth order was important. By the time of the second visit, children who had older siblings responded more negatively to peers' distress than did firstborn children with or without siblings. A majority of later born children showed negative reactions, as opposed to a minority of firstborn children. The tendency to show negative reactions to distress may possibly reflect imitation of the way their older siblings respond to them. In any case, it appears that, although exposure to older siblings may accelerate the development of theory of mind (Ruffman, Perner, Naito, Parkin, & Clements, 1998), it does not necessarily make younger siblings more empathic.

A Contextual Study of Empathy in Middle Childhood

My research then continued into the middle childhood years. The purpose of the study was to examine the affective and cognitive dimensions of empathy with respect to age and sex differences; the effects of the context in which distress occurred; and to provide a fuller picture of the nature of empathy and its relation to prosocial behaviour during the middle childhood years. The participants were 80 primary school children between 7 and 10 years of age. There were 20 children of 7, 8, 9 and 10 years of age, and each age group consisted of 10 girls and 10 boys. Although these four age groups were targeted, the study's intention was to make a direct comparison between the younger (7- and 8-year-old) and the older (9- and 10-year-old) children. A picture-story design was the principal method of enquiry and measures of empathy were discerned from the child's responses to the picture-stories. In particular, the child's understanding of portrayed distress and their reflection on what they would feel in such a situation, and in addition, children's other responses to the stories were examined for tendencies to advocate prosocial and also non-prosocial reactions to distress. Moreover, the research sought further evidence of the validity of the construct of empathy by using the Bryant Index of Empathy Measurement (Bryant, 1982), and Strength and Difficulties Questionnaire completed by teachers (Goodman, 1994).

Four picture-stories entitled *Toy*, *Sports-day*, *Teasing* and *P.E.* were devised for the purposes of the research. Each picture portrayed a distressed child and a protagonist—the latter either caused or witnessed the distress—and the corresponding stories were constructed to match the contents of each picture. The interview schedule probed for the feelings and thoughts of the distressed children in the photographs, attribution of blame, the possible course of action to be undertaken by the other child, and the course of action that the child would pursue under the circumstances. Of the four picture-stories, the Toy and Teasing picture-stories depicted distress which had been caused deliberately by the pro-tagonist (non-distressed child) in the picture; whilst the Sports-day and P.E. picture-stories reflected the distress of children which was witnessed by the other children in the pictures, as caused by a source other than themselves. Consequently, the former two stories were known as stories of *caused distress* and the latter two were known as stories of *witnessed distress*. Children were assessed through their understanding of distress (cognitive component of empathy) and also their feelings about distress (emotional component of empathy). Each of these two components of empathy comprised four reaction types that represented these aspects of the empathic construct. Helpful and aggressive responses were also exam-ined. The occurrence of these reactions is described in relation to differ-ences in age and sex. Also, investigations were conducted in order to establish whether children responded differently according to whether they viewed pictures of protagonists who were the same sex or opposite sex as themselves, and moreover whether they reacted differently if the protagonist had caused the distress or merely witnessed it.

Cognitive Empathy: The Understanding of Distress

Four response types to picture-story questions were focused on in order to measure the extent to which children understood the distress and the protagonist's likely reactions. Firstly, children were given a recognition of emotion score, hereafter referred to as *recognition*, which represented their inference that the protagonist reflected the other child's emotions. This was ascertained through the question "How is the girl/boy feel-ing?". Therefore, the child's understanding of the distress as seen through the non-distressed child in the picture was assessed. Secondly, in order to ascertain whether children had understood the story that was read to them, the causal understanding construct of *comprehension* was focused on which was represented by the question "Why does she/he think the girl/boy is crying?". Thirdly, the response type *complexity* was analysed in order to reflect the degree to which children referred to complex emotions. Lastly, the extent to which children used *evaluative statements* was examined as a feature that was a reflection of their understanding of the social and moral issues involved in the story. Children's overall ability to understand distress was ascertained through a composite score of their attributions of recognition, comprehension, complexity and evaluation. Children's overall understanding of portrayed distress increased with age. Previous studies have generally concluded that there is a greater degree of cognitive involvement by older children whose ability to focus on others' inner states is more advanced than younger children. However, overall understanding scores did not differ significantly between girls and boys.

There were no age or gender differences in recognition scores. Also girls' and boys' recognition of emotion did not differ significantly depending on whether they were shown protagonists who were the same or the opposite sex as themselves. However, children were more able to recognise emotions for picture-stories in which the protagonist was a boy. For example, an 8-year-old boy claimed that the boy in the P.E. picture-story would feel "Uncomfortable because his brother is crying". A 10-year-old boy felt that the boy in the Toy picture-story would be feeling that "He should share with the girl cos he thinks that she'll think he's bad unless he shares". Another 10-year-old boy simply said he'd feel "Really distressed". With reference to the Toy picture-stories, two 10-year-old girls said that the boy in the Toy picture-story would be "Feeling rotten with himself", and "He's sad inside that he snatched the toy". Another 10-year-old girl claimed that the boy of the P.E. picture-story would be "…feeling sad that his brother fell off and he feels that it should have been him instead of his brother". Despite only approaching statistical significance, a sex by responsibility trend on recognition indicated that whereas boys scored more highly on recognition for pictures in which the distress had been caused, girls scored higher for those pictures in which the distress had been witnessed. An example of this was given by a 10-year-old boy in response to the Teasing picture-story when he described the gratuitous behaviour: "She'd feel ashamed of herself because she's making other people feel sad, and if she was the girl who had been teased, she wouldn't have liked it". Moreover, in reply to questions for the Sports-day picture-story, a 7-year-old girl claimed that the girl would feel "Very sorry for the boy because he should have won a prize".

In general, children scored highly on the comprehension aspect of the picture-stories. Answers to questions such as "Why does he think his brother is crying?" in relation to the P.E. picture-story for example, took the form of "Because he fell off the apparatus", as given by a 7-year-old boy. Also in reply to the question in the Sports-day picture-story "Does she think she did anything to make him feel that way?", an 8-year-old girl replied "No, because she did win and that's just a way of life". Younger and older children did not differ significantly in their ability to comprehend the cause of the distress; and girls and boys did not differ in the extent to which they were able to identify the causal nature of the distress. Moreover, girls and boys did not differ in their comprehension of distress according to whether they were shown protagonists who were the same sex or opposite sex as themselves; and children did not respond with differential comprehension of the distress depending on whether the protagonist had caused the distress compared to instances where the distress had come about through other means.

Older children's responses were more complex in nature than those of their younger peers. An example of a complex response was reported by a 10-year-old girl who vacillated: "He might be feeling a bit sad about what he's doing, or maybe he doesn't care at all and is saying 'I don't care if she wants it, I want it now, so I want this toy and I'm having this toy.'" Despite the fact that girls' reports tended to reflect a greater amount of complex thought, as reflected in the difference in mean scores, they did not differ significantly in this respect to their male peers. And girls and boys did not differ significantly in the complex nature of their responses according to whether they were shown protagonists who were the same or the opposite sex as themselves. Also, children's complex comments did not differ depending on whether the protagonist had caused the distress compared to instances where the distress had been witnessed.

Older children were significantly more evaluative in their responses to the distress they observed in the pictures. This is illustrated by the following responses given by 10-year-olds: "Well, I'd feel a bit upset that he didn't win any prizes. But I'd think it's not really my fault and I shouldn't be really upset, but I would feel sorry for this boy"; and: "He can say 'sorry'. But the girl is very upset and I don't know whether sorry is enough"; and "I would say 'sorry that you've fallen…' because the friend might not have a very good sense of balance and so I would help him to get better. So if he entered a competition and he had to climb the apparatus and walk upside down, then he could complete it and have a good sense of balance". Moreover, a 10-year-old boy responded to the P.E. story with "I'd feel very sad for that boy because he fell off and he might not be able to walk again". The same boy went on to say: "… because sometimes when people fall over, no one comes to them and they feel really sad and it spoils part of their life". However, girls and boys did not differ to the extent to which they employed evaluative statements. Also, girls and boys did not differ significantly in their evaluative statements depending on whether they were shown protagonists who were the same or the opposite sex as themselves. And there was a trend of children giving more evaluative statements when the distress had been caused rather than witnessed. For example, a 7-year-old boy explained the Toy picture-story by saying that the protagonist would feel sad because the girl was "…playing with the toy first". Another 7-year-old boy concluded in response to the Teasing picture-story with "She's feeling unhappy with herself because she knows she's taking the mickey out of someone and it's not a nice thing to do". Such findings are in line with Hoffman (1975) who believed that a more complex empathic understanding of another's feelings emerges and develops after early childhood. More specifically, through their more complex and evaluative reactions, older children, who were on the threshold of the period of formal operations as characterised by Piaget, confirmed expectations that they would behave in more intricate ways. Whereas the younger children have the ability to recognise the emotion and comprehend the distress, sensitivity to complex emotion and an awareness of social norms and moral principles relevant to distress incidents seem to be the distinguishing characteristics of older children which sets them apart from their younger counterparts.

Emotional Empathy: Feelings About Distress

Four response types were focused on in order to acquire a sense of children's feelings about the distress in the picture-stories. Firstly, children were rated for their own feelings of *sadness* through identification with the protagonist. Children's own projected emotions were ascertained through the question "How do you think you would feel if you were the girl/boy?". In so doing, children's tendencies to feel along with the other were investigated. Secondly, children were scored on the extent to which they applied *personalisation* to their responses, where this reflected a tendency to relate the actions of the picture-stories with their own personal behaviour and experiences. Thirdly, children's responses were assessed for *futility*—another dimension which it was thought would give an indication of emotionality among children. Finally, *guilt* related responses were also focused on for the purposes of assessing children's feelings when they were confronted with pictures that depicted distress. Children's overall reference to emotion was ascertained through a composite score of their attributions of sadness, personalisation, futility and guilt. Overall references to emotion did not vary with age, which is in contrast to the cognitive components of empathy. Although Hoffman (1975) principally stresses cognitive change, this therefore brings into question his theory that the capacity for this type of responding continues to evolve into adolescence. This research is in agreement with Strayer (1993) who found only slight increases of affect match with age among 5- to 13-year-olds when they responded to the observed emotions of stimulus vignettes. Both Hoffman and Piaget would argue that more primitive emotions of this nature are apparent early on in life, which thereafter develop into emotional reactions that are more productive, less egocentric, and more contained, or are at least diluted down with the developing cognitive abilities. Overall, girls' total feeling score, which represented a composite of the four types of emotion, was significantly greater than that of boys, and overall reference to emotion was significantly greater among girls than boys. According to the literature, over-arousal to a peer's distress, which may be experienced to a greater degree among girls, should result in the display of vicarious reactions. Consequently, this has the potential to lead to egoistic concerns so as to render them to be self-focused and distressed.

Examples of responses to the questions: "How do you think you would feel if you were the girl/boy?", ranged from "Upset?" and "I'd probably be upset", to "I'd be sorry for making her sad…because I didn't know how she was on the inside…'cos it's not how you look on the outside, it's how you are on the inside" (10-year-old girl). The identical scores in the two age groups meant that there was no difference between age in terms of the degree to which children reported feeling sadness. There was also no difference between the expressions of sadness by girls compared to those of boys. However, pictures with boy protagonists elicited more sadness from children. For example, in responses to the Toy picture-story, a 10-year-old girl said "I would feel sad with myself". Another 10-year-old girl said in response to the Toy picture-story that she'd feel "…sort of bad inside… and lonely inside". Moreover, girls reported more sadness when they viewed pictures with girl protagonists and boys reported more sadness when they viewed pictures with boy protagonists. For example, a 9-year-old girl said of the Teasing picture-story that she'd feel "Really sad. Because if somebody just teased me, I wouldn't have liked it"; and an 8-year-old boy's response to the Toy picture-story was: "I'd feel unkind because I've done something naughty". Children also reported more sadness for pictures in which the distress had not been caused by the protagonist. Moreover, two trends revealed an interaction with age of the child and an interaction with sex of the child. The first of these showed that, whereas older children expressed more sadness towards distress that had been caused by the protagonist, younger children did so for distress that had been witnessed by the protagonist. The second result which approached significance showed that, whereas boys were more likely to express sadness for pictures in which the protagonist had caused the distress, girls were more likely to do this for scenarios where the distress had been witnessed by the protagonist. For example, a 7-year-old boy said that he'd "Feel miserable" if he were the protagonist of the Teasing picture-story; and on viewing the P.E. picture-story, an 8-year-old girl said: "I'd say 'could you stop crying please cos you're making me feel sad'". These results thereby concur with those of Stotland and Dunn (1963) and Feshbach and Roe (1968) which revealed a greater propensity for children to respond with emotional empathy towards distressed peers of the same sex to themselves. However, this result differs from others such as the Bryant (1982) empathy questionnaire which showed that, compared with 6-year-old and 12-year-old children who showed less empathy to opposite-sex stimulus figures, the 9-year-old girls showed more empathy for both same-sex and opposite-sex questions. Although my study differs from many that have focused on this issue in that children's responses were assessed according to their similarity by way of sex with the non-distressed child, and not the distressed child, it seems that children are more likely to be able to feel sadness for a peer of the same sex as themselves who themselves are confronted with distress.

Younger and older children did not differ in their use of phrases that made references to themselves. Despite the fact that girls on average gave a greater number of personalised statements in their responses to distress, they did not do this to a significantly greater degree than boys. An example of a response of this nature was given by a 9-year-old girl who responded in this way to the Sports-day picture-story: "I just feel very sorry for people when they're crying". In addition, although there was no significant interaction with the sex of child for personalised responses, there was a significant effect of the protagonist's sex. This showed that children employed more personalised responses for picture-stories in which boys were the protagonists. Examples of this type of response were given by an 8-year-old boy who replied to the Toy picture-story with: "Because when I want to play with my sister, I don't snatch, I ask her"; and a 10-year-old boy stated that the boy in the P.E. picture-story "… could say 'are you okay, do you need to go to the teacher and have it checked?' Because, when I was little, I hit my head on the door, we used to pretend that everything was alive and my mum said 'go and hit the door and tell him off', and so if that boy was me, I might go and say that". Children did not differ significantly in their incorporation of personalised responses depending on whether the distress was depicted as having been caused by the protagonist or by another source. There were more expressions of personalisation for stories in which boys were depicted as the protagonist. This result could reflect the different themes depicted in the stories, and perhaps gives a clue to the differential emphasis placed by children on various behaviours. For example, the boy protagonists of the

Toy and P.E. picture-stories could have produced more personalised responses due to the acknowledgement that taking a toy and having an accident respectively are aspects of everyday life that they themselves more frequently encounter, and are therefore able to give more thought-provoking personal responses to these. An example of the importance of being able to appreciate the situation in order to reflect on it was given by a 9-year-old girl who replied to the P.E. picture-story with: "I don't know how I'd feel because I haven't got a brother or sister – but I'm going to have one in June. Then I'd really try and make them better".

Younger and older children reflected similar levels of futility in their comments, and girls tended to report a greater degree of futility than boys. Also, children's responses of a futile nature did not differ according to whether they viewed pictures of girls or boys. But children expressed a sense of futility more often for distress that had been caused by the pro-tagonist compared to that which had been witnessed. For example, when responding to the Teasing picture-story question "Does she think there is anything she could say or do to make her feel better?", a 10-year-old boy replied "No, nothing. Because maybe that girl doesn't want her to sit with her in case she calls her names again, or something". Whereas older chil-dren were more likely to express futility for distress that had been caused, younger children were more likely to do this for witnessed distress. Also, whereas boys expressed more futility for distress that had been caused by the protagonist, girls were more likely to do this for distress which had been witnessed by the protagonist. An example of this was given by a 9-year-old boy in response to the Toy picture-story who felt there was nothing the protagonist could say or do to make the girl feel better: "If he gives her the toy back, she might stop crying. But if he doesn't give her the toy back, she'll still cry". Also, in reply to the P.E. scenario, a 10-year-old girl felt there was nothing the boy could do to make the other feel better "Cos he's hurt himself and words don't make up for if you've been hurt on the lip, or something".

There was not a significant difference between guilty reactions to the picture-stories of the younger compared with the older children; how-ever, girls responded more guiltily than boys when they viewed the pictures. An illustration of a guilty response was given by an 8-year-old girl when viewing the Toy picture-story: "I'd feel really guilty with myself and I'd give it back because I felt guilty". Another example of this is the response of a 9-year-old girl to the Sports-day picture-story to which she claimed: "I'd feel quite guilty and upset. I'd feel very pleased that I won, but I'd still feel a bit guilty: someone who's been practising ages and ages to do this, and someone who's just come along and pushed you out of the scene". Despite the absence of a sex of child by sex of protagonist interaction, there was a significant effect of the protagonist's sex, so that pictures in which girls were the protagonist evoked more guilty reactions. Thus, girls were generally more likely than boys to feel guilty, but both girls and boys expressed more guilt when the protagonist was a girl. In addition, children made more guilty comments when they were presented with picture-stories in which the distress had been caused rather than witnessed by the protagonist. For example, a 10-year-old boy claimed that the girl whose derogatory behaviour caused the distress in the Teasing picture-story would have feelings of self-recrimination "...feeling guilty because she wouldn't have liked it if some of her friends were bullying her and calling names". This result replicates that of Thompson and Hoffman (1980) who showed that children were more likely to suggest self-punitive behaviour when they were described explicit wrongful acts. The fact that girls' own likely sadness, personal references and expressions of futility did not differ significantly to those of boys challenges previous findings that girls continue to place a greater emphasis on the sympathetic component of empathy than boys do, at least during the middle childhood years. These results are in line with the greater emotional responsiveness by girls to crying infants (Fabes, Eisenberg, Karbon, & Troyer, 1994), and also with girls' more prevalent exhibitions of emotional intensity (Bryant, 1987). The fact that girls are more likely to express guilt and more feeling expressions in general corroborates other studies (Brody & Hall, 2008; Zahn-Waxler, Cole, & Barrett, 1991). There were also more guilty responses for pictures in which the protagonists were girls. Both the Sports-day and Teasing picture-stories represented these, and this finding reflects children's appreciation that both scenarios generate feelings of guilt, despite not necessarily having caused the distress oneself.

From Helpful Recommendations to Aggressive Suggestions to Distress

Helpful responses were derived mostly from the questions "Does she/he think there is anything she/he could say or do to make her/him feel better?" and "What do you think you would do if you were the girl/boy?" However, helpful reactions were also noted if they were given in response to any of the other questions. Although older children tended to report more helpful behaviour than the younger children, this finding was not significant. Boys tended to report more helpful recommendations than girls. But there was a significant effect of the protagonist's sex such that children were more likely to give helpful recommendations for pictures in which the protagonist was a boy. For example, a 10-year-old boy said that the boy in the P.E. picture could say "It's okay, the pain will go away one day". Moreover, a significant sex of child by sex of protagonist interaction showed that, whereas boys were more likely to recommend help for pictures in which the protagonist was a girl, girls were more likely to do so when they were shown pictures in which the protagonist was a boy. An example of a helpful response to the Teasing picture-story in which the protagonist was a girl was given by a 7-year-old boy who said he would ingratiate himself: "Sorry I bullied you. Let's be friends now and shake hands". And, an 8-year-old girl said that she would "cuddle" the distressed boy in the P.E. picture. When asked what he would do if he were the girl in the Sports-day picture-story, a 9-year-old boy replied: "I would probably help him gain his confidence"; and a 10-year-old girl claimed that the boy in the Toy picture-story should "Let her play with the toy and they can play with it together". Children were more likely to give helpful recommendations when they viewed picture-stories in which the protagonist was a bystander to the distressed child and had not caused the distress. For example, a 9-year-old boy responded to the Sports-day picture-story with: "She could teach him how to run the race and make him happy". Moreover, a helpful response given by a 10-year-old girl when she viewed the Sports-day picture-story was: "She could say 'Ah, maybe there will be a next time and next time you will be able to win it'. Put her arm around him and say 'It's alright, you did very well. I'm sure the judges thought that'". Other children suggested that they would acquire help indirectly. For example, a 9-year-old said in response to the P.E. picture-story that the boy should "…take him to the teacher to stop crying". Furthermore, some children suggested rather magnanimously that the girl should give the boy the winning rosette: "I'll say 'here you are, do you want my badge, because I don't want it'" (9-year-old girl), and others suggested the use of distraction tactics: "Tell a joke" to cheer up the boy in the P.E. scenario (8-year-old girl).

As well as children's helpful reactions to distress, the research sought to investigate aggressive reactions that the children might give in response to the picture-story questions. Children's aggressive reactions could have occurred in response to any of the questions posed to them and were most frequently given in response to the Toy picture-story. Older children expressed more aggression than their younger peers. Despite the fact that girls tended to incorporate more aggressive solutions in their responses, this difference was not significant. But a significant effect of the protagonist's sex reflected that children were more likely to respond aggressively when they were shown pictures in which the protagonist was a boy. For example, a 9-year-old boy replied to the Toy picture-story that the boy would feel "Angry. Because if he wants to play with the toy for a long time, she didn't let him play with it and he will feel angry inside". Also, a 10-year-old girl claimed that the boy in the Toy picture-story would be "…feeling, 'I want that toy' and now that he's got it, he's not going to give it back to the girl". In addition, a significant effect of the source of responsibility showed that children were more likely to make aggressive suggestions when they viewed picture-stories in which the protagonist had caused the distress. An 8-year-old girl claimed that the boy in the Toy picture-story would feel "Happy because he got the toy for once". A 9-year-old girl said of the Toy picture-story that the boy would be feeling "Happy because he's made the other person sad by taking the toy off her". A 10-year-old boy stated that the boy in the Toy picture-story would be "Feeling like he doesn't care. Because he's got the toy now and she can sit there now and watch him play with it". Another claimed that this boy would "…feel quite pleased with himself…because he got the toy off the girl and he's making her cry". A 10-year-old girl said that the boy in the Toy picture-story would feel "Happy that he's made her sad". An example of an aggressive response by a 10-year-old girl who viewed the boy protagonist of the Toy picture-story was: "…I don't care if she wants it, I want it now, so I want this toy and I'm having this toy". Another example is that of a 10-year-old boy's unabashed remarks towards the Toy picture-story: "He's probably thinking '*yes*, I've made her cry and I've got the toy and I'll go and play with it'".

Children's Reactions to Distress from Early to Middle Childhood

The findings of the early childhood study confirm the existence of prosocial reactions to a companion's distress in the toddler years. However, such interventions are not shown by all toddlers, and are influenced by contextual factors. To put things into perspective, the toddlers in this study responded prosocially to distress about as frequently as adults in airports responded to simulated requests for help (Latané & Darley, 1970). The fact that toddlers in day care centres respond even less frequently (Lamb & Zakireh, 1997) may mirror the diffusion of responsibility occurring among adults when multiple witnesses are present (Darley & Latané, 1968). In general, the contextual factors that affect adults' responses to distress (personal responsibility for, similarity to and relationship with the victim) also affect toddlers' responses to their distressed peers. Even very young children are equipped with an array of responses to their peers' distress, ranging from the very helpful to the blatantly belligerent, from benevolent to malevolent, depending on who is distressed and their personal responsibility for the peers' discomfort.

The research revealed that children experience discomfort and that they are capable of exhibiting an array of emotional and behavioural responses to another's distress. However, children rarely exhibited vicarious emotion and in so doing were similar to the 3-year-olds observed by Murphy (1937) of whom she said: "It was not characteristic for these children to be anxious when one of their number was in distress. Most frequently, they merely looked up, kept an eye on the crying child, and went on with their play" (p. 96). That said, the few instances of vicarious emotion in my study included an illustration of a host after he had caused the distress. Namely, he and his girl guest were sitting on tricycles side by side in the sitting room. In a somewhat sudden rampage, the boy host pulled his girl guest towards him and hit her abruptly on the face. The girl cried loudly and ran to her mother. The host looked on, looked towards his mother, and began to cry as loudly as his guest. Another example of vicarious emotion after causing distress occurred when a girl guest had been playing with building blocks at a table. Her boy host approached and knocked down the tower she had just built onto the floor. The girl cried and screamed and the boy cried instantaneously and screamed whilst looking at his guest. An episode of vicarious emotion displayed by a host after having had no role in the instigation of distress himself, occurred whilst two boys were playing in the sitting room with their mothers. The guest became restless as he needed to go to the toilet. Whereas neither mother acknowledged his discomfort, his boy guest looked on anxiously with a pained expression. A further illustration of vicarious emotion after a witnessed distress event occurred when two boys were playing with a toy on the sitting room floor. The guest caught his finger in the toy and said "ouch". Looking towards his guest, the boy host also said "ouch" and looked distraught.

Could the relatively infrequent exhibition of vicarious emotion therefore mean that children do not participate emotionally in their peers' distress? Alternatively, do they exhibit this arousal in another way that might not have been detected among these toddlers? According to Hoffman (1975), vicarious emotion during the toddler years should be rife, and subsequent studies have confirmed the emergence of these behaviours (Zahn-Waxler, Radke-Yarrow, et al., 1992). However, other studies have found that the likelihood of children becoming distressed is minimal. The present findings confirm that children of this age do respond with vicarious emotion. However, the frequency of this behaviour was low. Despite being paired with 'best friends', many guests were not as familiar to the hosts as other pairings, and the quality of friendship may have affected their inclination to respond vicariously to their distress. Also, and in accordance with the observations of Darley and Latané (1968) and Caplan and Hay (1989) and theory of diffusion of responsibility, the low frequency of this behaviour could be due to the fact that the children's mothers were present. However, further studies have shown that children at even younger ages are not only able to respond to distress with vicarious reactions and also prosocial responses, but also do so in the presence of their mothers, thereby providing evidence of empathic concern and prosocial behaviour in the first year of life. An example of this is Liddle, Bradley, and McGrath's (2015) study of baby empathy. They examined 8-month-old infants' responses to naturalistic peer distress and found that gaze towards the distressed infant was most commonly exhibited, followed by socially directed behaviours, including affect, with few instances of self-distress. Also, unlike previous studies, the presence of mothers did not impede babies' responses and in fact the babies prioritised their attention to the distressed peer after which they would typically seek out the distressed peer's mother, and thereafter their own mothers. Moreover, the study showed that infants' direct responses were successful in alleviating the distress for more than a third of the occurrences.

The girls and boys of the early childhood study did not show significant differences in their display of vicarious emotion, although there was a tendency for boys to be more prone to do this than girls. This result therefore contrasts with studies that have found girls to show more emotion than boys. However, the findings should be interpreted with caution as the occurrence of this behaviour was minimal. It could well be that children who are friends are unlikely to become emotionally involved in this way and instead show other behaviours when faced with distress. The children in their early childhood years did not vary their display of vicarious emotion according to whether they reacted to same-sex or opposite-sex peers. However, of the children in the middle childhood study, girls expressed more sadness when they viewed pictures of girl protagonists, compared with boys who did so towards boy protagonists. Of course, the limited display of vicarious emotion in the early childhood study does not allow us to conclude that children of this age are less biased according to the sex of the child to whom they respond. But it is clear that, by middle childhood, expressions of sadness are levelled to those of the same sex with whom the children seem to be identifying. Hoffman (1975, 1987) suggested that when children victimise others, they find themselves involuntarily experiencing the negative emotions of their victims.

Unlike the children in their early childhood years, who did not show differences in their exhibition of vicarious emotion depending on whether the distress had been caused by themselves or witnessed, the children of the middle childhood study expressed more futility and guilt for incidents in which the distress had been caused by the protagonist. Moreover, whereas older children and boys expressed more futility when the distress had been caused, younger children and girls did so when they were reporting about distress which the protagonist in the pictures had witnessed as an innocent bystander.

Although the toddlers were more likely to seek information about their peers' distress rather than to display vicarious emotion, this activity was not frequent. Perhaps this is not surprising as children's understanding of others' distress has been noted as emerging from 2 to 3 years of age. The findings are in line with studies that have found perspective-taking capacities to distressed others to be infrequent if not non-existent at these ages. Moreover, these results challenge other studies that have demonstrated that an empathic ability in the form of perspective-taking is apparent in children as young as 3 years of age when they appear to infer an emotion. An emphasis has been made on the second year as a time when there is a greater capacity to role-take (Campos, Campos, & Barrett, 1989; Nichols et al., 2014), when the beginning of representational thought and use of symbols have implications for children's abilities to infer others' perspectives and feelings. By 2–3 years of age, children have been shown to correctly distinguish between and to name various emotional states through facial and vocal expressions (Denham, 1986). Hoffman (1975) himself placed great weight on this period as a time when children's cognitive skills come to the fore and accompany the already present vicarious emotional reactions to ensure a more constructive empathic response.

Could it be that the children of the early childhood study were merely on the verge of being able to cognitively appreciate their peers' distress, hence the low levels of this behaviour? Would another year or so to their ages have shown more evidence of this type of empathy? Or could it be that, as Piaget and others have noted, this activity might not be apparent until much later? Given more opportunity to react in this way, children this young might have shown an aptitude for cognitively appreciating distress. Moreover, we may ask whether the seeking of information is the best means of detecting whether children are able to understand distress, or is there a better assessment of this behaviour? Certainly the observational setting restricts the investigation of this aspect of empathy, as it is not possible to ask the child directly how she or he feels about the distress they encounter. However, the observational procedure in a naturalistic setting in which mothers were present did provide an opportunity to observe whether a child would refer to mothers in order that they might gain a better understanding of the distress.

By the sixth to seventh years of middle childhood, the dissipation of self-centred egocentricity (Piaget & Inhelder, 1956), and the emergence of an authentic empathic understanding of another's feelings (Hoffman, 1975), ensures that children develop the capacity to think systematically, although this is only the case for concrete objects and activities. The study by Strayer (1993), for example, of 5- to 13-year-olds showed that a greater amount of perspective-taking was apparent with age. The 7- and 8-year-olds responded in self-relative ways according to their own experience compared with the older children who were more likely to focus on others' inner states, thereby confirming the thoughts of Hoffman and Piaget. In accordance with Piaget's claims about the ability to role-take with age, my research confirmed age as being a predictor for the occurrence of perspective-taking skills, at least in terms of children's ability to construct complex statements and make social and moral evaluations of the situation. Reactions such as these are arguably a result of decreased egocentrism and centration, increasing discrimination, recognition of emotion cues, inferential ability, and the facilitation of language. Moreover, whereas younger children view emotions in terms of external situations accompanied by behavioural reactions, older children possess a more mature understanding of emotion and use internal mental states to define their feelings.

During early childhood, girls and boys did not differ significantly from each other in their understanding of distress through seeking information about it, although a result that approached significance suggested that boys were more likely to do this. The majority of previous research has indicated that girls in particular are more likely to possess greater perspective-taking abilities (Zahn-Waxler, Radke-Yarrow, et al., 1992;

Zahn-Waxler, Robinson, & Emde, 1992). However, in keeping with other studies that have not shown differences among girls and boys (Murphy, 1937), the present findings are in agreement. By middle childhood, results are similar, with no difference between the sexes in their ability to understand distress. This finding conflicts with previous evidence of girls who have been shown to possess a greater ability to take the perspective of others (Eisenberg, Shell, Pasternack, Lennon, et al., 1987). Even sub-categories of what has previously and crudely been termed perspective-taking that represented this ability did not show girls and boys to perform significantly differently from one another. Therefore, unlike the differences that were found in children's understanding about distress with age, differences according to sex were not apparent. Overall, findings of my research show that girls and boys did not differ in their perspective-taking abilities to a significant degree during the early or middle childhood years. And neither study showed children to be any more likely to take the perspective of children of their own sex compared with those of the opposite sex, although the children in early childhood were more likely to make attributions about the emotions of boy rather than girl protagonists.

The results from both studies imply that children's ability to take the perspective of others in the form of seeking information about it or understanding it is related to their prosocial abilities as reported by their teachers and mothers. Conversely, the exhibition of vicarious emotion in early childhood and their own attributions of sadness as given in the study of middle childhood are related more particularly with non-prosocial behaviours outside the context of distress. This outcome conflicts with Barnett and Thompson's (1985) findings of vicarious emotion being related particularly to helpful behaviour, rather than perspective-taking abilities which did not. However, my research is in accordance with Eisenberg, Fabes, Schaller, and Miller (1989) who found that children's self-report of empathy when exposed to another person's distress was unrelated to their prosocial behaviour, suggesting that the sympathetic response requires a degree of emotional control to allow children to be other-oriented. Also, Eisenberg and Fabes (1992) concluded that children who experience personal distress when faced with empathy-inducing events are not likely to respond with sympathy because their emotional distress makes them self-focused. Therefore, empathic responding is not necessarily related to social competence, so that the overwhelming feelings of personal distress that usually accompany strong empathic responding may actually inhibit socially skilful behaviour.

The middle childhood study revealed that children's *feeling* responses in general, and in particular their guilty responses, were related to their scores on the Bryant (1982) empathy questionnaire. These findings validate the emotional empathy investigated as part of the picture-story measure, as the questionnaire was designed by Bryant to specifically tap this component of empathy. However, one of the emotional constructs that represented children's attributions of their *sadness* was negatively related with the emotional empathic component of guilt, and *sadness* was related with children's non-prosocial behaviour as assessed by their teachers. This suggests that this particular feature of emotional empathy may not be of a prosocial orientation, and could be described as being detrimental in terms of the likelihood of helping. Like many other studies that have attempted to pin-point empathy, this research has also distinguished between the two components of empathy that represent its cognitive and emotional nature. However, unlike other studies that have tackled this issue, the early childhood study revealed a need to differentiate further within these two components. Results show the importance of this. Whereas some forms of emotional empathy are related to prosocial behaviour, others are related to behaviour of a non-prosocial nature.

Generally therefore, the present findings substantiate past theories that empathy, and in particular its emotional component, facilitates social interaction (Mead, 1934). However, results from the Goodman (1994) questionnaire suggest that, whilst the cognitive appraisal of distress is associated with children's prosocial behaviour, there seems to be an association between their emotional reactions to distress and non-prosocial, even conduct-disordered, behaviour. Murphy (1937) stated that: "Sympathy…is intimately connected with all the other responses of a friendly and constructive nature that are the foundation of a cooperative society" (p. 3). Moreover, her observations of children's defence methods for the sympathetic assistance of other children, by children who were aggressive, led Murphy to say that: "Aggression, sympathetic responses, intelligence, and fears do not occur like books on a shelf, but the internal character of each conditions the other in specific ways…" (Murphy, 1937, pp. 280–2). Also, Hoffman (1976) claimed that: "The realisation that [the child's] feelings resemble those experienced independently by others in similar situations must inevitably contribute to a sense of 'oneness' which preserves and may even enhance the child's developing motivation to alleviate others' distress" (p. 136).

The children of the early childhood study often attempted to alleviate the distress of their peers, but did not always succeed. However, compared with the infrequent empathic reactions by children in their early childhood years, helpful activity was a more common type of reaction when they were observed in their homes, and therefore corroborates findings of helpful behaviour among toddlers in similar situations (Zahn-Waxler & Radke-Yarrow, 1982). Among the children in the middle childhood study, there were no differences in age. These findings are therefore similar to the results of studies that have found stability in the amount of children's helping with age in middle childhood (Eisenberg et al., 1987), rather than those that have either found age-related increases or decreases. Moreover, unlike the studies by Staub (1970) which found older children to offer less help for fear of disapproval, such a distinction was not apparent between the younger and older children of the middle childhood study. However, whereas Staub's research involved actual observations, the present study was confined to children's *reports* of helpful behaviour. Had the children of the research been required to be helpful rather than merely report on what they would do, the amount of helping might be considerably different.

By the second session of the early childhood study, boys were more helpful than girls, and although not significant, the study of middle childhood revealed that boys were slightly more helpful than girls. Therefore the present findings differ from studies of early childhood in which girls have been found to be more helpful (Zahn-Waxler, Robinson, et al., 1992), where girls and boys have not been found to differ in the amount of help they give (Murphy, 1937), and those of middle childhood where helpful behaviour is particularly prevalent among girls (Fabes et al., 1994). Boys of the early childhood study in particular showed a greater willingness to help, and are therefore similar to the boys of the Hoffman and Levine (1976) study who considered more action alternatives than girls. These findings, and also those in middle childhood, suggest that, when children are required to comment about helping, girls, whether through a greater willingness to talk, do so more than boys, but that when it comes to actually having to help, boys are able to do this as often, if not more often than their female counterparts. In contrast to the children of the early childhood study who did not show a preference for a particular sex peer during their helpful behaviour, the children of the middle childhood study gave more helpful recommendations when they viewed picture-stories in which the protagonist was a boy. Moreover, boys gave more helpful suggestions towards picture-stories in which the protagonist was a girl compared with girls whose helpful suggestions occurred mostly for picture-stories which depicted boy protagonists. Therefore, unlike children's same-sex expressions of sadness, their recommendations of helpful behaviour were more common towards protagonists of the opposite sex.

Compared with the first session in particular of the early childhood study, in which a greater amount of helpful behaviour took place after distress which the children caused themselves, the children of the middle childhood study gave more helpful suggestions when the protagonist was a bystander to the distress compared to episodes where the protagonist had actually caused the distress. Therefore, in contrast to studies that have found young children to be less likely to help with distress once they had caused it themselves (Zahn-Waxler et al., 1979), the findings of the early childhood research show that children were willing and able to help with distress they had caused themselves. However, this does not seem to be as likely when children are asked to report their helpful behaviours in middle childhood. Could it have been that the children of the early childhood study had yet to comprehend their role in the contravention and to feel quite unashamed about remedying the distress situation first instigated by themselves? Or do they have a sense of guilt which equips them with the need to rectify the misdeed? By middle childhood, the emphasis is placed on help after witnessing distress in particular. Do these children consider distress that has been caused beyond the scope for help? Thompson and Hoffman (1980) found that children in their middle childhood years particularly focus on distress that they have caused themselves with self-punitive thoughts. Could it be that these thoughts override any intentions they might have had to help, and thereby make them focus on witnessed distress instead, compared with the younger children, who perhaps out of ignorance of causation, tend to confront these situations more directly?

It was anticipated that because conflict is known to occur among children, aggressive reactions would result both from interactions between peers during early childhood and on viewing picture-stories that depicted conflict scenarios in middle childhood. Indeed, aggravating behaviour during the early childhood study was one of the most common types of behaviour when children were confronted with distress. This result therefore replicates studies that have been conducted with siblings (Dunn & Munn, 1986) and peers (Murphy, 1937). Other observations have not however shown aggression to be particularly prevalent when children are confronted with distressed peers. Of the children in their middle childhood years on the other hand, there was a tendency for older children to show more aggression than their younger peers.

The toddler study showed boys as being more aggressive, particularly during the first session, a finding that is in accord with results from previous research. By middle childhood, there does not seem to be a significant difference between girls and boys with respect to their aggressive suggestions. It is important to consider when comparing two different measures of observation and self-report that, being involved directly as in the former might evoke more aggression than simply relating fictional incidents of distress. Although it is not possible to compare the two studies directly, it seems that the gulf between girls and boys in their aggressive reactions was wider during the early childhood years when boys aggravated to a greater degree than girls. Whereas the boys of the early childhood study were particularly aggressive towards distressed girls, and in particular during the first session, the children of the middle childhood study were not aggressive to one sex more than another. However, the children of the latter study did make a greater number of aggressive suggestions when they viewed pictures in which boys were protagonists. The studies showed that children were more likely to actually aggravate distress and also suggest that they would be aggressive to distress that had been caused deliberately. Moreover, boys rather than girls in the early childhood study were more likely to aggravate distress they caused themselves. Instead, girls were more likely to aggravate distress they witnessed.

Associations Between Cognitive Understanding and Vicarious Emotion: Is Empathy a Valid Construct and Are We Studying Empathy After All?

Both studies indicated that children who show an understanding of distress, whether it be described to them through picture-stories or confronts them directly in the natural setting of the home environment, also tend to display vicarious emotion. The interrelation between the two components gives credence to theories that have described a "…cohesion between the cognitive [and] affective…aspects of the child' behaviour" (Feshbach, 1982, p. 320). Such results corroborate the multifaceted nature of the empathic response as comprising two very different but complementary ways of reacting, and highlights the fact that cognitive and vicarious responses are not mutually exclusive as people think about feelings as well as reacting emotionally to them. By operating in conjunction with one another, cognitive and affective processes serve to ameliorate the observer's assessment of what the other person is feeling. The empathic process may originate through simple mechanisms like conditioning, association and mimicry that arouse affect, followed by cognitive elaboration. Instead, there may be a more deliberate cognitive process that in turn triggers a vicarious affective reaction. Either way, the cues of the model's affective state serve as stimuli for arousing a similar affective state in the observer, which in turn provides the observer with information about the model's affective state. It could be argued that it is cognition that defines structural development and that affect may demonstrate stage-like properties through systematic shifts with age with its development being tied to cognition. Yet, as Piaget warned that neither affect nor cognition is causal for the other, the question about specific cognitive-affective links applicable to empathy development still remains.

In contrast to early formulations of empathy that were couched in either predominantly cognitive or affective terms, more recently: "Empathy means the experience of understanding and the emotional and intellectual sharing of another person's situation" (Kalliopuska, 1992, p. 1). In psycho-analytic perspectives, the child's social development depends on the gradual expansion of ego to include others, and if ego functions are to be adjusted to reality, they not only require cognitive but also affective-emotional differentiation of the self and non-self, of one's own experience and the experience of others. Since the 1970s, numerous debates about the integration of cognition and emotion have emerged and researchers have claimed that "…even though the abilities to take the role of the other and treat oneself as an object make role-taking emotions possible, these capacities are nearly useless for social control without their affective accompaniments" (Shott, 1979, pp. 1329–30). Also: "The study of relationships will suffer if relevant data from the cognitive domain are not integrated into the theory" (Hay, 1985, p. 152). Moreover, "…children' understanding of their partner' inner states…is crucially related to the emotional context of the interaction. [It is important] to frame our developmental questions in terms of both cognitive and emotional considerations" (Dunn, 1995, p. 200).

This study therefore questions theories and studies that compartmentalise the cognitive and emotional aspects of empathy and those that tend to focus on one or the other: as when for example a person can decentre and achieve understanding without necessarily feeling the same way as the other person. The conceptualisation of empathy as encompassing both cognitive and vicarious components is increasingly favoured. Research into the twofold nature of empathy has gradually replaced research that over the years has tended to focus solely on one or the other of the cognitive or emotional aspects of empathy. Even though Piaget and other cognitive psychologists acknowledged that affect is an integral part of human behaviour, they also assumed that once cognitive processes are in motion, they can be studied without recourse to affect. Theories such as this are valid for cognition in the physical domain, but should be reconsidered regarding the social domain, in which affect plays a prominent role. In addition to the ability to take on the role of another person, the affective response gives empathy its unique property. Results of this research point to the need to be sensitive to the particular aspects *within* each component in order to gain a wider picture of the concept we call empathy. Despite attempts to integrate the two components of empathy, the fundamental distinction has been maintained between the cognitive and affective elements. The capacity of the latter to mirror another's feelings and of the former's complex, not necessarily conscious process, empowers one with an awareness of what the other is feeling. Over time, psychological research into empathy has typically been predicated on one or the other of these general definitions. Therefore, whilst some stress only cognitive components of comprehension of social situations or role-taking ability, others underscore affective arousal, which entails the matching of one's own feelings and emotions with someone else's. Alternatively, others accept any definition as long as it has some reference to an individual's ability to feel, perceive and sense from another person's viewpoint. It is only relatively recently that theory has attended to the need to include both affect and cognition in predicting prosocial behaviour and hence move away from the segregation of affect and cognition.

Despite attempts to target responses that reflect empathy, both the early and middle childhood studies lead us to speculate about what children were really feeling and thinking at the time of the research. Instead, it seems we have come full circle to Lipps's (1903) *Einfühlung*, with its meaning of 'feeling into another', used by him to refer to 'interpersonal knowledge', 'inner participation' and 'self-activation', perhaps a more accurate reflection of the type of empathy tapped in the middle childhood study. These descriptions invoke an empathy in which the cognitive and affective aspects are not mutually exclusive. Instead, they evoke a synthesis and a conceptualisation of empathy similar to that of Greenson (1960), whose observation of empathy was a form of 'emotional knowing' which results from experiencing another's feelings through perception and emotion. Of primary concern with the middle childhood study is the fact that, unlike the early childhood study, in which children's reactions to real distress were observed directly, children's reactions were in the form of verbal reports that may not necessarily have been a true reflection of their reactions, and therefore merely represent children's *recommendations* for various behaviours. Therefore, whilst children's responses are the next best thing to actually observing them, it is vital to take heed that children's responses may not necessarily represent their actions if they were to find themselves in the situations described to them.

How much of the empathic capabilities of young children therefore have been tapped? Such is the elusive nature of empathy that the findings prompt the question whether it is empathy that is being measured. Indeed, can it be defined? Can empathy be measured? And are physiological techniques, structured assessments and observational procedures warranted? What is clear from my research are findings of, on the one hand, detached responses from the picture-story technique, and on the other, few responses that are subject to misinterpretation during the observational procedure. The distress stimulus prompted children to display significant involvement in many ways in the emotional lives of others, both as causes and as bystanders, as well as inducing them to talk knowledgeably about the feelings and thoughts of others. On the one hand, they expressed concern, attempted to comprehend or experience the situations and engaged in behaviours directed towards alleviating distress in others. Children were also unresponsive and indifferent, and sometimes found others' distress amusing, and under some circumstances became distressed or aggressive. Overall, both studies showed that: "Humans react to their distressed companions in many different ways: with wonder, disinterest, repugnance, or pity, to name but a few possibilities" (Hay & Demetriou, 1998, p. 224). However, it also seems to be the case that "…young peers influence each other's behaviour, but the extent to which they do so depends, as it does for older persons, on situational constraints and enhancements" (Hay, Nash, & Pedersen, 1983, p. 561). Also, there "…are increases, no changes, and decreases depending on the prosocial behaviour, the research methods, and the ages studied" (Radke-Yarrow, Zahn-Waxler, & Chapman, 1983, p. 42).

It seems that preschool children are not only egocentric, selfish and aggressive but are also perceptive and respond prosocially across a broad spectrum. Of all reactions shown by the early childhood children, the majority were attentive behaviours during which children oriented towards their distressed peers, ceased their current activity and approached peers. These results are reminiscent of previous research such as Murphy's (1937), whose illustrations of sympathetic behaviour were confined to the most active responses, since the less definite ones, such as merely watching, were more frequent and more ambiguous. At both time points, but especially during the first visit, boys became more involved with their peers' distress, compared with girls who were less likely to react to their peers' distress. The involvement of boys took the form of helpful and, at the other extreme, aggressive behaviours, which was perhaps as a result of the overall greater amount of attention paid by boys rather than girls to peers once they became distressed. An example of the less inhibited behaviour displayed primarily by boys occurred when a boy in the early childhood study was amused by the distress of his girl peer. The children had attached felt-tip pen lids to the ends of their fingers and were improvising, showing off their 'long fingers'. The boy prodded the girl with one of his 'fingers' on her neck. The girl cried and the boy stared at her whilst saying despairingly "oh, girls, girls…". Observations such as this have prompted developmentalists to suggest that: "Boys are often cruel, not because they wish to cause suffering, but merely because they enjoy seeing the victim make queer motions without once thinking how it feels" (Kirkpatrick, 1908, p. 121). The apparent absence of a sympathetic reaction from this boy could therefore be attributed to a lack of experience and imagination.

Hume (1751) felt that it was perfectly natural for people to empathise more with those who are familiar to them than with strangers and that doing this was not necessarily incompatible with being moral. Girls and boys of both studies tended to react more empathically and more favourably towards children of the same sex as themselves compared with those of the opposite sex. Furthermore, boys were as likely to react to both distress that they caused and that which they witnessed, with perhaps a greater tendency to become involved after they themselves caused the distress. Girls, however, tended to react and in particular to aggravate distress which they had witnessed as innocent bystanders. This pattern was repeated in the middle childhood study where, compared with the tendency for boys to recognise the distress that had been caused by protagonists, girls exhibited a greater understanding for distress when they were shown pictures in which the protagonist had witnessed the distress as an innocent bystander to it.

If affective responses appear in tandem with cognitive role-taking skills, then it appears that empathic responsiveness emerges during the preschool period. If an infant's cries in response to a peer crying are considered as empathic behaviour, then empathy can be said to emerge almost congenitally. But is this latter behaviour 'true' empathy or a precursor to later empathic behaviour? Despite the definitional issue and the fact that data in this area are far from complete, a number of generalisations can be made. It seems that children at a very early age are able to discriminate between emotional signs in others, that empathy begins early but becomes more differentiated and purposeful with additional years, and that not all children are equally responsive or equally empathic. Due to the low numbers of children who responded in this way, it is only possible to hint at the fact that boys react with more vicarious and cognitive empathy during early childhood. By middle childhood, it was girls who showed a greater aptitude in their vicarious and cognitive empathic responses, thereby implying that with age, convention seems to dictate that empathy plays a greater role in the social repertoire of girls rather than boys. Also, aggression among girls is associated with reparation for their own aggressive misconduct, but is not associated with a generally greater sensitivity to another's distress. Feelings of guilt may be a precursor of altruism in girls. In order to heighten a sense of responsibility, guilt is induced for interpersonal aggression and transgressions. There seems to be a gradual refinement of gender from its initiation as an over-generalised concept in early childhood after which time diversified paths lead to the gulf between girls and boys in their middle childhood years. Distinctions between the two types of empathy are particularly important where sex differences are concerned. Could it be that the increasing prevalence of sex differences with age is the result of the ways in which we construct ourselves through the world of our social relations through the expectations of others and the social rules which govern these relations? My findings implied that this is the case.

There is empirical support for the multidimensional feature of empathy proposed long ago by Adam Smith, which manifests itself in affective, behavioural and symbolic domains of expression. As well as Hoffman's (1975) postulation of a biological preparedness for empathy that is already present in infancy, evolutionary and neuroscience perspectives emphasise the value for the individual and species of a capacity for empathy. Furthermore, genetic factors have been implicated in children as early as the second year of life (Zahn-Waxler, Robinson, et al., 1992). To relate empathically to other people usually involves a certain effort, as empathy is an attitude that requires a temporary setting aside of one's feelings and needs, and a partial stepping outside of oneself with the result that it constitutes the basis of our ability to develop and to maintain mature relationships with other people. To a degree, my research confirmed the early origins of this capacity. By studying both cognitive and affective aspects of empathy, it is clear that neither one of these components alone is sufficient to represent empathy. The importance of distinguishing between these two dimensions of empathy was highlighted in the study of middle childhood when children responded differently to the picture-stories to questions that required a recognition of the protagonist's emotion compared with those that aimed at tapping the children's own sadness. An example of this is a response by a child to one of the picture-stories, who, on the one hand said that the protagonist would be "Happy because he's got the toy he wanted", but that he himself would be "Sad cos I made the girl cry". Even Piaget (1981) acknowledged the importance of affects that "…by being represented…last beyond the presence of the object that excites them" (p. 44). Therefore, emotions do not simply happen and then disappear, but are instead routinely included as part of our representation of a wide variety of events, and are therefore stored as part of our basic cognitive representation.

Additional research is needed in natural settings in order to investigate the affective components of empathic responding, its duration, nature of emotional contagion of the parties regarding affect, and empathic responses to that affect. Moreover, in order to acquire a more representative picture of the developmental progression of children's reactions when they encounter distress, it is necessary to assess children in between these two age groups with observational and structured assessments. This is especially interesting as researchers have highlighted the period between 4 and 7 years as a time when a child is particularly prone to "…assume the part of some other person…and acts out the character to some extent" (Kirkpatrick, 1908, p. 138). In view of the multidimensional nature of emotional and cognitive processes involved in the empathic process, and the changes in empathy likely to occur with the emergence of new cognitive structures (Hoffman, 1975), it is evident that these processes should be studied longitudinally in the very young child through to the preadolescent child in order to understand and describe developmental changes in empathy. In fact, the need for more research of this kind cannot be underestimated as "…despite its acknowledged importance as a major interpersonal dimension, empirical research on empathy does not parallel its theoretical salience" (Feshbach, 1978, p. 2).

Both studies explored issues of stability, interconnections and possible mediators of behaviours, as well as focusing on early patterns of sex differences. These differences include the fact that whereas girls seem to internalise their emotions, boys externalise theirs and take a generally aggressive stance towards peer conflict. Girls therefore tend to adhere to a more socially acceptable approach, suppressing their anger and aggressive tendencies, thereby mirroring the difference found in observational studies of conflict in preschool classrooms. The research investigated general trends and also individual differences as: "It is not legitimate to assume that a sample of behaviour in one situation tells much about a child…Any behaviour must be sampled in a variety of situations over a period of time, along with other aspects of behaviour, and as this is done, its actual relation to the personality in both subjective and objective terms must be observed in detail" (Murphy, 1937, p. 280). However, as well as children's own reasoning powers and emotional responsiveness, the importance of including information about the quality of their social relationships should be incorporated in future research. The process of understanding feelings observed in others begins through affect that is often aroused vicariously in humans through involuntary, minimally cognitive mechanisms. Arguably, empathy has the potential to enable someone to respond in a helpful, responsible way, or in a destructive way. It has both affective and cognitive elements so that one feels what the other feels and then, through a complex, not necessarily conscious process, becomes aware what the other is feeling. Above all, empathy epitomises a benevolence, which in the words of Kalliopuska (1992) "…can be considered the primary stage of social tact on the way towards humanity" (p. 134). Such early appearances of empathic behaviour allude to a combination of genetic predisposition for empathy as well as influential environmental effects. But what role does nature play compared with its nurture counterpart? The focus will now shift to address the biological and social influences on the development of empathy.

References

Barnett, M. A., & Thompson, S. (1985). The role of perspective-taking and empathy in children's Machiavellianism, prosocial behaviour, and motive for helping. *Journal of Genetic Psychology, 146,* 295–305.

Brody, L. R., & Hall, J. A. (2008). Gender and emotion in context. In M. Lewis, J. M. Haviland-Jones, & L. F. Barrett (Eds.), *Handbook of emotions* (3rd ed., pp. 395–408). New York: The Guilford Press.

Bryant, B. K. (1982). An index of empathy for children and adolescents. *Child Development, 53*, 413–425.

Bryant, B. K. (1987). Mental health, temperament, family, and friends: Perspectives on children's empathy and social perspective-taking. In N. Eisenberg & J. Strayer (Eds.), *Empathy and its development*. Cambridge, UK: Cambridge University Press.

Campos, J. J., Campos, R. G., & Barrett, K. C. (1989). Emergent themes in the study of emotional development and emotion regulation. *Developmental Psychology, 25*, 394–402.

Caplan, M. Z., & Hay, D. F. (1989). Preschoolers' responses to peers' distress and beliefs about bystander intervention. *Journal of Child Psychology and Psychiatry, 30*, 231–242.

Darley, J. M., & Latané, B. (1968). Bystander intervention in emergencies: Diffusion of responsibility. *Journal of Personality and Social Psychology, 8*, 377–383.

Demetriou, H. (1998). *Reactions of girls and boys to the distress of their peers in early and middle childhood*. PhD dissertation. King's College, University of London.

Denham, S. A. (1986). Social cognition, prosocial behaviour, and emotion in preschoolers: Contextual validation. *Child Development, 57*, 194–201.

de Waal, F. B. M. (2005, October 8). The empathic ape. *New Scientist*, pp. 52–54.

Dunn, J. (1993). *Young children's close relationships: Beyond attachment*. London: Sage.

Dunn, J., & Munn, P. (1986). Siblings and the development of prosocial behaviour. *International Journal of Behavioural Development, 9*, 265–284.

Dunn, J. F. (1995). Children as psychologists: The later correlates of individual differences in understanding of emotions and other minds. *Cognition and Emotion, 9*, 187–201.

Dunn, J. F., & Brown, J. R. (1994). Affect expression in the family, children's understanding of emotions, and their interactions with others. *Merrill-Palmer Quarterly, 40*, 120–137.

Duveen, G., Lloyd, B., & Smith, C. (1988). A note on the effects of age and gender on children's social behaviour. *British Journal of Social Psychology, 27*, 275–278.

Eisenberg, N., & Fabes, R. A. (1992). Emotion, self-regulation, and social competence. In M. Clark (Ed.), *Review of personality and social psychology* (Vol. 14). Newbury Park, CA: Sage.

Eisenberg, N., Fabes, R. A., Schaller, M., & Miller, P. A. (1989). Sympathy and personal distress: Development, gender differences and interrelations of indexes. *New Directions in Child Development, 44,* 107–126.

Eisenberg, N., Shell, R., Pasternack, J., Lennon, R., et al. (1987). Prosocial development in middle childhood: A longitudinal study. *Developmental Psychology, 23,* 712–718.

Fabes, R. A., Eisenberg, N., Karbon, M., & Troyer, D. (1994). The relations of children's regulation to their vicarious emotional responses and comforting behaviour. *Child Development, 65,* 1678–1693.

Farver, J. M., & Branstetter, W. H. (1994). Preschoolers' prosocial responses to their peers' distress. *Developmental Psychology, 30,* 334–341.

Feshbach, N. D. (1978). Studies of empathic behaviour in children. In B. A. Maher (Ed.), *Progress in experimental personality research* (Vol. 8). New York: Academic.

Feshbach, N. D. (1982). Sex differences in empathy and social behaviour in children. In N. Eisenberg (Ed.), *The development of prosocial behaviour* (pp. 315–338). New York: Academic.

Feshbach, N. D., & Roe, K. (1968). Empathy in six- and seven-year-olds. *Child Development, 39,* 133–145.

Goodman, R. (1994). A modified version of the Rutter parent questionnaire including extra items on children's strengths: A research note. *Journal of Child Psychology and Psychiatry, 35,* 1483–1494.

Greenson, R. (1960). Empathy and its vicissitudes. *International Journal of Psychoanalysis, 41,* 418–424.

Hay, D. F. (1985). Learning to form relationships in infancy: Parallel attainments with parents and peers. *Developmental Review, 5,* 122–161.

Hay, D. F., & Demetriou, H. (1998). The developmental origins of social understanding. In A. Campbell & S. Muncer (Eds.), *The social child.* Hove, UK: Psychology Press.

Hay, D. F., Nash, A., & Pedersen, J. (1981). Responses of six-month-olds to the distress of their peers. *Child Development, 52,* 1071–1075.

Hay, D. F., Nash, A., & Pedersen, J. (1983). Interaction between six-month-old peers. *Child Development, 54,* 557–562.

Hoffman, M. L. (1975). Developmental synthesis of affect and cognition and its implications for altruistic motivation. *Developmental Psychology, 11*, 607–622.

Hoffman, M. L. (1976). Empathy, role-taking, guilt and development of altruistic motives. In T. Lickona (Ed.), *Moral development and behaviour: Current theory and research*. New York: Holt, Rinehart & Winston.

Hoffman, M. L. (1987). The contribution of empathy to justice and moral judgement. In N. Eisenberg & J. Strayer (Eds.), *Empathy and its development*. New York: Cambridge University Press.

Hoffman, M. L., & Levine, L. E. (1976). Early sex differences in empathy. *Developmental Psychology, 12*, 557–558.

Hume, D. (1751). *An inquiry concerning the principle of morals* (Vol. 4). New York: Liberal Arts Press.

Kalliopuska, M. (1992). *Empathy – The way to humanity*. Edinburgh, UK: The Pentland Press Ltd.

Kirkpatrick, E. A. (1908). *Fundamentals of child study: A discussion of instinct and other factors in human development with practical implications* (2nd ed.). London: Macmillan.

Lamb, S., & Zakireh, B. (1997). Toddlers' attention to the distress of peers in a daycare setting. *Early Education and Development, 8*, 105–118.

Latané, B., & Darley, J. M. (1970). *The unresponsive bystander: Why doesn't he help?* New York: Appleton-Century-Crofts.

Legault, F., & Strayer, F. F. (1991). The emergence of sexual segregation and behavioural differences in preschool children. *Behaviour, 119*, 285–301.

Liddle, M. J., Bradley, B. S., & McGrath, A. (2015). Baby empathy: Infant distress and peer prosocial responses. *Infant Mental Health Journal, 36*, 446–458.

Lipps, T. (1903). *Empathy, inner imitation, and sense-feelings*. In Rader, *Aesthetics*, (pp. 291–304). Translated from Einfühlung, inner Nachahmung, und Organ-empfindungen. *Archiv fur die gesamte Psychologie, 2*, 185–204, by Rader and M. Schertel.

Maccoby, E. E. (1988). Gender as a social category. *Developmental Psychology, 24*, 755–765.

Mead, G. H. (1934). In C. M. Morris (Ed.), *Mind, self, and society*. Chicago: University of Chicago Press.

Murphy, L. B. (1937). *Social behaviour and child personality: An exploratory study of some roots of sympathy*. New York: Columbia University Press.

NICHD Early Child Care Research Network. (2001). Before head start: Income and ethnicity, family characteristics, child care experiences, and child development. *Early Education and Development, 12*, 545–576.

NICHD Early Child Care Research Network. (2003). Does quality of child care affect child outcomes at age 4½? *Developmental Psychology, 39*, 451–469.

Nichols, S. R., Svetlova, M., & Brownell, C. A. (2014). Toddlers' responses to infants' negative emotions. *Infancy, 20*, 70–97.

Piaget, J. (1981). *Intelligence and affectivity. Their relationship during child development*. Palo Alto, CA: Annual Reviews.

Piaget, J., & Inhelder, B. (1956). *The child's conception of space* (trans: F. J. Langdon, & E. L. Lunzer). London: Routledge & Kegan Paul.

Radke-Yarrow, M., Zahn-Waxler, C., & Chapman, M. (1983). Children's prosocial dispositions and behaviour. In P. H. Mussen (Ed.), *Handbook of child psychology (Vol. 4). Socialisation, personality, and social development*. New York: Wiley.

Rose, A. J., & Rudolph, K. D. (2006). A review of sex differences in peer relationship processes: Potential trade-offs for the emotional and behavioural development of girls and boys. *Psychological Bulletin, 132*, 98–131.

Ruffman, T., Perner, J., Naito, M., Parkin, L., & Clements, W. A. (1998). Older (but not younger) siblings facilitate false belief understanding. *Developmental Psychology, 34*, 161–174.

Sagi, A., & Hoffman, M. L. (1976). Empathic distress in the newborn. *Developmental Psychology, 12*, 175–176.

Shott, S. (1979). Emotion and social life: A symbolic interactionist analysis. *The American Journal of Sociology, 84*, 1317–1334.

Simner, M. L. (1971). Newborn's response to the cry of another infant. *Developmental Psychology, 5*, 135–150.

Sippola, L. K., Bukowski, W. M., & Noll, R. B. (1997). Dimensions of liking and disliking underlying the same-sex preference in childhood and adolescence. *Merrill-Palmer Quarterly, 43*, 591–609.

Staub, E. (1970). A child in distress: The influence of age and number of witnesses on children's attempts to help. *Journal of Personality and Social Psychology, 14*, 130–140.

Stotland, E., & Dunn, R. E. (1963). Empathy, self-esteem, and birth order. *Journal of Abnormal and Social Psychology, 66*, 532–554.

Strayer, J. (1993). Children's concordant emotions and cognitions in response to observed emotions. *Child Development, 64*, 188–201.

Thompson, R. A., & Hoffman, M. L. (1980). Empathy and the development of guilt in children. *Developmental Psychology, 16*, 155–156.

Warden, D., & MacKinnon, S. (2003). Prosocial children, bullies and victims: An investigation of their sociometric status, empathy and social problem-solving strategies. *British Journal of Developmental Psychology, 21*, 367–385.

Zahn-Waxler, C., Cole, P. M., & Barrett, K. C. (1991). Guilt and empathy: Sex differences and implications for the development of depression. In J. Garber & K. Dodge (Eds.), *The development of emotion regulation and dysregulation* (pp. 243–272). Cambridge, UK: Cambridge University Press.

Zahn-Waxler, C., & Radke-Yarrow, M. (1982). The development of altruism: Alternative research strategies. In N. Eisenberg-Berg (Ed.), *The development of prosocial behaviour*. New York: Academic.

Zahn-Waxler, C., Radke-Yarrow, M., & King, R. A. (1979). Child rearing and children's prosocial initiations towards victims of distress. *Child Development, 50*, 319–330.

Zahn-Waxler, C., Radke-Yarrow, M., Wagner, E., & Chapman, M. (1992). Development of concern for others. *Developmental Psychology, 28*, 126–136.

Zahn-Waxler, C., Robinson, J. L., & Emde, R. N. (1992). The development of empathy in twins. *Developmental Psychology, 28*, 1038–1047.

5

Nature Versus Nurture: The Biology and Psychology of Empathy

Empathy has dimensionality through its various forms, from direct experiencing of vicarious emotion to having an understanding of others' perspectives. As such, through its agency, empathy can enable unlimited appreciation of another's perspective and 'sing' to us through its ability to reach others. Empathy facilitates the development of social competence and enhances the quality of relationships to give meaning and purpose to them. Conversely, the presence of deficits in empathy is related to emotion dysregulation, which in turn has shown to increase the risk of psychopathology and aggression through childhood to adulthood (Schipper & Petermann, 2013). As we have seen, empathy can be experienced emotionally and/or cognitively and can begin at an early age, with very young infants showing some responsiveness to other infants' distress and evolving from self to other oriented reactions as well as helpful behaviours. There is evidence to suggest that these early dispositions towards empathy and prosocial behaviour may be consistent and stable over time. But when and how do these empathic behaviours emerge? Moving on from the variety of reactions and responses, including empathic ones, that children are able to offer others in distress, this section explores the internally programmed biological and externally influenced social forces

© The Author(s) 2018
H. Demetriou, *Empathy, Emotion and Education*,
https://doi.org/10.1057/978-1-137-54844-3_5

that allow for this empathy to emerge in the first place and flourish—or not—as the case may be. Some believe that environmental and genetic influences exist in equal measure, as cited by Rich (2015): "You inherit your environment just as much as your genes". But where empathy is concerned, are we born with an innate empathy system as per the nature debate, or does the emergence of empathy depend on the influence of other people during our upbringing as propounded by the nurture argument? By internal influences, I am emphasising the 'nature' side of the debate. Are we hard-wired for empathy and to what extent? The external influences that will follow in this section reflect the 'nurture' side of the argument and the people that influence our upbringing, the attachments we form, and the effect of these attachments on our empathy development. As we will see, genes, brain, cognition, behaviour and the environment all play a part.

Neuroscience, the Brain and Genetics

What role do biological processes play in the aetiology and development of empathy? Smith (2006) debated the association between cognitive and emotional empathy and the effect of natural selection on human evolution and how it might have acted on variation in the relationship between cognitive and emotional empathy thus resulting in two separate but complementary systems. Hoffman considered mechanisms such as classical conditioning and motor mimicry as giving rise to the empathic response and this theory is consistent with views of the adaptive nature of empathy from evolution and neuroscience. Neuroscience holds a key in its representation of the brain for our mental states, thoughts, feelings, beliefs and desires. Are there specific areas in the brain that harbour our empathic centres? Science has also investigated the role of genes in empathy (Chakrabarti, Kent, Suckling, Bullmore, & Baron-Cohen, 2006) as well as the effect of foetal testosterone in determining sex differences in empathy (Knickmeyer, Baron-Cohen, Raggatt, Taylor, & Hackett, 2006).

In its efforts to investigate empathy, neuroscience has unveiled its origins in certain brain structures. The limbic system is an area of the brain that houses emotional experiences. The primitive limbic cortex has strong neural connections with the hypothalamus which plays a basic role in integrating emotional expression with viscero-somatic behaviour, and with the prefrontal cortex which functions in "…helping us to gain insight into the feelings of others…[and]…receives part of this insight – the capacity to see with feeling – through its connection with the limbic brain" (MacLean, 1973, p. 58). The limbic system is differentiated enabling it to process different types of empathy-related emotional stimuli and where for example, the amygdala is triggered during the observation of faces expressing fear or distress (Decety, 2011). The cognitive component of empathy of perspective-taking is enabled through the activation of areas within the frontal and parietal lobes involved in executive functioning. Moreover, there are neural mechanisms within areas of the brain including the right temporo-parietal junction, the posterior cingulate and the precuneus that enable us to experience empathy in a controlled way so that we so do not become overwhelmed with our own internalised distress for the situation. This perspective-taking, self-other differentiation allows a distancing of the situation, thus enabling the potential to help (Jackson, Brunet, Meltzoff, & Decety, 2006), during which time areas of the temporal lobe are also activated, thereby accessing long-term memories that may relate to the situation. The neural foundations of empathy have also been investigated in relation to other altruistically related skills such as fairness and indicated that such characteristics emanate from similar brain regions. For example, functional magnetic resonance imaging (fMRI) has shown the anterior insula and anterior cingulate cortex respond to situations involving issues of fairness, and these same brain regions are also implicated in empathy when responding to others' pain or disgust.

Research has also shown that we are literally wired for empathy via specialised motor neurons known as 'mirror neurons', and such empathy neurons help us to connect with others' feelings (Gallese, Rochat, Cossu, & Sinigaglia, 2009; Singer et al., 2006). Evidence of a mirror neuron system lies in the premotor and surrounding areas of the frontal and parietal lobes (Iacoboni, 2008). The mirror neuron system contributes to providing a neural basis for connecting our own and others' experiences. Empathic reactions are instigated when mirror neurons communicate with other areas of the brain. The insular cortex connects premotor mirror neurons to the limbic system, which stimulates the emotional aspects of empathy (Carr, Iacoboni, Dubeau, Mazziotta, & Lenzi, 2003). Mirror neurons are believed to have generated in evolving man a relatively recent 100,000 years ago and thereby sparked the onset of skills such as tool use, fire making, shelter building, but also language and importantly the cognitive component of empathy in the form of theory of mind and perspective-taking. The Perception-Action Model of empathy by de Waal highlights the significance of mirror neurons for the development of and basis for higher levels of empathy whereby viewing another's emotional state prompts a trigger for one's own personal associations with that state, initiating responses similar to those one would apply to oneself (de Waal, 2008). These mirror neurons have been labelled 'Gandhi neurons' by Ramachandran (2000) who claimed: "I predict that mirror neurons will do for psychology what DNA did for biology: they will provide a unifying framework and help explain a host of mental abilities that have hitherto remained mysterious and inaccessible to experiments." Researchers (Burkett et al., 2016) have also shown the hormone oxytocin as being linked with empathy-related behaviours in prairie voles whilst comforting another in distress through emotional contagion. However, when the oxytocin receptors in the anterior cingulate cortex were blocked, very uncharacteristically the voles did not console the other in distress. According to the researchers, such findings of the role of oxytocin have implications for psychological disorders such as autism and schizophrenia where a person is typically unable to recognise and respond to others' emotions. Additionally, hormones such as oxytocin and vasopressin have been implicated in empathy's capacity to elicit aggressive behaviours towards perpetrators who cause distress to others (Buffone & Poulin, 2014).

What if anything does genetics contribute to the development of empathy? Some have attributed empathy with 68% heritability (Chakrabarti & Baron-Cohen, 2013). Twin studies comparing identical (monozygotic) with fraternal (dizygotic) twins are particularly powerful for investigating genetic influences, as heredity is indicated with similarities and differences in the gene pool. Furthermore, longitudinal twin studies have proved to be even more effective, an example of which is the twin study by Emde et al. (1992) that compared emotion in 200 pairs of identical and fraternal twins at 14 months of age and discovered a significant genetic empathy effect. The longitudinal study conducted by Zahn-Waxler and her colleagues (1992) comparing identical and fraternal twins' responses to simulated distress at 14 and 20 months of age found that at 14 months, infants exhibited significant heritability for a range of empathic responses, including prosocial behaviour, empathic concern, enquiry through hypothesis testing and unresponsive/indifferent behaviour. By 20 months, empathic concern and unresponsive/indifferent behaviour continued to suggest genetic influences. Such empathy-specific findings of the emotional component of empathy but also for the unresponsive/indifferent component, suggest an early, innate responsive and developed form of empathic responding. Knafo et al.'s (2008) focus on 24 and 36 months found that the genetic contribution decreased with age indicating the interweaving of genetic influences with increasing environmental factors on the development of empathy. The degree to which environment and genetics contribute towards children's prosocial behaviour was also investigated by Knafo and Plomin (2006) using longitudinal genetic analysis among pairs of twins as rated by their parents at the ages of 2, 3, 4 and 7 years and by their teachers at age 7 years. Results showed that genetic effects are responsible for both change and continuity in prosocial behaviour across this age span.

The ability to empathise therefore develops via a variety of variables ranging from biologically related systems, structures and mechanisms that include genes, hormones, areas of the brain such as the mirror neuron system and the limbic system, and not forgetting personality factors such as child temperament. A malfunction in any one or more of these structures may contribute to empathy deficits and lead to autism spectrum disorders, with their limitations to take the perspective of others; or psychopathy, with its inhibitions to respond to others' emotions. The flip side reveals other influences that may dictate the development of empathy in the individual, such as parenting factors of security, attention, warmth, parent-child synchrony and other qualities of the parent-child attachment relationship. It is to these nurture-related environmental influences that we now turn our attention.

Attachments and Their Effect on Social, Emotional and Cognitive Functioning

My mother is 1 of 12 children. She remembers one of her siblings asking their mother (my grandmother) which of them all she loved the most. My grandmother responded by using the analogy of her fingers as representing her children, saying that whichever finger is cut off, it hurts just the same, thereby conveying that all her children were loved equally. Theories and research in attachment abound from psychotherapy to developmental psychology to neuroscience, and all relay a common theme. When a baby is attended to with affection and care, that baby typically develops and responds positively, with the same affection and care, but is also able to develop emotionally, cognitively and socially healthily. What follows is a brief dip into attachment history.

'Too Much Mother Love' was the title of a chapter by John Watson (1928) as a warning to mothers. In it he wrote: "When you are tempted to pet your child remember that mother love is a dangerous instrument. An instrument which may inflict a never-healing wound, a wound which may make infancy unhappy, adolescence a nightmare, an instrument which may wreck your adult son or daughter's vocational future and their chances for marital happiness. …Never hug and kiss them, never let them sit in your lap. If you must, kiss them once on the forehead when they say goodnight. Shake hands with them in the morning" (p. 87). Such a stark and apocryphal view of parenting was subsequently outnumbered and overruled by a flurry of theorists and researchers. Citing, with little scope for leniency, Sigmund Freud (1940) reflected on the nature of the mother-child relationship emphasising its profound influence in later life, as forming the blueprint and determining the nature of all future relationships for the child: "… unique, without parallel, established unalterably for a whole lifetime…and as the prototype of all later love relationships…" (p. 45). Many of Freud's followers were in favour of the effect of nurturing as were other famous names associated with attachment-related theories including Bowlby, Ainsworth, Harlow and Fonagy, whose works resonate with the importance of the infant's first emotional attachment to a caregiver as a prerequisite for subsequent healthy capacity to empathise and thus, in turn, form healthy relationships of their own.

These sections examine childhood attachments at a variety of points along the lifespan and their implications for developing a healthy and balanced individual. The underlying principle of empathy and theories of attachment are that an individual matters. Empathy requires an interest in the other person, a way of understanding their thoughts and emotions. In order to form secure attachments with a child, the child must matter and come first. Alice Miller (1995) claimed that: "A child can experience her feelings only when there is somebody there who accepts her fully, understands her, and supports her. If that person is missing, if the child must risk losing the mother's love or her substitute in order to feel, then she will repress emotions" (p. 9). Such attachment function or dysfunction has an effect on the infant's social, emotional and cognitive functioning and implications for empathy-related behaviours. The ability to empathise is important for facilitating and maintaining meaningful relationships from birth through childhood to adulthood. Kohut's (1957) 'self psychology' emphasised the role of empathy as 'vicarious introspection' in the infant's development and claimed that primary empathy which is rooted in the early symbiotic relationship between mother and infant "prepares us for the recognition that to a large extent the basic inner experiences of other people remain similar to our own" (p. 451) and enables us to grasp *an appreciation of the meaning* (p. 461). Hoffman (1987) claimed that emotional attachments to family members have the effect of facilitating emotional sharing and lead to "an affective response more appropriate to someone else's situation than to one's own" (p. 48). Also, empathic concern and perspective-taking have been linked to aspects of attachment such as trust and comfort, as well resolving conflict (de Wied, Branje, & Meeus, 2007).

Babies are able to establish cohesive attachments that will go on to permeate their lives, including their relationships with siblings, peers, friends and teachers. The latter group of people—teachers—whom every child will encounter is also vital to a child's sense of self and learning. Related to this is the important principle underlying pupil voice, of respecting the views of students and forming connections between teachers and pupils in order to enhance teaching and learning. What is apparent and important within all these practices across the lifespan is that children are listened to and respected in ways that enhance their emotional, social and academic development, their involvement generally, and importantly their self-esteem. The foundation for all these is encapsulated by Montessori's view of the potency of love. Throughout children's development, they encounter influential individuals with whom they form attachments. Research has shown that the quality of childhood attachments has a significant effect on a child's ensuing relationships with others throughout their lives. More than that, research has also shown the effect of secure attachments on children's eventual social, emotional and cognitive development. Using different methods and indeed species, from geese to monkeys to humans, first impressions have been shown to count, and the following passages will describe some of the work in this area by some well-known researchers in the field.

The observation of animals in a naturalistic setting has revealed instinctive, innate, emotional bonds as noted by the Nobel prize-winning Austrian zoologist Konrad Lorenz (1973) who considered "…early childhood events as most essential to a man's scientific and philosophical development" (p. 1). A pioneer in the study of animal behaviour, known as ethology, Lorenz recognised the initial bond that is formed between a newborn and its caregiver. His naturalistic investigations demonstrated that if he was their first observable object, immediately on hatching, geese would naturally form attachments with him, despite being of a different species, and moreover the geese would treat him as their primary caregiver. Lorenz referred to this behaviour as 'imprinting', where the image of the 'mother' is imprinted on to the babies' consciousness for the purposes of survival. Because this behaviour happens so automatically upon hatching, it implies somewhat hard-wired origins that instinctively lead the hatchlings to the first caregiver they see. However, it also implies that attachments and the instinctive need for them are formed early, indeed from birth; and as will be seen, the nature of the attachments thereafter are also important for the consequences of the developing infant.

Listening to Margaret Mead's accounts of her journey to the South Pacific Islands, Benjamin Spock was inspired. She recounted her observations of mothers out working whilst carrying their babies in a sling. Whenever the babies cried, the mothers would stop and feed them, and then continue with their work. Such feeding and attending on demand was a far cry from the preaching of John Watson but impressed itself on Spock and propelled him to understand and communicate to parents the instinctive and emotional nature of children. He espoused that affection was as important as the more practical concerns of child-rearing. Spock based much of his advice on Freud's theories, but unlike Freud's work, which sought to cure neuroses, Spock was of the thinking 'prevention is better than cure' and sought to advise parents on aspects of child development with the aim of averting emotional issues later in life. Spock also incorporated the views of John Dewey, and although within education rather than psychology, these translated well to the Spockian treatment of children, giving them a voice and a role and treating each child as an individual, so that parent, teacher and child can work in synchrony. In his 1968 revised edition of *Baby and Child Care* Spock wrote:

> We know for a fact that the natural loving care that kindly parents give their children is a hundred times more valuable than their knowing how to pin a diaper on just right or how to make a formula expertly. ...Every time you pick your baby up, even if you do it a little awkwardly at first, every time you change him, bathe him, feed him, smile at him, he's getting a feeling that he belongs to you and that you belong to him. (p. 3)

In direct contrast to Watson and his warnings about hugging and kissing a baby, Spock urged parents to trust their instincts, show affection and not be afraid to kiss their babies. Reflecting the mood of the day, fathers were also encouraged to take part in their children's upbringing, a concept which was a relatively unknown quantity for a role that was seen as predominantly the mother's. Another of Spock's revolutionary insights, which he did with great empathy, and especially as he wasn't female or a mother, and moreover was still trying to understand his own detached maternal upbringing, was his advice to mothers of the importance of looking after themselves physically and emotionally.

Using experiments that drew on the dynamics and evaluated the effects of motherhood, Harry Harlow's 1960s controversial but revealing research with rhesus monkeys showed the adverse effects on monkeys when deprived of maternal love and thereby leading him to the conclusion that love matters. He said: "If monkeys have taught us anything it's that you've got to learn how to love before you learn how to live" (1961). Not only did these maternally deprived monkeys display signs of anxiety and depression, but he found that those raised with a surrogate model monkey mother made of cloth showed no signs of engaging in play with other monkeys. Harlow concluded: "The surrogate mother can meet the infant monkey's need for an object of affection…but it cannot teach the infant to groom itself or others, as the real mother does. Nor can it replace the mother and the other members of the monkey group, young and old, in providing the variety of social rules that the young monkey needs to make its way in the monkey world" (p. 193). Despite being kept clean, fed, warm and away from harm, the unresponsiveness of the cloth mothers proved limiting, incomplete and potentially destructive through lack of interaction, expression of emotion and display of social skills. Moreover, the profound impact of physical contact for the monkeys was highlighted in experiments when they displayed a preference for the cloth monkey mother despite not providing the monkey with milk, compared with a wire monkey mother counterpart who was equipped with milk, thereby prioritising comfort over food.

Further experiments demonstrated the detrimental effects of extreme conditions of isolation, devoid of social and emotional intelligence, which led to psychopathologies that perpetuated the cycle. Of note, Harlow showed that monkey mothers who had never experienced any love themselves, were deficient in love for their infants. Most of these mothers ignored their infants and in extreme cases, seemingly unable to understand the concept of love and loving, they physically injured and sometimes destroyed their own infants. However, the effects of maternal deprivation were not necessarily irreversible. Further experiments by Harlow's student Rosenblum (1971) showed the powerful restorative effects of friendship. When baby monkeys raised by cloth mothers visited other baby monkeys, the compensatory effect on the maternally deprived monkeys was noticeable. The young monkeys formed friendships and were excited to see one another. Moreover, as adults, the baby monkeys were quite unlike their cloth mothers and more similar to their peers who had grown up with their biological mothers, in that they were socially adept, outgoing and socially skilled, thereby demonstrating that exposing the monkeys to a typical environment with peers could facilitate them to flourish within normal relationships and overcome the deficits of life with a cloth monkey mother.

Despite these startling and somewhat disconcerting findings of animated and interactive beings having a positive impact on young monkeys, Harry Harlow showed that beauty is in the eye of the beholder in that a mother's face is always beautiful to its infant, even the incongruously inanimate red-eyed, green-mouthed face of a cloth mother. The fact is that, and in accordance with Lorenz, whichever face is exposed to the young being, that is the face that becomes imprinted. Despite the limitations of an inanimate mother, to the infant monkey it represents a stability, constancy, continuity and commitment. So in keeping with Freud, Harlow found that the first relationship, which is most likely to be with the mother, is the first important building block, indeed foundation, that determines the success and security of future relationships, and moreover helps to prevent potential psychopathologies. Like some other proponents of attachment theory such as Benjamin Spock, who practically reviewed and reassessed his own childhood through his writings, it is often the case that the initial interest in a topic of investigation, and in this case attachment, stems from an often unconscious desire to understand the researcher's own negative experience. In the case of Harlow, his own mother was present physically but their relationship was not emotionally close. He said: "…I may have lost some percentage time of maternal affection, and this deprivation may have resulted in consuming adolescent and adult loneliness" (Blum, 2002, p. 11). From man to monkey, their loneliness and limitations stemmed from the same common cause.

John Bowlby was a student of Harlow and friend of Lorenz whose shrewd observations of a hard-wired connection between mother and child paved the way to Bowlby's own conceptualisation of attachment theory. In accordance with Lorenz, Bowlby (1988) proposed an evolutionary theory of attachment where children arrive in the world biologically pre-programmed to form attachments and he claimed: "…The propensity to make strong emotional bonds to particular individuals is a basic component of human nature" (p. 3). Along with his colleagues, Bowlby spoke thus of the effects of deprivation "…young children, who for whatever reason are deprived of the continuous care and attention of a mother or a substitute-mother, are not only temporarily disturbed by such deprivation, but may in some cases suffer long-term effects which persist" (Bowlby, Ainsworth, Boston, & Rosenbluth, 1956, p. 211). Bowlby (1969) coined the phrase 'internal working models' to reflect the increasingly complex internal working models of the world and the significantly influential people in it, including the self, as constructed by the child. In keeping with theories of psychoanalysis, John Bowlby agreed with Freud that mental health and behavioural problems were direct outcomes of early childhood experiences, and in particular, attachment issues. Specifically, Bowlby drew a positive correlation between children with disruptive, neglectful or abusive upbringing, and whose future resulted in weak emotional relationships and an inability to empathise with others, thus highlighting the significance of our earliest emotional attachment for the development of a healthy empathy. However, in slight discordance with Freud who envisioned the mother as the person with whom the child forms attachments in order to achieve a successful lifetime of relationships, Bowlby's visions were more flexible as he claimed that as long as the child formed secure attachments with one main caregiving source, it need not necessarily be the mother herself in order for the child to succeed in their lifespan of relationships.

Influenced by John Bowlby, Mary Ainsworth studied relationship quality in the context of the security of a child's attachment. She measured this 'attachment security' using a procedure she named the 'Strange Situation', during which children's reactions to a series of separations from and reunions with their parent are assessed and represent the level of attachment between mother and child (Ainsworth, Blehar, Waters, & Wall, 1978). Three types of attachment were initially identified: Secure Attachment, Ambivalent Attachment, Avoidant Attachment, with the subsequent addition of Disorganised Attachment. Whereas Secure Attachment describes a secure child, the other styles define types of insecurity. In so doing, Ainsworth was able to classify children according to the security of their attachments. Securely attached children typically display behaviours consistent with a trusting, loving relationship with their parent. Such behaviours include being upset by the parent's absence and being reassured by the parent's presence, but feeling comfortable enough to explore their surroundings. By contrast, insecurely attached children may ignore their parent upon their return, remain upset and clingy, or exhibit a disorganised strategy of re-engaging with the parent. As a result of her research, Ainsworth and her colleagues, in agreement with her predecessors such as Spock, advised mothers never to miss an opportunity to give attention and show affection to their babies. The now ubiquitous use of the Strange Situation has since been developed widely and modified as a tool for assessment of child attachment.

Now we bring attachment and empathy together whilst also coming full circle from the days of Freud in the field of psychoanalysis. Peter Fonagy and colleagues (see Fonagy & Bateman, 2012) have demonstrated that having a secure attachment to a parent or caregiver enables children to develop the ability to understand their own and others' thoughts and feelings. Naming this capacity 'mentalisation', it is transferrable from caregiver to child, not genetically, but rather through the quality of the childcare itself. Mentalisation involves the interaction of the imagination from one's own feelings, thoughts, motives, intentions, beliefs, desires and needs, to those of others. Research via theory of mind and false-belief experiments has contextualised developmental psychopathology within attachment relationships and applied mentalisation within psychotherapeutic techniques for borderline personality disorders. People with difficulties in emotion regulation and impulse control, and their ensuing unstable relationships and self-image were often previously regarded as untreatable, until the advent of mentalisation-based treatment. Such treatments have huge implications for conditions such as autism and psychopathology where cognitive or emotional empathy components are lacking; whilst also having the power to override even hard-wired conditions and thereby providing further evidence through therapy for the power of nurture over nature.

The Domino Effect: From the Sensitive Caregiver to the Sensitive Child

As well as the previously described research that led to their respective attachment theories, studies typically reveal the inextricable link between a secure parent-child attachment and the child's ensuing social, emotional and cognitive nature as reflected in traits such as self-esteem, empathy and language development. Such exposure to a parent is reminiscent of the conditioning theories of those such as John Watson (1924) who famously said "Give me a dozen healthy infants, well-formed, and my own specified world to bring them up in and I'll guarantee to take any one at random and train him to become any type of specialist I might select – doctor, lawyer, artist, merchant-chief and, yes, even beggar-man and thief, regardless of his talents, penchants, tendencies, abilities, vocations and the race of his ancestors" (p. 104). Quite a claim—and reminiscent of Aristotle's declaration around 300 BC of: "Give me a child until he is 7 and I will show you the man".

Studies have unveiled the significant influential powers of caregivers on an infant's development. But extreme experiences of maternal privation or deprivation have also shown the potential of the restorative powers of others to override such experiences, as seen by peer monkeys and adoptive families. An example of an early naturalistic case study was conducted by Freud's daughter Anna Freud and her colleague Sophie Dann (1951). In 1946, they observed the behaviour of six infant orphans who had been rescued from a concentration camp in the Czech Republic and who had suffered severe privation, never experiencing attachments with adults, although they had formed close bonds with each other since the age of around 6 months. The research was known as the 'Bulldogs Bank' study, named after their accommodation in West Sussex. The children became very attached to each other and they refused to be separated. Moreover, they displayed hostility and aggression towards adults and even their carers who described being able to tend to their physical wellbeing but unable to form any kind of emotional attachment (Moskovitz, 1985). A barrier had been created by the children and as part of their coping skills, they had learnt to survive without the adults. Fortunately, eventually the children recovered from their early deficits in learning to speak and play and they even formed emotional attachments with adults. Anna Freud is often overshadowed by her father Sigmund Freud. However, through her own observations and also her therapeutic approaches with children whom she felt, in keeping with adults, should be recognised as personalities in their own right, she has also rightly established a name for herself in the field of child psychoanalysis.

Stanley Coopersmith (1967) investigated the powerful effect of a parent's unconditional positive regard on the development of self-esteem and the importance of that self-esteem in turn for that child's development. In his study, the self-esteem of hundreds of 9- to 10-year-old boys was measured, and he found the boys with high self-esteem to be the most expressive and active but also the most successful and confident group, both academically and socially. In addition to this, Coopersmith found that these boys were also the ones who received positive affection from parents with firm boundaries on acceptable behaviour; whereas low self-esteem was related to harsh or unloving parenting with a lack of parenting restrictions. Moreover, the longitudinal dimension of this research into adulthood revealed that it was the high self-esteem boys who were the most successful in their careers and relationships; thus confirming that secure, healthy attachments during childhood are positively associated with more balanced and successful individuals, but also provide the blueprint with which children can go on to form their own successful relationships and life events.

A case in the 1970s of a girl who was given the name 'Genie' for purposes of anonymity was a striking example of the effects of attachment deprivation on physical, social, emotional and cognitive development. Isolated by her father from birth in an upstairs room, Genie was finally released from captivity at the age of 13 years not knowing any other way of life. She exhibited rudimentary behaviours, was barely able to stand upright or to communicate with others, and was fearful of those she encountered. Despite the enormous amount of help and support she received, it took a long time for Genie to establish a trust and confidence in others. Moreover, very significantly her language development was impaired with a vocabulary that consisted of 20 words, to the degree that as a result of Genie's case, a 'critical period' was mooted for the development of language function (Curtiss, Fromkin, Krashen, Rigler, & Rigler, 1974). It is claimed that after a certain time of non-exposure to language and interaction with other people, the critical period when the brain is receptive to language acquisition lapses, resulting in difficulties thereafter in procuring language. Similar to Harlow's monkey experiments, which today would be deemed completely unethical an undertaking as a research approach, fortunately too, Genie's experience was an exceptional case. Despite the very unfortunate nature of these cases, such exceptional occurrences allow us to understand more fully the effects of attachment deprivation. Specifically, what such experiments and observations have shown is that children and monkeys alike have sufficient cognitive development to distinguish their own psychological selves from others and to reflect upon themselves in relation to others; however, their experiences have also shown that, when deprived of parental love and communication, there is a point after which the brain shuts down and even trying to make up for the lost time becomes an insurmountable task. Whereas Genie experienced great difficulty establishing a variety of cognitive, emotional and social abilities, some examples of individuals with early deprived experiences reveal that such situations can be reversed, as is the case in 1976 when Koluchová reported the discovery of 7-year-old Czechoslovakian twin boys. They had been locked in a cellar, maltreated and beaten, and were unable to form attachments. Similar to Genie, on discovery, the boys had very little speech and communicated via gestures. However, they were fostered by two sisters, and by the age of 14 years they were on a developmental par with their peers and, moreover, by the age of 20 had above average intelligence, attended university and were able to form good friendships and relationships.

In his book entitled *Maternal Deprivation Reassessed* (1972), Michael Rutter expanded on Bowlby's concept of 'maternal deprivation' distinguishing separation from loss versus failure to develop with an attachment figure and viewing them as having differing developmental trajectories. He also built on the theory by adding the term 'privation': a situation in which there has been an absence of attachment; in contrast with deprivation where there is a loss or damage to an attachment relationship. Privated individuals have for whatever reason failed to form an attachment in the first instance and typically do not show distress when separated from a familiar figure, thereby indicating a lack of attachment. Rutter's research showed that such individuals typically display clinging, attention-seeking behaviour, and in later life they have difficulty in keeping rules, forming long-term relationships or feeling guilt. Rutter and colleagues have also found a link between early severe institutional deprivation and adult attention-deficit hyperactivity disorder (Kennedy et al., 2016). Rather than assigning causation of such problems to a lack of attachment with a mother figure as Bowlby would have done, Rutter also believed that the quality as well as the quantity of intellectual and social stimulation were contributing factors to the nature of the attachment relationship. But also, as was shown in his Isle of Wight study of 1964–1974, Rutter and colleagues (see Rutter, Tizard, Yule, Graham, & Whitmore, 1976) assessed 2000 boys of 9–12 years and found that an atmosphere of family discord resulted typically in the children subsequently developing antisocial behaviours.

Also, and corroborating Rosenblum's compensatory effect of Harlow's monkeys using friendships of peer monkeys, Rutter identified effective attachment interventions where deficiencies can be reversed, as well as finding certain critical ages before which reversal is easier. Researching Romanian orphans, Rutter (1998) showed that the earlier the children were adopted, the smoother their transition and faster their developmental progress. Subsequent research (Rutter et al., 2007) monitored children adopted into UK families having been raised in deprived Romanian institutions and added support to the thesis of a critical period and the importance of early intervention after privation for the prevention of long-term cognitive and behavioural deficits. Rutter compared a group of orphans before 6 months of age and a group who were older than 6 months of age at the time of adoption at the ages of 4, 6 and 11 years. The children who were adopted younger than 6 months developed as per typical British adoptees, whereas those adopted after the 6 month cut-off age exhibited random attachments and problems with peer relationships, thereby suggesting that the negative effects of privation after 6 months are more difficult to overcome. Therein lies further evidence for the soft-wired architecture of the brain and its structures and the effects that privation can have on them. When PET scans were administered to the Romanian adoptees (Chugani et al., 2001), there was evidence of neuro-cognitive impairment, impulsivity and attention and social deficits in the orbital frontal gyrus, prefrontal cortex and hippocampus areas, the amygdala and the brain stem. Such damage was thought to be linked to the stress of early deprivation and potentially linked to the long-term cognitive and behavioural deficits. Longitudinal studies continue to reveal associations such as the findings from the Avon Longitudinal Study of Parents and Children (ALSPAC: Golding, Pembrey, & Jones, 2001), which began gathering data in 1991–1992 from more than 14,000 children and their families. In addition, the Millennium Cohort Study (MCS) comprised a sample of 19,000 children and their families born across the UK around the turn of this century identifying the beneficial effects of a stimulating early home-learning environment, and as Rutter espoused, not only placing emphasis on attachments that are secure in nature, where there is privation or deprivation, but also those in which there is adequate intellectual stimulation and so that quality was deemed equally as important as the quantity of attachment (Parsons, Schoon, & Vignoles, 2014). All the evidence points to the impact of others and the environment on the previously disadvantaged individual, a clue to the malleability of the individual, and that recovery at least to a certain degree is possible.

Other research has shown a profound impact of mothers' interactions with infants' mental states at 6 months of age as predicting the quality of their infant's joint attention at 12 months (Roberts et al., 2013). Moreover, studies have shown the significant effects of maternal emotional expression towards their infants as being a predictor of anti-social behaviour problems (Caspi et al., 2004). And even by 7 months of age, filmed assessments of mothers with their infants at home have revealed that flat and withdrawn maternal affective expression is associated with infant distress (Cohn & Tronick, 1989). Studies have also revealed mothers' postnatal depression (PND) as interfering with infants' imitation development, as in the study by Perra, Phillips, Fyfield, Waters, and Hay (2015) who showed that 12-month-old infants whose mothers were diagnosed with PND were less competent at imitation, as well as showing the influence of mother-child interaction at 6 months of age for imitation competence later at 12 months of age. Studies are also discovering children's perceptions of their intelligence mindsets as being either fixed or with the potential for growth as a result of their parents' failure mindsets that have a significant effect on their children's beliefs about their own ability; so that parents who view failure as negative rather than a learning experience, have children who themselves believe that intelligence is fixed with little scope for improvement (Haimovitz & Dweck, 2016). And an overarching meta-analytic study within the field of attachment has shown that early security predicts later social competence (Groh, Fearon, van Ijzendoorn, Bakermans-Kranenburg, & Roisman, 2016).

This takes us back to the aforementioned social referencing exhibited by babies crawling along the visual cliff in the hope that the clear plastic surface is a safe option for crossing based on their mothers' expressions. Babies typically scan faces for answers to questions: Am I doing the right thing? Am I making you happy? Are you paying attention to me? Am I safe? These are excellent examples of the power of non-vocal emotion emission and understanding and a test of trust and faith in another person. When this trust, faith, security and positivity are breached, as in the studies of neglected, abused, privated or deprived children, such studies reveal that these children typically by default see a still-face or an angry face, no matter what the expression when shown photos of facial expressions. Ultimately, such findings show how secure attachments can support and sustain us: they can offer the best, or alternatively their absence can result in the worst outcomes. Indeed, love, and the lack of it, changes the young brain forever, and this includes its capacity for empathy.

Attachment and Empathy

The quality of the attachment relationship has also been shown to have an effect on the quality of empathy, thereby implying that empathy can be learnt through observation (Britton & Fuendeling, 2005). Research by Kestenbaum, Farber, and Sroufe (1989) found that securely attached preschoolers engaged in more empathic responding than their insecurely attached counterparts who were anxious-avoidant. Studies reflect that training in attachment security leads to more empathic and fewer personal distress reactions (Mikulincer et al., 2001). There is also evidence that empathy is influenced by an interaction between factors within the child itself and relationship factors. For example, research by van Der Mark, van Ijzendoorn, and Bakermans-Kranenburg (2002) that examined the impact of temperament and attachment styles on girls' empathic responding found that it was only among the girls who were temperamentally fearful that an insecure attachment style resulted in reduced empathic concern for a stranger. Children who are shy or fearful tend to engage quickly with others' distress, but then become overwhelmed with their own internalised distress. However, the secure environment may compensate for the shyness, as the children are then less likely to become dumbfounded by their own distress, and equip them to engage empathically with others' distress.

Kochanska (2002) investigated a particular aspect of the parent-child relationship, known as mutually responsive orientation (MRO) and showed that young children with more responsive parents and where there was a working model of a cooperative relationship of shared positive affect, were more likely to respond empathically to a person in distress. Kochanska measured the degree of responsiveness and shared positive affect during naturalistic interactions between mother and child at home and in the laboratory, and her studies have also found that MRO has a direct effect on children's moral emotions, showing that the quality and quantity of maternal responsiveness during infancy predicted the amount of empathic distress in toddlers when they were 22 months of age (Kochanska, Forman, & Coy, 1999). As well as this, MRO was able to predict guilty reactions when children were 45 months of age (Kochanska, Forman, Aksan, & Dunbar, 2005). Such studies indicate that when children experience genuine warmth and responsiveness during their early development, such values are likely to be perpetuated and lead to their own development of empathy and a moral conscience. However, it is important to note that as well as the major contributions of our early experiences of attachment with a caregiver, more recent acknowledgements of biology through neuroscience and genetics have also contributed to our knowledge of empathy, and supersede Freud's original concept of the 'archaeology of the mind'. For example, genetic and physiological explanations of the conditions of autism and Asperger syndrome can have repercussions for empathy development (Baron-Cohen et al., 2000; Dapretto et al., 2006).

Studies have shown the significance of maternal responsiveness to a baby during playful interactions, such that if a mother responds more sensitively to her baby, then the developing toddler is less likely to develop callous, indifferent and unresponsive behaviour. Such implications for maternal sensitivity were seen in the longitudinal study by Bedford, Pickles, Sharp, Wright, and Hill (2015) who found that greater maternal sensitivity had an impact at 5 months, when infants exhibited a preference for a person's face compared with an object of a red ball; and by toddlerhood, when the children were two and half years old, they exhibited fewer callous and unemotional behaviours (as defined by a lack of guilt and empathy) and were better able to understand emotions in general. Such studies have implications for the importance of the social world at an early age, but also a social world in which the cues are positive, engaging and encouraging. The powerful effect of maternal warmth in fostering empathy development has been shown through studies that have revealed greater empathy among infants whose parents display more warmth towards them during interactions at home and laboratory conditions (Zhou et al., 2002). The quality and style of conversation by parents has also been found to affect their children's empathy, in that the more parents help their children label emotions and emotional concern for others, as well as the degree to which parents provide explanations for the causes and consequences of emotions, the greater the child attempts to understand others' emotions (Dunn, Brown, & Beardsall, 1991; Dunn, Brown, Slomkowski, Tesla, et al., 1991).

Kochanska's work involving MRO has since been developed by others who have been equally keen to examine the socialising influence of caregivers on their children's ensuing empathic development. The concept of 'synchrony', as defined by complementary behaviours between mother and child, has been explored through a longitudinal study by Feldman (2007). Results showed that the quality of mother-infant synchrony as measured at 3 and 9 months of age was reflected in the subsequent levels of empathy when the children reached 6 and 13 years of age. Mother-infant face-to-face play in infancy in particular seemed to govern the degree of empathy in the child as measured through their conversation with their mothers during their subsequent middle childhood and adolescent years. Of further interest in these findings was that the amount of synchrony was related specifically to the emotional rather than cognitive aspects of empathy. Added to this is the facilitative effect of maternal empathy on perspective-taking and prosocial behaviour (as well as emotional empathy) in early childhood (Farrant, Devine, Maybery, & Fletcher, 2011) and the influence of mothers' mental state utterances on later theory of mind understanding (Paine & Hay, 2017; Ruffman, Slade, & Crowe, 2002). Such findings are indicative of the potential of parenting practices for a full complement of empathy. Other researchers have explored the origins of mother-infant brain-to-brain synchrony and its implications for cognitive and emotional development. For example, Leong and Goswami (2015) have shown that mothers and their infants share a bond of communication and empathy as displayed through 'behavioural synchrony' where postures, mood and gestures are mirrored, and they showed moreover that when these bonds are severed, they can result in long-term negative effects. Such powerful findings from longitudinal studies highlight the impact of the early mother-infant relationship in expediting the child's subsequent degree of empathy. From imitation during infancy such as tongue protrusions of infant humans (Meltzoff & Moore, 1997) and monkeys (Simpson, Miller, Ferrari, Suomi, & Paukner, 2016) in response to adults, to the two-way exchanges of affective synchrony, children internalise early the emotions of others through their expressions during the interaction process. This platform for engaging with emotions educates the child about the transference of feelings and has consequences for their moral and helpful behaviour.

The biological and psychological worlds of empathy have collided. And that includes empathy in both its affective and cognitive guises and their respective neural functioning in relation to parental empathic dispositions. With echoes of Harlow, researchers have begun to show the potentially powerful effects of even the simple action of maternal physical touch, which in itself has been shown to activate the social brains of infants and thereby enhance their mentalising and perspective-taking abilities (Brauer, Xiao, Poulain, Friederici, & Schirmer, 2016). This led the researchers to speculate that the greater the amount of touch, the greater the mentalising aspect of the 'social brain', which in turn triggers an interest in others' mental states. In the field of affective neuroscience, touch has also been recommended as a biological necessity in the teacher-pupil relationship and children's ensuing brain development (McGlone, Wessberg, & Olausson, 2014). Whilst in the field of cognitive-behavioural neuroscience, higher levels of parent cognitive empathy is related to left frontal brain activation during perspective-taking (Decety, Meidenbauer, & Cowell, 2017). In order to experience empathy, a child needs to be able to value, and in order to value, the child needs to be valued in the first instance. Parents who provide a progressive, positive, interactive and sensitive environment are most likely to have more empathic children.

Such relationships that take into account the social, personal, emotional, moral and academic development and welfare of the child, in turn serve to nurture these qualities. What is more is that these qualities are inter-linked and interdependent. And in keeping with the array of theories and research on attachment that advocate the interrelatedness of these quali-ties for a healthy and balanced upbringing, so is the importance of high-lighting their relationship in the discourse on successful schools (Gray, 1990; Rutter, Maughan, Mortimore, Ouston, & Smith, 1979). A respect for, or valuing of the other person leads to that person also being able to value other people. Thereby the contagious nature of values leads to a chain reaction and this is evident in the school context too (McLaughlin, 2008). Through respecting and reacting effectively to both the emotional and cognitive factors of development, parents and teachers alike appreci-ate the whole child. Such holistic approaches are similar to theories that combine emotion and cognition, from developmental psychology, such as Vygotsky's transformational processes that occur from the interper-sonal to the intrapersonal, firstly socially between people and then trans-posed internally within the individual; to education, where Dewey envisioned effective learning as emanating from a level playing field of social interactions between pupil and teacher.

References

Ainsworth, M., Blehar, M., Waters, E., & Wall, S. (1978). *Patterns of attach-ment: A psychological study of the strange situation*. Hillsdale, NJ: Erlbaum.

Baron-Cohen, S., Ring, H., Bullmore, E., Wheelwright, S., Ashwin, C., & Williams, S. (2000). The amygdala theory of autism. *Neuroscience and Behavioural Reviews, 24*, 355–364.

Bedford, R., Pickles, A., Sharp, H., Wright, N., & Hill, J. (2015). Reduced face preference in infancy: A developmental precursor to callous-unemotional traits? *Biological Psychiatry, 78*, 144–150.

Blum, D. (2002). *Love at Goon Park. Harry Harlow and the science of affection*. New York: Perseus Publishing.

Bowlby, J. (1969). *Attachment. Attachment and loss: Vol. 1. Loss*. New York: Basic Books.

Bowlby, J. (1988). *A secure base: Parent-child attachment and healthy human development*. New York: Basic Books.

Bowlby, J., Ainsworth, M., Boston, M., & Rosenbluth, D. (1956). The effects of mother-child separation: A follow-up study. *British Journal of Medical Psychology, 29*, 211–249.

Brauer, J., Xiao, Y., Poulain, T., Friederici, A., & Schirmer, A. (2016). Frequency of maternal touch predicts resting activity and connectivity of the developing social brain. *Cerebral Cortex, 26*, 3544–3552.

Britton, P. C., & Fuendeling, J. M. (2005). The relations among varieties of adult attachment and the components of empathy. *Journal of Social Psychology, 145*, 519–530.

Buffone, A. E. K., & Poulin, M. J. (2014). Empathy, target distress, and Neurohormone genes interact to predict aggression for others-even without provocation. *Personality and Social Psychology Bulletin, 11*, 1406–1422.

Burkett, J. P., Andari, E., Johnson, Z. V., Curry, D. C., de Waal, F. B. M., & Young, L. J. (2016). Oxytocin-dependent consolation behaviour in rodents. *Science, 351*, 375–378.

Carr, L., Iacoboni, M., Dubeau, M. C., Mazziotta, J. C., & Lenzi, G. L. (2003). Neural mechanisms of empathy in humans: A relay from neural systems for imitation to limbic areas. *Proceedings of the National Academy of Sciences of the USA, 100*, 5497–5502.

Caspi, A., Moffitt, T. E., Morgan, J., Rutter, M., Taylor, A., Arseneault, L., et al. (2004). Maternal expressed emotion predicts children's antisocial behaviour problems: Using monozygotic-twin differences to identify environmental effects on behavioural development. *Developmental Psychology, 40*, 149–161.

Chakrabarti, B., & Baron-Cohen, S. (2013). Understanding the genetics of empathy and the autistic spectrum, chapter 18. In S. Baron-Cohen, H. Tager-Flushberg, & M. V. Lombardo (Eds.), *Understanding other minds: Perspectives from developmental social neuroscience*. Oxford: Oxford University Press.

Chakrabarti, B., Kent, L., Suckling, J., Bullmore, E., & Baron-Cohen, S. (2006). Variations in the human cannabinoid receptor (CNR1) gene modulate striatal responses to happy faces. *European Journal of Neuroscience, 23*, 1944–1948.

Chugani, H. T., Behen, M. E., Muzik, O., Juhász, C., Nagy, F., & Chugani, D. C. (2001). Local brain functional activity following early deprivation: A study of post-institutionalized Romanian orphans. *NeuroImage, 14*, 1290–1301.

Cohn, J. F., & Tronick, E. Z. (1989). Specificity of infants' response to mothers' affective behaviour. *Journal of the American Academy of Child and Adolescent Psychiatry, 28*, 242–248.

Coopersmith, S. (1967). *The antecedents of self-esteem.* San Francisco: W. H. Freeman & Co.

Curtiss, S., Fromkin, V., Krashen, S., Rigler, D., & Rigler, M. (1974). The linguistic development of genie. *Language, 50,* 528–554.

Dapretto, M., Davies, M. S., Pfeifer, J. H., Scott, A. A., Sigman, M., Bookheimer, S. Y., et al. (2006). Understanding emotions in others: Mirror neuron dysfunction in children with autism spectrum disorders. *Nature Neuroscience, 9,* 28–30.

de Waal, F. B. M. (2008). Putting the altruism back into altruism: The evolution of empathy. *Annual Review of Psychology, 59,* 279–300.

de Wied, M., Branje, S. J. T., & Meeus, W. H. J. (2007). Empathy and conflict resolution in friendship relations among adolescents. *Aggressive Behaviour, 33,* 48–55.

Decety, J. (2011). The neuroevolution of empathy. *Annals of the New York Academy of Sciences, 1231,* 35–45.

Decety, J., Meidenbauer, K. L., & Cowell, J. M. (2017). The development of cognitive empathy and concern in preschool children: A behavioural neuroscience investigation. *Developmental Science.*

Dunn, J., Brown, J., & Beardsall, L. (1991). Family talk about feeling states and children's later understanding of others' emotions. *Developmental Psychology, 27,* 448–455.

Dunn, J., Brown, J., Slomkowski, C., Tesla, C., et al. (1991). Young children's understanding of other people's feelings and beliefs: Individual differences and their antecedents. *Child Development, 62,* 1352–1366.

Emde, R. N., Plomin, R., Robinson, J. A., Corley, R., DeFries, J., Fulker, D. W., et al. (1992). Temperament, emotion, and cognition at fourteen months: The MacArthur longitudinal twin study. *Child Development, 63,* 1437–1455.

Farrant, B. M., Devine, T. A. J., Maybery, M. T., & Fletcher, J. (2011). Empathy, perspective-taking and prosocial behaviour: The importance of parenting practices. *Infant and Child Development, 21,* 175–188.

Feldman, R. (2007). Mother–infant synchrony and the development of moral orientation in childhood and adolescence: Direct and indirect mechanisms of developmental continuity. *American Journal of Orthopsychiatry, 77,* 582–597.

Fonagy, P., & Bateman, A. (Eds.). (2012). *Handbook of mentalising in mental health practice.* Arlington, VA: American Psychiatric Publishing.

Freud, A., & Dann, S. (1951). An experiment in group upbringing. *Psychoanalytic Study of the Child, 6,* 127–168.

Freud, S. (1940). *An outline of psychoanalysis.* London: Hogarth Press. 1979.

Gallese, V., Rochat, M., Cossu, G., & Sinigaglia, C. (2009). Motor cognition and its role in the phylogeny and ontogeny of intentional understanding. *Developmental Psychology, 45*, 103–113.

Golding, J., Pembrey, M., & Jones, R. (2001). ALSPAC: The Avon longitudinal study of parents and children. *Paediatric and Perinatal Epidemiology, 15*, 74–87.

Gray, J. (1990). The quality of schooling: Frameworks for judgement. *British Journal of Education Studies, 38*, 204–233.

Groh, A. M., Fearon, R. M. P., van Ijzendoorn, M. H., Bakermans-Kranenburg, M. J., & Roisman, G. I. (2016). Attachment in the early life course: Meta-analytic evidence for its role in socioemotional development. *Child Development Perspectives, 11*, 70–76.

Haimovitz, K., & Dweck, C. S. (2016). What predicts children's fixed and growth intelligence mind-sets? Not their parents' views of intelligence but their parents' views of failure. *Psychological Science, 27*, 859–869.

Harlow, H. F. (1961). The development of affectional patterns in infant monkeys. In B. M. Foss (Ed.), *Determinants of infant behaviour* (pp. 75–97). London: Methuen.

Hoffman, M. L. (1987). The contribution of empathy to justice and moral judgement. In N. Eisenberg & J. Strayer (Eds.), *Empathy and its development*. Cambridge, UK: Cambridge University Press.

Iacoboni, M. (2008). *Mirroring people*. New York: Farrar, Straus & Giroux.

Jackson, P. L., Brunet, E., Meltzoff, A. N., & Decety, J. (2006). Empathy examined through the neural mechanisms involved in imagining how I feel versus how you feel pain. *Neuropsychologia, 44*, 752–761.

Kennedy, M., Kreppner, J., Knights, N., Kumsta, R., Maughan, B., Golm, D., et al. (2016). Early severe institutional deprivation is associated with a persistent variant of adult attention-deficit/hyperactivity disorder: Clinical presentation, developmental continuities and life circumstances in the English and Romanian adoptees study. *Journal of Child Psychology and Psychiatry, 57*, 1113–1125.

Kestenbaum, R., Farber, E. A., & Sroufe, L. A. (1989). Individual differences in empathy among preschoolers: Relation to attachment history. In N. Eisenberg (Ed.), *Empathy and related emotional responses. No. 44, New directions for child development series*. San Francisco: Jossey-Bass, Inc.

Knafo, A., & Plomin, R. (2006). Prosocial behaviour from early to middle childhood: Genetic and environmental influences on stability and change. *Developmental Psychology, 42*, 771–786.

Knafo, A., Zahn Waxler, C., VanHulle, C., Robinson, J. L., & Rhee, S. H. (2008). The developmental origins of a disposition toward empathy: Genetic and environmental contributions. *Emotion, 8*, 737–752.

Knickmeyer, R., Baron-Cohen, S., Raggatt, P., Taylor, K., & Hackett, G. (2006). Foetal testosterone and empathy. *Hormones and Behaviour, 49*, 282–292.

Kochanska, G. (2002). Mutually responsive orientation between mothers and their young children: A context for the early development of conscience. *Current Directions in Psychological Science, 11*, 191–195.

Kochanska, G., Forman, D., Aksan, N., & Dunbar, S. (2005). Pathways to conscience: Early mother-child mutually responsive orientation and children's moral emotion, conduct and cognition. *Journal of Child Psychology and Psychiatry, 46*, 19–34.

Kochanska, G., Forman, D., & Coy, K. C. (1999). Implications of the mother-child relationship in infancy for socialization in the second year of life. *Infant Behaviour and Development, 22*, 249–265.

Kohut, H. (1957). Introspection, empathy, and psychoanalysis. *Journal of the American Psychoanalytic Association, 7*, 459–483.

Leong, V., & Goswami, U. (2015). Acoustic-emergent phonology in the amplitude envelope of child-directed speech. *PLoS One, 10*(12), e0144411.

Lorenz, K. (1973). *Analogy as a source of knowledge*. Nobel Lecture, December 1973: Nobel Foundation.

MacLean, P. D. (1973). *A triune concept of the brain and behaviour*. Toronto, ON: University of Toronto Press.

McGlone, F., Wessberg, J., & Olausson, H. (2014). Discriminative and affective touch: Sensing and feeling. *Neuron, 82*, 737–755.

McLaughlin, C. (2008). Emotional well-being and its relationship to schools and classrooms: A critical reflection. *British Journal of Guidance and Counselling, 36*, 353–366.

Meltzoff, A. N., & Moore, M. K. (1997). Explaining facial imitation: A theoretical model. *Early Development and Parenting, 6*, 179–192.

Mikulincer, M., Gillath, O., Halevy, V., Avihou, N., Avidan, S., & Eshkoli, N. (2001). Attachment theory and reactions to others' needs: Evidence that activation of the sense of attachment security promotes empathic responses. *Journal of Personality and Social Psychology, 81*, 1205–1224.

Miller, A. (1995). *The drama of being a child*. UK: Virago.

Moskovitz, S. (1985). Longitudinal follow-up child survivors of the holocaust. *Journal of Child and Adolescent Psychiatry, 24*, 401–407.

Paine, A., & Hay, D. F. (2017). *Caregivers' references to thoughts fosters children's understanding of second-order false belief in middle childhood.* Poster: British Psychological Society Developmental Section Annual Conference, September.

Parsons, S., Schoon, I., & Vignoles, A. (2014). Parental worklessness and children's early school achievement and progress. *Longitudinal and Life Course Studies, 5*, 19–41.

Perra, O., Phillips, R., Fyfield, R., Waters, C. S., & Hay, D. F. (2015). Does mothers' postnatal depression influence the development of imitation? *Journal of Child Psychology and Psychiatry, 56*, 1231–1238.

Ramachandran, V. S. (2000). Mirror Neurons and imitation learning as the driving force behind 'the great leap forward' in human evolution. *Edge, 69.*

Rich, J. (2015). *The human script: A novel in 23 chromosomes.* UK: Red Button Publishing.

Roberts, S., Fyfield, R., Baibazarova, E., Culling, J. F., van Goozen, S., & Hay, D. F. (2013). Parental speech at 6 months predicts joint attention at 12 months. *Infancy, 18*(Supplement 1), 1–15.

Rosenblum, L. A. (1971). Infant attachment in monkeys. In R. Schoffer (Ed.), *The origin of human social relations* (pp. 85–113). New York: Academic.

Ruffman, T., Slade, L., & Crowe, E. (2002). The relation between children's and mothers' mental state language and theory of mind understanding. *Child Development, 73*, 734–751.

Rutter, M. (1972). *Maternal deprivation reassessed.* Harmondsworth, UK: Penguin.

Rutter, M. (1998). English Romanian Adoptees (ERA) study team. Developmental catch-up, and deficit, following adoption after severe global early privation. *Journal of Child Psychology and Psychiatry, 39*, 465–476.

Rutter, M., Beckett, C., Castle, J., Colvert, E., Kreppner, J., Mehta, M., et al. (2007). Effects of profound early deprivation: An overview of findings from a UK longitudinal study of Romanian adoptees. *European Journal of Developmental Psychology, 4*, 332–350.

Rutter, M., Maughan, B., Mortimore, P., Ouston, J., & Smith, A. (1979). *Fifteen thousand hours: Secondary schools and their effects on children.* London/Boston: Open Books/Harvard University Press.

Rutter, M., Tizard, J., Yule, W., Graham, P., & Whitmore, K. (1976). Research report: Isle of Wight studies, 1964–1974. *Psychological Medicine, 6*, 313–332.

Schipper, M., & Petermann, F. (2013). Relating empathy and emotion regulation: Do deficits in empathy trigger emotion dysregulation? *Social Neuroscience, 8*, 101–107.

Simpson, E. A., Miller, G. M., Ferrari, P. F., Suomi, S. J., & Paukner, A. (2016). Neonatal imitation and early social experience predict gaze following abilities in infant monkeys. *Scientific Reports, 6.*

Singer, T., Seymour, B., O'Doherty, J. P., Stephan, K. E., Dolan, R. J., & Frith, C. D. (2006). Empathic neural responses are modulated by the perceived fairness of others. *Nature, 439,* 466–469.

Smith, A. (2006). Cognitive empathy and emotional empathy in human behaviour and evolution. *The Psychological Record, 56,* 3–21.

Spock, B. (1968). *The common sense book of baby and child care.* New York: Duell, Sloan and Pearce.

van Der Mark, I. L., van Ijzendoorn, M. H., & Bakermans-Kranenburg, M. J. (2002). Development of empathy in girls during the second year of life: Associations with parenting, attachment and temperament. *Social Development, 11,* 451–468.

Watson, J. B. (1924). *Behaviourism.* New York: People's Institute Publishing Company.

Watson, J. B. (1928). *Psychological care of infant and child.* New York: Norton.

Zahn-Waxler, C., Robinson, J. L., & Emde, R. N. (1992). The development of empathy in twins. *Developmental Psychology, 28,* 1038–1047.

Zhou, Q., Eisenberg, N., Losoya, S. H., Fabes, R. A., Reiser, M., Guthrie, I. K., et al. (2002). The relations of parental warmth and positive expressiveness to children's empathy-related responding and social functioning: A longitudinal study. *Child Development, 73,* 893–915.

6

Attachment and Empathy from the Home to the Classroom: Listening to Learners

Attachment and empathy have come a long way from their roots in parenthood, and can be considered just as important for teachers in the realm of teaching and the classroom. In fact, the Freudian concept of transference, where emotions are passed from client to therapist, is arguably just as valid from child to parent and from pupil to teacher. The post-behaviourist era of John Watson gave way to a breath of fresh air of anti-traditional, progressive, child-centred thinking. To the mere presence of a parent was added emotional availability (Sorce & Emde, 1981) and has been fortified further by adding empathy's cognitive component of perspective-taking (Farrant, Devine, Maybery, & Fletcher, 2011). In the educational arena, John Dewey prioritised the needs of the child when considering the curriculum and his dramatic astronomical analogy places the child centre stage in education:

> The change which is coming into our education is the shifting of the centre of gravity. It is a change, a revolution, not unlike that introduced by Copernicus when the astronomical centre shifted from the earth to the sun. In this case the child becomes the sun about which the appliances of education revolve; he is the centre about which they are organised. (Dewey, 1899, p. 151)

© The Author(s) 2018
H. Demetriou, *Empathy, Emotion and Education*,
https://doi.org/10.1057/978-1-137-54844-3_6

The importance of this is now reflected in present-day teaching with recognition by Ofsted (2016) that considers the quality of attachments in children among its inspection framework. Lev Vygotsky's notion of the *zone of proximal development* and Jerome Bruner's *scaffolding* reflect the social nature of learning where teachers provide the help, structure and support to develop pupils' skills and goals. Research has found that for pupils and teachers alike, and in keeping also with the aforementioned ground-breaking theories of attachment, it is vital that a person feels valued by those around them to ensure a feeling of safety and security. In keeping with research that focuses on understanding student motivation, if a person feels that they are deemed worthy then they are more likely to do well (Seifert, 2004). Research has shown that the simple act of listening to the voice of the learner has a profound impact on the learner and their learning. Moreover the role of empathy and emotion in education has been advocated through listening to learners, as emphasised by James Park's 'Antidote' campaign establishing a 'listening culture' and an effective dialogue "…talking together in ways that allow individuals to understand the thoughts, feelings and values of each other" (Park, 2000, p. 11). Just as the mere act of paying attention, listening and responding appropriately to the growing infant in the home has been shown to impact positively on their development, so listening to the child in the classroom can do the same. Attachment beyond and/or concurrently with the caregiver is, it seems, as important in school as it was and is in the home.

An evolution has taken place regarding the people who are most influential in a child's life: from Freud's declaration that the mother was the one and only significant being in a child's emotional upbringing, to Bowlby extending the definition to the effectiveness of other caregivers, to the more recent awareness of other relationships in a child's life, such as those with siblings, friends and teachers, as having significant effects on children's social, emotional and cognitive development. The research into siblings, for example, has uncovered the wealth of learning that takes place within these relationships (Dai & Heckman, 2013; Paine, Pearce, van Goozen, & Hay, 2018). Siblings set and maintain standards and provide role models for each other, through which both develop and practise social-interactional skills and serve as confidants and sources of non-judgemental social support during difficult times (Lamb, 1978). Other researchers have suggested that social interactions, including the more negative ones such as teasing that occur in the context of early sibling relationships, boost learning and propel social understanding, perspective-taking and moral development (Dunn & Munn, 1986).

I will now move on to citing research, including my own, on the effects of such relationships on children's development; and indeed, as all relationships are reversible, how children in turn can also affect the lives of others. Much of the research has elicited pupil voice. In keeping with theories of attachment that have highlighted the importance of a secure relationship with the child as promoting exploration but at the same time maintaining authority, the concept of pupil voice enables discussions with children at the centre so that they can engage freely and fully in their education. They are thus afforded a voice with which to express their thoughts and feelings. Such avenues of expression empower children with confidence and offer them the respect that makes them want to become involved and interested in their education. My research that started within the discipline of developmental psychology in London, to educational research in Cambridge, began with a focus on the extent to which toddlers and children in their middle childhood years are able to empathise with their peers. The research continued with children's friendships and the factors that affect them. Pupil voice then came on the scene. The research ranged from children's friendships and their learning and also in particular the role of friendships during school transfer and transition (Demetriou, Goalen, & Rudduck, 2000), to why boys underachieve in modern foreign languages (Jones, Jones, Demetriou, Downes, & Rudduck, 2001), to establishing why there might be a performance dip in certain year groups (Doddington, Bearne, Demetriou, & Flutter, 2001), to advocating a toolkit for teachers for pupil consultation (MacBeath, Demetriou, Rudduck, & Myers, 2003), to children's concepts of fairness in school (Demetriou & Hopper, 2007), to finding ways of sustaining newly qualified teachers (Wilson & Demetriou, 2007), to my current research on the effects of empathy on creativity. All these studies, some of which will be described more fully, have in common the underlying principle and approach of listening to and eliciting pupil voice. I will recount my research looking at pupil voice itself, and its potential in harnessing the thoughts and feelings, the cognitive and affective nature of pupils, and ultimately the aim of achieving effective and affective teaching and learning.

Effective and Affective Teaching and Learning

My father was a lecturer in organic chemistry who was passionate about his subject but also keen to inspire his students. The impact he made was apparent at his funeral, as his students formed a long line around the perimeter of the cemetery to pay their respects. He treated each student as an individual and for months afterwards we would find notes from his students at his graveside. One wrote: "You said I would get a First, and I did. Thank you". Recently, I found a book in his collection entitled: 'What's the use of lectures?' by Bligh (1971). One section entitled *The lecture method alone is rarely adequate* cautions the reader about the limitations of rote-style lectures for stimulating thought or changing attitudes. There is no denying the importance of being able to teach effectively with the desired outcomes of transmitting knowledge and learning. But recent research has shown some of the most effective ways in which teachers teach and in which pupils learn are not purely down to transmitting the knowledge. Before we mention the recent research, it is important to show that this thinking isn't particularly new. Three notable figures who have propounded the ways in which children should be taught will be mentioned, one perhaps lesser known than the other two, and four centuries apart.

A French philosopher named Michel de Montaigne, born in 1533, wrote about the psychological aspects of educating children, their teaching, learning and motivation. Education in Montaigne's time focused primarily on the reading of classics and learning, and purely through books. His essays are a critique of this approach to learning, both the content and the execution, believing instead that it was necessary to educate children in a variety of ways. But more than that, Montaigne felt that such inflexible and dictatorial teaching denied learners the chance to think for themselves, to question or query what they were learning, rather than taking it 'as read', and thereby being critical about teaching and learning. Indeed, Montaigne was ahead of his time. Today increasingly, what we encourage in our learners, known as 'critical thinking', is what he was advocating—a way of taking the information presented to learners and making it their own through formulating their own opinions and making and taking the time and space to teach themselves. With the student as inquisitor, using independent thought and social interaction such as dialogue, discussion and debate as part of their learning, Montaigne claimed: "Learned we may be with another man's learning: we can only be wise with wisdom of our own" (1603, Essays, I, 25). His thesis was quite revolutionary in the 16th century and turned the ethos of teaching on its head. It was by learning through mistakes and reinventing the information they learn that students were thought to gain a new perspective on that information. At the same time as assimilating the information, students learn new concepts but also learn about themselves as learners and the mechanisms and mechanics that propel their learning. In the words of Winston Churchill: "Success is stumbling from failure to failure with no loss of enthusiasm"; whilst Albert Einstein advocated: "Anyone who has never made a mistake has never tried anything new". And I happened to catch some more wise words on the radio: "…make friends with your failures – they may be the best teachers you've got" (Blue, 2011).

Some 400 years later, and with observations reminiscent of today's parents and teachers also, Dewey (1916) commented, "…parents and teachers often complain – and correctly – that children 'do not want to hear, or want to understand'. Their minds are not upon the subject precisely because it does not touch them; it does not enter into their concerns. This is a state of things that needs to be remedied, but the remedy is not in the use of methods which increase indifference and aversion" (p. 73). Echoing the criticisms of Montaigne, Dewey was also referring to the limitations of rote learning. Around the same time as Dewey, Maria Montessori's focus on the preschool child advocated similar methods in the centre she established in 1907 called the Casa dei Bambini, which I visited in the summer of 2016 whilst on holiday in Rome. The courtyard is now surrounded by apartments, but a plaque at the entrance commemorates Montessori's work. This was a school similar to the one created by Portsmouth's previously mentioned John Pounds which attracted disadvantaged children, this time from the slums of Rome. Montessori recommended that the teacher should take a step back to observe the child whilst at the same time guide, facilitate, direct and attend to specific needs so that children take the lead in their explorations and learning and thereby taking responsibility for themselves. As such, Montessori's emphasis on tailoring education to the individual aligns with Dewey's approach. Montaigne, Dewey and Montessori would be pleased to know that today we seem to have reached the goal in education they were striving for, where child and curriculum overlap and interact, where the result is self-determination and self-realisation of the individual learner. The evolutionary process at work again, pupil voice research and practice has escalated over the last few years and demonstrated the effectiveness of involving pupils to an even greater extent in their teaching and learning.

Involving Children and Young People

Can and should we be talking with pupils about their teaching and learning? This section is all about the potential and effectiveness of collaboration of empathy and emotion between teachers and pupils in order to make strides in teaching and learning. Stenhouse (1975) claimed that only teachers could "…change the world of the classroom" (p. 208) and that: "It is teachers who in the end will change the world of the school by understanding it" (1981, p. 111). However, the nature of learning can only really be understood through taking the time to listen to pupils about their experiences. Through such teamwork, teachers and educators form attachments, not unlike those secure attachments that parents form with their children, and where empathy and respect can flourish. Linking up psychology to education, we now extend the powerful concept of attachment theory to teaching. The attentive, patient and supportive nature of parenting which results in securely attached and confident children now shifts to the domain of teaching. This is all about listening to learners, hearing the pupil voice and thereby forming constructive and purposeful attachments with teachers, thus benefitting both pupils and teachers. Empathy in this domain has been found to be contagious. Such teacher empathy in turn has been shown to elicit pupil empathy—an empathy for pupils of their work, and also their social and emotional life, and these three factors are intrinsically interconnected, thereby helping and understanding the developing child. In a nutshell, when given choice and voice, pupils flourish. But it doesn't stop there, as teachers benefit and learn too.

The United Nations Convention on the Rights of the Child (1989) and the subsequent Children's Act emphasised the importance of children's views being heard and taken seriously. In fact, four of its basic principles include children's right to be heard, including article 12: The views of the child which asserts: "Every child has the right to say what they think in all matters affecting them, and have their views taken seriously".

Various organisations have since drafted charters ensuring that young people are more fully involved in matters that concern them, both within and beyond schools. And Ofsted is now formally asking schools about the extent of their procedures for consulting pupils and extending their involvement. The UK's Government Department for Education states in its mandate (2014): "The Government is committed to the promotion and protection of children's rights, in line with the United Nations Convention on the Rights of the Child. It believes that children and young people should have opportunities to express their opinion in matters that affect their lives. Some of the benefits of involving children and young people in decision making are that: It encourages pupils to become active participants in a democratic society – by holding youth parliaments and school councils which develop skills such as cooperation and communication and encourage them to take responsibility. …It contributes to achievement and attainment – young people involved in participative work benefit in a range of different ways. Increased confidence, self-respect, competence and an improved sense of responsibility have all been reported by young people who contribute in school. Schools also report increased motivation and engagement with learning". As a direct result of a plethora of research, practice and discussions with schools, the DfE (2014) has acknowledged and instilled the concept into its ethos and recommendations and its website reads:

> The term 'pupil voice' refers to ways of listening to the views of pupils and/ or involving them in decision-making. You may also hear the expressions 'learner voice' or 'consulting pupils'. …A feature of effective leadership is engaging pupils as active participants in their education and in making a positive contribution to their school and local community.

So, how and where did the concept and practice of pupil voice begin, and what has been discovered that has resulted in schools and policies worldwide changing their approaches to teaching and learning to include and involve their learners? Since the pioneering research at the University of Cambridge's Faculty of Education that focused on the effects of pupil consultation, funded by the Economic and Social Research Council (ESRC) as part of its Teaching and Learning Research Programme and coordinated by Jean Rudduck (Rudduck et al., 2005), the concept of pupil voice, listening to the words and ideas of pupils, has propelled itself into policy limelight and become integrated within education. Students, as a consequence of this approach to teaching and learning, are themselves the agents of pedagogical change. The result is a transformed and democratically aligned school structure in which students are proactive agents in their learning (Storey, 2007).

Pupil Voice: Children Should Be Seen and Heard

A while back, one of my children was working on trigonometry when I commented that the topic had always confused me. On hearing this he said: "let me go through this example with you. It will help me learn it at the same time". He proceeded to explain the process systematically in a way that made sense to me, and in a way that he claimed helped him too. I was a sounding board, giving my son an audience, a free rein to talk through the maths so he could make sense of it. That instance with me listening and him explaining, seemed to help his learning, and this rings true of the concept of pupil voice, where there is often a two-way interaction between teachers and pupils for the benefit of both concerned.

So what do we actually mean by 'pupil voice' or 'student voice'? The phrases are now widely used, from policy makers to schools. But the coining is relatively recent. It is in fact the means by which learners are enabled to express themselves on the mechanics as well and the substantive nature of learning: the how and the what, thereby becoming involved in their education, and thus empowered and effective agents of change. Among the statements that have triggered such practices include:

What would happen if we treated the student as someone whose opinion mattered? (Fullan, 1991, p. 70); and

Somehow educators have forgotten the important connection between teachers and students. We listen to outside experts to inform us, and, consequently overlook the treasure in our very own backyards, the students. (Soo Hoo, 1993, p. 389)

Such epiphanic comments have inspired researchers to investigate the means by which pupil voice can be tapped for its potential powers in teaching and learning. In order to manage school improvement and confront the underlying structures and values that are embodied within a school, the focus has switched to the pupils themselves as active participants through tuning in to their views and experiences. The need has been highlighted for teachers to be trained to listen to their students, to enable children to express their learning needs and thereby respect the participation rights of the child (Rudduck & Flutter, 2000). As Rudduck (2004) said: "Pupil voice is the consultative wing of pupil participation. Consultation is about talking with pupils about things that matter in school. It may involve: conversations about teaching and learning; seeking advice from pupils about new initiatives; inviting comment on ways of solving problems that are affecting the teacher's right to teach and the pupil's right to learn; inviting evaluative comment on recent developments in school or classroom policy and practice" (p. 1).

Research has shown how such strategies of 'respecting children's voices' (Flutter, 2015) have impacted on teaching and learning in the classroom. An example of this by Flutter (2007) examined the relationship between pupil voice and teacher development and led to her conclusions: "...in a range of different settings, from small, rural primary schools, to large, inner city comprehensive schools facing challenging circumstances. ... The relationship between pupil voice and teacher development demonstrates how pupil voice strategies have enabled teachers to gain a deeper understanding of the teaching and learning processes and have helped them to change the way they think about pupils and their learning" (p. 343). Overall, research has highlighted the clear advantages of listening and talking to students in order to gain their opinions and perspectives on classroom teaching and learning (Rudduck, 2004). As a direct consequence of this research, many teachers have been consulting their pupils to help them find ways of improving the teaching and learning of their own classrooms. For example, McIntyre, Pedder, and Rudduck (2005) investigated the experiences of six teachers and their year 8 pupils. Findings reflected pupils' preferences for more interactive teaching and greater collaboration with peers which they believed gave them a greater ownership of their learning. Teachers' reacted to these ideas as sensible, practical and educationally desirable. Such research shows that when pupil consultation is successful, the results are striking. But how can we relate most effectively with pupils and indeed, how can they relay their thoughts to us in ways that are comfortable and they enjoy? The following section provides some suggestions for the involvement of pupils in their learning.

The 'Toolbox'

Tools come in a variety of forms. The obvious examples are those you might find in a toolbox for DIY tasks around the home. The importance of having a full complement of tools is invaluable for ensuring that every task is completed successfully, after all, as the expression goes: "a workman is only as good as his tools". Speaking metaphorically, Maslow (1966) said: "I suppose it is tempting, if the only tool you have is a hammer, to treat everything as if it were a nail" (p. 15). Tools are a means to an end. They come in all shapes and sizes, can be physical or virtual, but ultimately they are a conduit through which information is relayed and a goal is reached. Conceptualising life as a toolbox in which the tools equip and enable children to resolve issues they encounter, Vygotsky set humans apart from other species as a consequence of being able to use cultural tools such as language, art, stories, posters and models in order to make sense of the world.

Similarly, within education, there are a variety of resources to help gain information for teaching and learning. In constructing a 'toolkit' with my colleagues (c.f. Demetriou, 2009) we recommended a number of ways in which pupils can relay information about their learning. Our reasons for creating a resource for gathering information from pupils was that thitherto, there was comparatively little within the literature on tools with which to dig for the buried treasure, despite the growing acceptance of the idea that students should have a say about learning (and even more challengingly about teaching) and that such tools would be welcomed by teachers. These 'tools' have enabled and empowered pupils so that they can be consulted and communicate issues and aspects of their teaching and learning. Once unlocked, this power has the potential to enhance the quality of teaching and learning and transform the dynamics in the classroom for the benefit of all concerned, not least the students. Consulting students can take a variety of forms and the effectiveness of the tools was demonstrated through the action research we conducted in a variety of schools as implemented by the schools themselves. Instead of placing the tools haphazardly into the toolbox, we classified them into sections, so that like an actual toolbox, when we need a particular tool, we would know where to find it. The virtual toolbox contains a range of instruments designed for a range of users that may be selected for use in different contexts. Despite a wealth of tried and tested approaches to consultation, the present research recognised the need for more varied and fine-grained tools. Our concern was to enhance the confidence of teachers themselves in engaging with students whilst consulting them about teaching and learning. Unlike tools in a household toolbox, these need to be adapted to suit the task and the context, including the age of the students to be consulted.

The final toolbox (see MacBeath et al., 2003) includes a snapshot of approaches, samples of questionnaires and interview schedules that schools have found useful and realistically achievable, enabling teachers to decide on the approach that best fits their purpose and to see how they might adapt it for their context. The array of approaches to consultation using tools from the toolbox has, since its publication, been extensively used and adapted for use by schools. The tools typically involved 'direct', 'prompted' or 'mediated' approaches to consultation, each with its own set of tools that ranged from questionnaire-based, more open forms of writing, minimum of writing, talk-based approaches to creative approaches. Such approaches enabled teachers and pupils to understand each other's viewpoints for the first time. For example, the talk-based approach was particularly effective for one school when the head teacher developed, over time, a conversational style with her combined class of year 5 and 6 students, talking to them in lessons about their learning, listening sensitively to their viewpoints, encouraging them to talk openly about their strengths and weaknesses as learners and the things that helped them to learn and that got in the way of their learning. The head teacher sat at the level of the students on a small chair like theirs and established an adult, non-patronising tone during the conversation. Students learned to feel increasingly comfortable in talking, individually and collectively, about their successes and their problems in learning and about things that would help them to learn more effectively.

Consultation, Participation and Pupil Research

The powerful Chinese proverb, "Tell me, I'll forget; show me, I may remember; involve me, and I'll understand", extolls the virtues of learning first hand through a hands-on, collaborative experience. Within the realms of education, it rings true of the power of dialogue with the learner and respecting pupils enough so as to involve them in their learning. Having described means and ways where pupils were able to act as researchers themselves using a variety of 'tools' in order to gather information on which to discuss and potentially act, there is vast potential in consulting pupils and strengthening their participation in school and classroom matters. In particular it highlights what pupils can achieve by taking on 'researcher' roles, disseminating their findings on a variety of levels and to a variety of audiences, and discussing issues that concern them whilst planning and managing constructive ways of responding. Of course, pupil involvement in research is not new as school councils often provide an agenda for pupil research which has triggered a growing willingness to encourage research undertaken by pupils themselves (Demetriou & Rudduck, 2004). Whilst national policy has provided an increasingly urgent framework for involving pupils in improving their own learning, the pioneering work has been done by teachers in this country and abroad and shared within and across schools.

There are three overlapping ideas of consultation, participation and pupil research. *Consultation* is about talking with pupils about things that matter in school, through: conversations (discourse), building a habit of easy discussion; seeking advice (planning), about policies or other initiatives; and inviting comment (evaluation), on recent developments or changes in school or classroom, policy or practice. *Participation* is about involving pupils more closely in important aspects of their lives in school. At classroom level, participation is about giving pupils more opportunities for making decisions and greater choice and involving pupils in thinking about their own learning priorities and their progress in learning. At school level, participation is about inviting pupils to be members of teams, working parties and discussion groups that focus on real issues, events, problems or opportunities and enabling pupils to take on a wider range of roles and responsibilities—for instance, as mediators, peer tutors and, of course, as pupil researchers. And *Pupil research* is about involving pupils in identifying something that troubles them and that needs action, as well as in gathering data that will open up or solve a problem. Alternatively, the 'research' might focus on the evaluation of a new initiative through enquiries conducted by teams of pupils. It can be carried out in relation to problems at school or classroom level. 'Pupils as researchers' assumes that pupils can undertake serious and significant work and they have skills and knowledge about teaching and learning based on their daily experience of schools and classrooms. Typically, 'pupils as researchers' projects involve specific groups of pupils who identify and investigate issues related to their schools and their learning that they see as significant. The projects aim to enable pupils to work with teachers in bringing about change, or even to take the lead, with teachers supporting and facilitating the process. Rather than being a passive data source, simply ticking boxes on a survey designed by adults, they become a significant 'voice' and significant agents, shaping the form and direction of research. 'Pupils as researchers' seeks to *involve*, not merely to *use* young people, viewing them not just as recipients or targets, but as resources and producers of knowledge.

'Pupils as researchers' projects generally fall into three categories: they are about *teaching and learning, school and curriculum policy*, and *school organisation and environment*. Pupils have researched: what makes a good teacher; what makes a good lesson; what helps and hinders learning; starting lessons effectively; the effect of environment on learning; aspects of assessment; the extent of bullying and different ways of intervening; ways of rewarding achievement that pupils value; investigating the buddy system; pupils as mediators; playground layout and design; school meals; safe and unsafe places within school; pupils' recreational needs; and refurbishing toilets and social areas. Pupils generally gather data through questionnaires that they themselves have designed or helped design; through talking with other pupils individually or in small groups (with one of them making notes); or through carefully focused observation. It is important to be aware of topics that pupils find comfortable to explore. In one school, for instance, it took time for pupils to gain confidence to comment on what goes on in the classroom, the remit of which they saw as belonging to the teacher and which they had no right to comment on:

> I wanted them to tell me about how to teach maths or reading, but the children hadn't got the feeling that that was their territory. The playground very definitely was their territory, so we went with it. (Primary deputy head)

The success of 'pupils as researchers' projects depends on a number of practical issues, namely: finding time for pupils to meet; availability of some minimal resources; building trust; guidance in straightforward ways of gathering and analysing the data; and guidance in ways of summarising and communicating the findings to others (whether to other pupils, teachers or governors). Communication and sharing of findings can be both formal and informal through announcements in staff meetings or at morning briefings; via newsletters for parents, governors and staff; through presentations by pupils to other pupils—at assemblies, in classes—and to staff; through the intranet and emails if available; through posters and displays; making a film or a photographic record; and by word of mouth. Trust and openness are a pre-condition of 'pupils as researchers' activities. Sharing the data and/or offering feedback to pupils is also important. Pupils need to know what is happening as a result of what they have investigated as well as knowing what is not possible and why. Participation is sometimes restricted to 'representatives' or 'enthusiasts', so it is important therefore to listen and involve a range of pupils. Also, the term itself 'pupils as researchers' could be seen to trivialise professional research by implying that anyone with minimal training can do it. Some have argued that it may be more appropriate to think of pupil research as 'inquiry'. However, the term that is used is perhaps unimportant, provided that the activity is handled with proper respect for the nature of evidence; pupils involved think seriously about how 'findings' that indicate a diversity of views can lead to action; and young people's interest in and commitment to help make schooling better is recognised and respected.

Overall, evidence suggests that 'pupils as researchers' projects have a positive impact on pupils, not only on those involved as researchers but on the whole class, year group and even school. These include developing a positive sense of self and agency, developing inquiring minds and learning new skills, developing social competence and new relationships, being able to reflect on their own learning and a chance to be active and creative. Pupil researchers also develop 'civic' skills such as those of running meetings—including drawing up an agenda, taking minutes, chairing and turn-taking:

> The year 5s do minuting, it sounds very grand, but what they would do basically is use note-taking and where else in the curriculum do they get the chance to do real note-taking? It's all real-life stuff! (Primary deputy head)

'Pupils as researchers' projects often involve getting to know pupils of different ages and abilities, understanding their perspectives and valuing their contributions:

> We have opportunities to work, play and help younger children. This helps me to get on with people. It calms me down and helps me to get to know them and for them to get to know me. (year 6 researcher)

Working together on a 'real' task can be an exciting, communal experience:

I would love to think that it would stay with them for life, that feeling of what you can achieve if you work together, what you can achieve if you try your best. (Primary head teacher)

And another teacher said this:

They had a real sense of collective ownership, thinking 'It's up to us to make this work, it's up to us to make this interesting'. ...And you can tell from all that sense of joy in learning that the process of working together worked effectively. (year 6 teacher)

Learning from the Student Perspective: The Transformative Potential

Just as the disengaged infant is typically a product of the disengaged parent, so pupil disengagement results from schools and teachers who do not involve their students closely. School improvement is about enhancing engagement through achieving a better fit between young people and the school as an institution. It is not just about raising the profile of a school's test scores; it is, literally and logically, about the *improvement of schools*, their organisational structures, regimes and relationships of 'the conditions of learning' (Demetriou & Rudduck, 2001; Fielding & Bragg, 2003; Rudduck & Flutter, 2004). Achieving change in the basic conditions of learning in schools, as Watson and Fullan (1992) have said, "will not happen by accident, good will or …. ad hoc projects. It requires new structures, new activities, and a re-thinking of the internal workings of each institution" (p. 219). Just as Bowlby's 'internal working model' as fashioned by the child of its mental representations for understanding the self and others is dependent on the nature of attachments, the internal workings of a school are similarly fashioned based upon the people and input it receives. As observed by Robinson (2014): "Pupils in schools where a rights-respecting approach had been developed stressed that they felt valued, cared for, respected and listened to in school, and they recognised that staff were genuinely concerned for their well-being" (p. 5). And, as so succinctly put by Oscar Wilde: "With conversation, talking is the craft, listening is the art".

Listening to pupils has proved to be a powerful way forward. Hearing students talk about their experiences as learners in schools has challenged assumptions, provoked reflection and has led to changes, both nationally and at school level. These changes are a clear testament to the importance of what pupils have to say as expert witnesses in discussions of teaching, learning and schooling. As Rudduck (2002) noted: "From an early age in school young people are capable of insightful and constructive analysis of social situations and if their insights are not harnessed in support of their own learning then they may use them strategically to avoid learning in school and conspire unwittingly in the process of their own underachievement" (pp. 123–124). Increasingly, listening to the student voice, as proposed in the Cambridge Primary Review (Alexander, Doddington, Gray, Hargreaves, & Kershner, 2010) has shown that involving students more in the day to day business of the school as a learning community is likely to enhance their engagement with learning and their progress as learners. Gray, Hopkins, Reynolds, Farrell, and Jesson (1999), drawing on correlational analyses of school effectiveness studies, have suggested that schools achieving more rapid progress were those which 'had actively sought pupils' views as well as giving them more prominent roles' in school. But "moreover…the transformative potential of student consultation and participation goes beyond the usual confines of school effectiveness and improvement to affect school regimes; it challenges traditional images of 'childhood' … and enables young people to develop more positive identities as learners" (Rudduck, Demetriou, & Pedder, 2003, p. 276).

What's in it for Pupils, Teachers and Schools?

First, a broad and predictable response: being heard is important and necessary to young people. A survey in a national newspaper in England (Birkett, *The Guardian*, June 2001) asked students (aged 5–16) to describe 'The school I'd like'. There were over 15,000 responses. Nine key features were identified and two were about consultation. Top of the list were these: 'A beautiful school; A comfortable school; A safe school'. Fourth in the list was this: 'A listening school, with students on governing bodies, class representatives and the chance to choose teachers'. And seventh on the list was 'A respectful school, where children and adults can talk freely and student opinion matters'. These ratings confirm the data from our interviews with young people that being able to voice an opinion matters. But more than that, young people want teachers to take action on what they have heard or, if there are differences of view within the pupil group, to explain why some actions are preferred or why only limited action is possible. In conversations with 11-year-old pupils who had failed to gain a place in the high schools they wanted to move to and whose comments revealed the pain and stigma of rejection, one said, "You know you've asked us if there is anything we'd like to change? (Well) If there's anything that they can do (about it), will it happen?" (Urquhart, 2001, p. 86).

Our data, across the projects, suggest that being able to talk about your experiences of learning in school and having your account taken seriously offers students four things: a stronger sense of membership: *the organisational dimension*—so that they feel positive about school; a stronger sense of respect and self-worth: *the personal dimension*—so that they feel positive about themselves; a stronger sense of self-as-learner: *the pedagogic dimension*—so that they are better able to manage their own progress in learning; and a stronger sense of agency: *the political dimension*—so that they see it as worthwhile becoming involved in school matters and contributing to the improvement of teaching and learning. These are all things that could make a difference to pupils' engagement with learning; the transformative potential is considerable but there are dangers, and students can be short-changed. In the acoustic of the school, whose voice gets listened to (Fielding & Rudduck, 2002)? A student claimed: "Sometimes I wish I could sit down with one of my teachers and just tell them what I exactly think about their class. It might be good, it might be bad, it's just that you don't have the opportunity to do it" (Shultz & Cook-Sather, 2001). If the school claims to be supporting student voice, can students be certain that the familiar dividing practices are not still operating? Students will be justifiably cynical if, within a framework of promise, attention and respect there is a bias towards a select group of students.

There are two possible gains for teachers, namely: a sharper awareness of young people's capabilities; and a practical agenda for improvement. Teachers are the gatekeepers of change in school. To unlock the transformative potential of student perspective and participation we have to help teachers 'see' students differently (Cook-Sather, 2014). During our boys' achievement project (Jones et al., 2001) we received the reply that 12- to 13-year-old students were 'too young to express an opinion'. What helps teachers to see students differently? Quite often it is reading the insightful comments on teaching and learning in reports on research into student voices, and even more compelling are the comments from their own students. In another of our projects, "How teachers respond to and use pupil perspectives to improve teaching and learning", the team worked with teachers to develop consultation practices in different subjects. Here the head of maths in a secondary school talks about her work with 12- to 13-year-old students; she had been using feedback on her maths lessons:

> One girl in particular clearly seemed to understand, better than I did!—how she learned. Some, interestingly, were immediately reflective in a highly sophisticated way, beyond my expectation, but nobody had known that before because nobody had asked them. (Webb, 2001)

Another of our projects set out to identify manageable strategies for talking about learning in both primary and secondary schools (MacBeath, Myers, & Demetriou, 2001). The head of a small primary school commented on the early stages of building a school-wide commitment to involving her young students in talking about learning:

> I started to look with the children at what they thought learning was. ... They told me that if they're told what to do, they just listen and then do it. But as soon as they had to be responsive, then they would realise that their understanding wasn't as good as they thought it was. ...I think that was really important because there's now two-way exchange most of the time in the classroom.... Children very freely now say, 'Can you go over that again, I don't understand it'. .... They need that freedom to come back. (Primary head teacher, 2001)

This head teacher has since become a schools' inspector, and I hope and am sure that she has taken her work ethic with her into her new role.

Comments from students can challenge assumptions and lead the teacher to 'see' students as they are and not as they have been historically, and conveniently, constructed to fit the regimes of schooling. They are their own advocates but they are supported now by a range of other voices that remind us of the need to see, value and use students' capacities. For example, Apple and Beane (1999) contend that educators should help young people to research and voice a range of their own ideas. Soo Hoo (1993) argued that "Traditionally students have been overlooked as valuable resources in the re-structuring of schools" (p. 392). And Hodgkin (1998) said: "The fact is that pupils themselves have a huge potential contribution to make, not as passive objects but as active players in the education system. Any legislation concerning school standards will be seriously weakened if it fails to recognise the importance of that contribution" (p. 11). As teachers see students differently, so they are more likely to respect and trust them and offer more opportunities for them to take responsibility for learning and for the management of their learning. And as it happens, this is what students say they want.

The discussion on the importance of 're-profiling' students in teachers' eyes should not underestimate the practical value of student commentaries on teaching and learning: what helps them to learn and what gets in the way of their learning. The commentaries may be elicited by direct questioning or they may be identified more casually by teachers simply 'tuning in' to the messages students send that are not always heard. For instance, teachers learned a lot when 15- to 16-year-old male students, in interviews about what turned them off learning, started to talk about the difficulty of changing from being a 'dosser' to a 'worker'. They communicated vividly the difficulty of shifting an image that was held in place by various people's expectations. One talked about becoming 'addicted' to messing about and the difficulty of kicking the habit; another talked about how his friends were disappointed if he didn't continue to muck about in lessons; another said that most teachers never forgot the bad things he'd done and that his favourite teacher was the one who said that every lesson was a clean slate for her—a forgetting rather than a remembering; another described how little praise he got because of his reputation as a nuisance in classes:

> No one's praised me in quite a long time actually. But I think they're used to me being a trouble-maker and they don't want to go back on themselves by praising me. I'd faint if they did. No, I'd be happy 'cos I would have done something and they've like, praised me for it.

And another, showing a greater empathy for teachers than they seem to have shown him, said this:

> Me personally, I've brought a reputation upon myself. I'm known to be the class clown, and it's got me in a lot of trouble. And so I've decided to change and it's just really hard to, like, show the teachers that… and when I went on report and I got A1, A1, best, top marks, but there's just been some lessons where it's slipped and they're like 'Oh, he's still the same'. I can understand how they feel about that.

Such comments help us towards a better understanding of the support that students need and the difficulties that students face who want to settle down to work but feel trapped by the negatively biased images others hold of them. Student commentaries have enabled us to 'read' the messages that schools send out about what matters in school and how this influences their investment of effort; they have helped us re-balance the emphasis at transfer from primary to secondary school on the social and the academic aspects of induction; they have enabled us to understand how important it is to have time for dialogue with someone they trust about problems with learning; they have made us aware how frustrating it is not to be able to complete a task they are committed to because of the boundaries of lesson times. They offer an agenda that is rooted in the realities of *their* everyday world.

It is perhaps not surprising that teachers, anxious to escape the increasing bureaucratisation of their work, see student consultation as a way of bringing the relationship of learner and teacher together, restoring it to its rightful place at the centre of professional practice. The energy and ebullience that emanates from building a productive partnership with students is exemplified in the words of an English teacher from our project, which focused on how teachers in different subjects use pupil commentaries on their lessons to improve teaching and learning:

> You know, that's what made me enthusiastic because I suddenly saw all that untapped creativity really…. You can use pupils' ideas in a very valid, interesting way and it can make the pupil excited, the teacher excited and you know obviously the lessons will take off from there. …. Although you do a

bit of collaborating together with other teachers, there's not that much time any more so, you know, if you can actually collaborate with pupils it's equally - I didn't realise it – it's equally exciting isn't it? (Pedder, 2001)

For teachers, tuning in to what students, rather than what policy makers, say is a professionally re-creative act. There are two main gains for schools, namely, a stronger sense of the school as a learning community and a commitment to 'enacting' and not merely 'teaching about' citizenship. Aoki (2004) said that in order to learn in school, it is necessary to "…venture forth together" (p. 6). But we all know that it is so often not the case. The traditional power regimes can mark out an 'us' and 'them' relationship between students and teachers; the familiar dividing practices separate out the students whose achievement is valued by the school and those whose work is not valued. Schools need support in the task of "reshaping long standing structures that have fostered disconnection, separateness, division", features that have prevented teachers and students in schools from "sharing powerful ideas about how to make schools better" (Warsley, Hampel, & Clark, 1997, p. 204). The transformative desire, with its increasingly intrusive agenda, seeks to change the status and sense of agency of students, bringing them in from the margins so that their voices can be heard. This means establishing processes whereby dialogue with students would become part and parcel of the way a school functions (Fielding, 1997); there might be a requirement that pupils would be partners in regular dialogues, providing advice and feedback so that "…schools should be more explicitly, more imaginatively and more profoundly committed to the enactment of democracy as a way of living and learning together 'as an inclusive human order'" (Fielding, 2016, p. 2).

Ensuring that students see themselves as stake-holders in the institutional enterprise of learning is key. But we know that it takes time for teachers and students to learn to work together to build a climate in which they feel comfortable in managing a constructive review of the teaching and learning in their schools. If we appreciate how much young people value being consulted, how it gives them a stronger sense of their school as an inclusive learning community and how insightful and constructive their points of view can be, then we may give serious thought to reviewing the traditional structures of schooling in ways that are appropriate to the maturity and analytic insight of young people today. The politically acceptable justification for student consultation is of course school improvement, but the renewal of interest in citizenship education supports the principle of student voice within an empowerment frame. Here, we have to distinguish between teaching *about* citizenship and ensuring that in the daily life of schools, pupils *experience* citizenship: the meaning of democracy has to be demonstrated and lived, not merely described. The next step, then, is to build more opportunities for participation and consultation into the fabric of school, and whilst we may see the school council as the vehicle for 'delivery', the council only works well if it is at the centre of school-wide democratic practice. If the school council does not go beyond the predictable agenda of uniform and school dinners (important as these are in the school lives of young people) to take on issues of teaching and learning and the conditions of learning, then it can become merely a way of channelling student complaints—an exercise in damage limitation rather than an opportunity for real and constructive debate.

Language for Learning, Ownership of Learning and School as a Democratic Community

Teachers increasingly see the merit in giving pupils ownership and leadership when it comes to their learning. When he was in year 4, my youngest son was awarded the weekly medal in assembly for his role in helping another child in the class understand a concept in maths. The certificate read that he 'supported his partner in learning a new method of multiplication'. When I talked about this with my son, he said "I basically acted as the teacher". This was the same boy who, as a toddler said I was being daft over daffodils. He was correct then and was correct subsequently at 9 years of age, recognising that he was taking the role of the teacher.

Research in the social sciences has asked powerful questions about the status of young people both in and outside schools. Young people are constantly presented, they argue, in a state of *becoming* rather than as *being* actors in their own right. This view of young people as 'inadequately socialised' future adults (James & Prout, 1997, p. xiv) still retains a powerful hold on the structures of schooling. Schools have been described as a period of 'quarantine' between childhood and adulthood (Aries, 1962), and a period during which young people remain as 'uneasy, stranded beings' (Silver & Silver, 1997). Research into student voice enables us to confront the implications of a situation that we have for too long seen as 'the natural order of things'. If there are concerns, it is with the 'fashionableness' of student voice. Consulting students has in the words of Rudduck et al. (2003) "…become so popular that in a climate of short-termism the interest may burn out before its transformative potential has been fully understood" (p. 285). So, "…despite the climate of performativity, where students' grades matter more than their engagement with learning, teachers and students together may be able … to construct a new status and a new order of experience for students in schools" (p. 274).

As pupils develop a more 'professional' language for discussing their learning, they are less likely to disengage; they are able to contribute effectively to the agenda for school improvement; and are more committed and effective learners. But it is important to have a good relationship with pupils in which both teachers and learners can establish confidentiality, trust, respect and empathy. Results of consultation have shown that: pupils recognise ownership of their work and their learning; merely asking pupils about their learning improved it; pupils feel empowered; it equips them with a sophisticated dialogue; pupils respond better to staff; and pupils view consultation as an entitlement. As two pupils told us:

> We make the targets for us now…and that's better because I think we know more about ourselves than the teachers…in a way, because we know more what our strengths and weaknesses are. (year 7 girl)

> It's not just for the adults to do everything, the children get involved too. (year 8 boy)

Teachers also shared with us their genuine surprise at the process and outcomes of pupil consultation:

I've been amazed about how much children want to talk about their learning.

I think what's been so interesting about this project has been the children's perceptions…actually listening and taking account of children's views. We tend to make assumptions and think 'Oh that's fine for them' or 'That's hard for them' and we don't necessarily get their views right. I think the project's shown that children really think far more than we give them credit for. (head teacher)

Listening to the student voice enables students to take on an active role in their own education, where they are able to work directly with school leaders and teachers to develop better learning experiences. Some teachers mentioned the empowering effect of pupil voice and its transformational potential in harnessing teachers' views about important issues in school:

Merely the expectation that their views will be listened to and acted upon empowers pupils. They become aware of their capacity to change teacher perceptions and that teachers will listen to their views on the curriculum. (head teacher)

Pupil feedback has definitely made me think about my teaching.

It gives pupils a chance to shine…but it also really does matter what they say.

One of the biggest surprises that we've had is the power that pupil voice can have on the rest of the staff.

Our levels of achievement at the end of the cohort year were truly tremendous…I know this was due to the work we had been undertaking as part of this project because these children saw themselves as successful and had developed considerably their self-esteem. Three years ago, just after I arrived at the school, the results were some of the worst in the County (17% at Level 4 in maths and English). This year we were fourth in the National League tables.

> I think it's essential to consult pupils about their learning…it's educational in its own sense, it develops their ability to take responsibility for their learning.

Teachers also stated how their perceptions of pupils' capabilities had changed as a result of talking with them about some of the taken-for-granted aspects of teaching and learning. They reported a much more positive view of pupils' capacities for observation and constructive analysis:

> I know I shouldn't be (but) I'm still astounded at the depth of their honesty. And about how much if we listen we can learn and influence what's happening with them and be part of what's happening with them. (Secondary teacher)

As well as establishing effective relationships between pupils and teachers, instilling confidence and delivering an ownership for learning, pupil involvement in decision-making has received acclaim from teachers who have witnessed its impact on improved exam performance. In Canada under the leadership of Jean Courtney (2008), the student voice initiative has been used by Ontario's Ministry of Education, where since 2014, their SpeakUp projects have awarded 7000 grants to 800 schools. Another example of the international acclamation of student voice is in Africa where Ngussa and Makewa (2014) have highlighted its impact on curriculum change. Using a constructivist approach to learning, these researchers showed how an active and involved approach to learning enables learners to connect their newly acquired knowledge to existing ones through decision-making processes about what and how they learn. Such a sideways shift by teachers as a result of heeding the voices of pupils enables teachers to revisit their teaching as well as empowering students to take ownership, responsibility and understand themselves and their learning. And a study in Kenya (Mati, Gatumu, & Chandi, 2016) showed that pupils' responsibility, ownership and involvement in decision-making had a direct impact on their academic achievement; as did the cooperation between parents, teachers and pupils, whilst at the same time increasing teachers' creativity and quality of teaching.

Also, both teachers and pupils concur that: pupils are more able to talk about their learning and are more aware and accepting of their learning needs; pupils are more confident about telling their teacher if they don't understand something; pupils have a greater sense of why they are doing a particular task and a stronger sense of ownership; and pupils are more ready to become involved and to take initiatives. Such comments from teachers who were involved in the research reflect the genuine surprise and appreciation that pupil consultation can bring to teaching. Whereas teachers reaped the benefits of consultation, the process was primarily in favour of the pupils, who took centre stage. Such research that has focused on teachers' thinking has thus far alerted them to the ways in which they might think about education and encouraged them to ask questions of their own practice, the attachments they make and the empathy they incorporate.

Whichever way pupil consultation is achieved, the result is that of a school with a democratic ethos. Pupil consultation has generally proved to be an effective experience for both pupils and teachers. It has shown that, through listening and learning from the pupil's perspective, there are educational benefits for all concerned, not least the teachers. Fielding (1997) wrote: "A transformative approach to student involvement would be one in which the process of involving students was seen as part of the normal way in which a school goes about its daily work" (p. 7). As a result of their research, Rudduck and McIntyre (2007) claimed that: "Pupil consultation can lead to a transformation of teacher-pupil relationships, to significant improvements in teachers' practices, and to pupils having a sense of themselves as members of a community of learners". The research, which consisted of six projects culminated in its publication in 2004, and its findings have been disseminated widely, with the desire for schools to consult their students escalating ever since. Indeed, in England, young people's views have found a place on the government agenda. This may be ascribed to political expediency, an instrumental view about improving standards, or indeed a: "…growing recognition that young people have a right to be heard and have something worthwhile to say about their school experiences. Policy makers internationally are thinking differently … about the contribution of young people to today's and tomorrow's world" (Rudduck, 2003, p. 1). There is a changing social context, a slow swell of opinion about the place of children and young people in today's and tomorrow's world, a climate in which young people are less willing to be taken for granted and in which they are physically becoming adults whilst still in their middle years of schooling. The growing prominence of citizenship education in the school curriculum is another source of support. There is an extensive and growing literature on student voice, not entirely disconnected from its ascendancy on the policy agenda. Several strands run through that literature. These include: an historic neglect of students as a source of evidence; the shortfall when seeing students simply as sources of data; the role of students in school self-evaluation; the potential contribution of students to school improvement; and the role of students as partners in their own learning. Through engaging with pupils, taking their perspective and learning from their perspective, teachers can learn about what makes pupils tick, but also learn about themselves as teachers. Schools therefore should be encouraged to engage with their learners and enable them to express themselves about their experiences of school, thereby involving them in a partnership within a democratic community that inspires both teachers and learners alike and results in a transformative approach to teaching and learning.

References

Alexander, R. J., Doddington, C., Gray, J., Hargreaves, L., & Kershner, R. (2010). *Children, their world, their education: Final report and recommendations for the Cambridge primary review.* London: Routledge.

Aoki, T. (2004). *Curriculum in a new key: The collected works of Ted T. Aoki* (W. F. Pinar, & R. L. Irwin, Eds.). Routledge: New York/London.

Apple, M. W., & Beane, J. A. (Eds.). (1999). *Democratic schools: Lessons from the chalk face.* Buckingham, UK: Open University Press.

Aries, P. (1962). *Centuries of childhood.* London: Jonathan Cape.

Birkett, D. (2001, June 5). The children's manifesto. *The Guardian.*

Bligh, D. A. (1971). *What's the use of lectures?* Exeter, UK: B. Bligh.

Blue, L. (2011). Thought for the day. *Radio 4. BBC.*

Cook-Sather, A. (2014). The trajectory of student voice in educational research. *New Zealand Journal of Educational Studies, 49,* 131–148.

Courtney, J. (2008). *SpeakUp* project. Ontario, Canada.

Dai, X., & Heckman, J. J. (2013). Older siblings' contributions to young child's cognitive skills. *Economic Modelling, 35*, 235–248.

de Montaigne, M. (1603). *Montaigne's essays.* Translation by John Florio (1533–1625).

Demetriou, H. (2009). 'Accessing students' perspectives through three forms of consultation' (chapter 6). In A. Cook Sather (Ed.), *Learning from the student's perspective: A sourcebook for effective teaching.* Boulder, CO: Paradigm Publishers.

Demetriou, H., Goalen, P., & Rudduck, J. (2000). Academic performance, transfer, transition and friendship: Listening to the student voice. *International Journal of Educational Research, 33*, 425–441.

Demetriou, H., & Hopper, B. (2007). 'Some things are fair, some things are not fair and some things are not, NOT fair': Young children's experiences of 'unfairness' in school. In D. Thiessen & A. Cook-Sather (Eds.), *International handbook of student experience of elementary and secondary school* (pp. 167–192). Dordrecht, The Netherlands: Springer Science.

Demetriou, H., & Rudduck, J. (2001). Transforming our perceptions of pupils. *ESRC/TLRP Newsletter*, schools edition.

Demetriou, H., & Rudduck, J. (2004). Pupils as researchers: The importance of using their research evidence. *Primary Leadership Paper: Teaching as a research informed profession, 11*, 31–34 (For the National Association of Head Teachers).

Dewey, J. (1899). *The school and society.* Chicago: University of Chicago Press.

Dewey, J. (1916). *Democracy and education. An introduction to the philosophy of education* (1966 ed.). New York: Free Press (Classic discussion of education for democracy).

DfE. (2014, January). *Listening to and involving children and young people.* Department for Education, UK.

Doddington, C., Bearne, E., Demetriou, H., & Flutter, J. (2001). 'Testing, testing, testing…can you hear me?' Can year 3 pupils tell us anything we don't know already about assessment? *Education 3–13 The Professional Journal for Primary Education, 29*, 43–46.

Dunn, J., & Munn, P. (1986). Siblings and the development of prosocial behaviour. *International Journal of Behavioural Development, 9*, 265–284.

Farrant, B. M., Devine, T. A. J., Maybery, M. T., & Fletcher, J. (2011). Empathy, perspective-taking and prosocial behaviour: The importance of parenting practices. *Infant and Child Development, 21*, 175–188.

Fielding, M. (1997). Beyond school effectiveness and school improvement: Lighting the slow fuse of possibility. *Curriculum Journal, 8*, 7–27.

Fielding, M. (2016). Why and how schools might live democracy 'as an inclusive human order'. In S. Higgins & F. Coffield (Eds.), *An invited contribution to John Dewey's democracy and education: A British tribute*. London: UCL IOE Press.

Fielding, M., & Bragg, S. (2003). *Students as researchers: Making a difference*. Cambridge, UK: Pearson Publishing.

Fielding, M., & Rudduck, J. (2002). *The transformative potential of student voice: Confronting the power issues*. Paper given at the BERA Annual Conference, University of Exeter.

Flutter, J. (2007). Teacher development and pupil voice. *The Curriculum Journal, 18*, 343–354.

Flutter, J. (2015, February). *Respecting children's voices*. Cambridge Primary Review Trust.

Fullan, M. G. (1991). *The new meaning of educational change*. London: Cassell Educational.

Gray, J., Hopkins, D., Reynolds, D., Farrell, S., & Jesson, D. (1999). *Improving schools: Performance and potential*. Buckingham, UK: Open University Press.

Hodgkin, R. (1998). Partnership with pupils. *Children UK, 17*.

James, A., & Prout, A. (1997). *Constructing and reconstructing childhood*. London: Falmer Press.

Jones, B., Jones, G., Demetriou, H., Downes, P., & Rudduck, J. (2001). *Boys' performance in modern foreign languages – Listening to learners*. London: CILT.

Lamb, M. E. (1978). Interactions between eighteen-month-olds and their preschool-aged siblings. *Child Development, 49*, 51–59.

MacBeath, J., Demetriou, H., Rudduck, J., & Myers, K. (2003). *Consulting pupils: A toolkit for teachers*. Cambridge: Pearson Publishing.

MacBeath, J., Myers, K., & Demetriou, H. (2001). Supporting teachers in consulting pupils about aspects of teaching and learning and evaluating impact. *Forum, 43*, 78–82.

Maslow, A. H. (1966). *The psychology of science*. New York: Harper & Row.

Mati, A., Gatumu, J. C., & Chandi, J. R. (2016). Students' involvement in decision making and their academic performance in Embu west sub-county of Kenya. *Universal Journal of Educational Research, 4*, 2294–2298.

McIntyre, D., Pedder, D., & Rudduck, J. (2005). Pupil voice: Comfortable and uncomfortable learnings for teachers. *Research Papers in Education, 20*, 149–168.

Ngussa, B. M., & Makewa, L. N. (2014). Student voice in curriculum change: A theoretical reasoning. *International Journal of Academic Research in Progressive Education and Development, 3*(3), 23–37.

Ofsted. (2016). *School inspection handbook*. Ofsted inspections of maintained schools.

Paine, A., Pearce, H., van Goozen, S. H. M., & Hay, D. F. (2018). Late, but not early, arriving younger siblings foster firstborns' understanding of second-order false belief. *Journal of Experimental Child Psychology, 166*, 251–265.

Park, J. (2000). The dance of dialogue: Thinking and feeling in education. *Pastoral Care in Education, 18*, 11–15.

Pedder, D. (2001, September). *How teachers respond to and use pupil perspectives to improve teaching and learning: Summary of issues*. Paper given as part of the Consulting Pupils Network Project Symposium, BERA Annual Conference, University of Leeds.

Robinson, C. (2014). Children, their voices and their experiences of school: What does the evidence tell us? *Cambridge Primary Review Trust*. Research Reports, Pearson.

Rudduck, J. (2002). The transformative potential of consulting young people about teaching, learning and schooling. *Scottish Educational Review, 34*, 123–137.

Rudduck, J. (2003). Consulting pupils about teaching and learning. *Teaching and Learning Research Briefing*, 5, TLRP.

Rudduck, J. (2004). *Pupil voice is here to stay*. Futures, meeting the challenge: QCA.

Rudduck, J., Arnot, M., Bragg, S., Demetriou, H., Fielding, M., Flutter, J., et al. (2005). *Consulting pupils about teaching and learning: TLRP research briefing* (Vol. 5). London: TLRP.

Rudduck, J., Demetriou, H., & Pedder, D. (2003). Student perspectives and teacher practices: The transformative potential. *McGill Journal of Education, 38*, 274–288. (Spring).

Rudduck, J., & Flutter, J. (2000). *Consulting young people in schools*. Teaching and Learning Research Programme, p. 1, ESRC.

Rudduck, J., & Flutter, J. (2004). *How to improve your school: Giving pupils a voice*. London: Continuum.

Rudduck, J., & McIntyre, D. (2007). *Improving learning through consulting pupils*. London/Hoboken, NJ: Routledge/Taylor & Francis.

Seifert, T. L. (2004). Understanding student motivation. *Educational Research, 46*, 137–149.

Shultz, J., & Cook-Sather, A. (Eds.). (2001). *In our own words: Students' perspectives on school*. Latham, NY: Rowman & Littlefield.

Silver, H., & Silver, P. (1997). *Students – Changing roles, changing lives*. Buckingham, UK: SRHE and Open University Press.

Soo Hoo, S. (1993). Students as partners in research and restructuring schools. *The Educational Forum, 57*, 386–393.

Sorce, J. F., & Emde, R. N. (1981). Mother's presence is not enough: Effect of emotional availability on infant exploration. *Developmental Psychology, 17*, 737–745.

Stenhouse, L. (1975). *An introduction to curriculum research and development.* London: Heinemann.

Stenhouse, L. (1981). What counts as research? *British Journal of Educational Studies, 29*, 103–114.

Storey, A. (2007). Cultural shifts in teaching: New workforce, new professionalism? *The Curriculum Journal, 18*, 253–270.

United Nations. (1989, November 20). *Convention on the rights of the child.* General Assembly Resolution 44/25.

Urquhart, I. (2001). 'Walking on air'? Pupil voice and school choice. *Forum, 43*(2), 83–86.

Warsley, P. A., Hampel, R. L., & Clark, R. W. (1997). *Kids and school reform.* San Francisco: Jossey-Bass.

Watson, N., & Fullan, M. (1992). Beyond school-district-university partnerships. In M. Fullan & A. Hargreaves (Eds.), *Teacher development and educational change* (pp. 213–242). Lewes, UK: Falmer Press.

Webb, L. (2001, September). A teacher working with Project 1. *Communicating* (The ESRC Network Project Newsletter), *2*, 1.

Wilson, E., & Demetriou, H. (2007). New teacher learning: Substantive knowledge and contextual factors. *The Curriculum Journal, 18*, 213–229.

7

A Tale of Two Studies: Features of Friendships and Awareness of Fairness

Research using some of the aforementioned tools for pupil consultation is in its element and has elicited pupil voice in order to investigate areas and issues that affect children's learning. The two areas of investigation that follow are the effects of friendship on aspects of school life; and children's perceptions of fairness. Within this framework of friendships and fairness through listening to pupils' voices, apparent once again is the essential complementarity of emotion and cognition working together for successful teaching and learning.

Features of Friendships

Friendships are multi-functional resources for our social, emotional and cognitive lives. They facilitate fun, ensure enjoyment in school, manage stress, aid the acquisition of knowledge, enable the fostering of a sense of community and identity, and in extreme cases come to the rescue as seen with Rosenblum's (1971) deprived monkeys and Freud and Dann's (1951) orphaned children, with their compensatory effects of attachment and facilitation of empathy. Indeed, "Friendship is a living thing that lasts only as

© The Author(s) 2018
H. Demetriou, *Empathy, Emotion and Education*,
https://doi.org/10.1057/978-1-137-54844-3_7

long as it is nourished with kindness, empathy and understanding" (anonymous). As observed by Hartup (1996): "…friends provide one another with cognitive and social scaffolding" (p. 1). This is because friends share a variety of resources and develop mutual dependence (Bukowski & Sippola, 2005; Dunn & McGuire, 1992). Moreover, children as young as 4 years of age with close friendships characterised by high levels of pretend play show relatively mature levels of moral orientation (Dunn, Cutting, & Demetriou, 2000). The experience of sustaining friendships can form the basis of a democratic, autonomy-enhancing school community: "…The understanding of what a friend should be like implies a direct reciprocity of trust – sharing, playing properly, being with you, not showing off" (Pollard, 1985, p. 48). Children of 6 years of age have been shown to bring sensitivity and understanding to their friendships (Howe, 2010; Howes, 2009). Indeed, by middle childhood, friends feature highly in children's lists of the most important people in their lives and of people they turn to when in difficulty. This is because friends have a more immediate and intuitive understanding of what peer disputes are like, and they can act as confidants in matters that children feel unable to discuss with parents or other adults.

The importance of friendships when starting school and at transfer from primary to secondary school has been well documented. Ladd (1996) showed that pupils as young as 5 years with more classroom friends on entering school had more favourable perceptions of school, and children who maintained their friendships increasingly favoured school as the year progressed. Moreover, sustaining friendships or developing new friendships with peers who were interested in schoolwork has been associated with increased school performance; and early rejection by peers led to less favourable perceptions of school, higher levels of avoidance of school, and lower performance levels. Several authors have highlighted the importance of friendships for motivating children to attend school. Overall, the evidence supports the outcome that friendship is a source of confidence and that "… developing new friendships can help reduce uncertainty and thus help adjustment to school" (Blatchford, 1998, p. 88). Break times in particular have been highlighted as providing opportunities for children to learn and practise social skills with their peers (Blatchford, Pellegrini, & Baines, 2016), and therefore provides an 'extended classroom' in which social skills are learned. Moreover, positive peer interaction in the playground has been shown to be an indicator of adjustment to school more generally.

Some research suggests that interactions with friends (rather than with peers who are acquaintances) are more influential for children's learning. For example, a study by Newcomb and Brady (1982) required school-aged children to explore a 'creativity box' with either a friend or alternatively a classmate who wasn't a friend. Results showed that there was more extensive exploration and more rigorous and mutually oriented conversation among friends. Moreover, when the children were tested individually, those who explored the box with a friend remembered more about it later. Research by Chauvet and Blatchford (1993) investigated whether pupils of 7 years of age become more involved in classroom tasks in the presence of their friends and whether a greater knowledge of each other produces more effective collaboration. The study showed that children in friendship groups showed greater task involvement and increased performance.

It seems that friendships may not only enhance social and communicative skills and schoolwork (Demetriou, 2003) but also benefit pupils who experience problems with learning (Day, 1996). For children of 10 years of age, the definition of a friend is likely to be someone who helps you, rather than someone who plays with you. This can take the form of practical help such as showing someone how to spell words they don't know, and also psychological support such as listening when someone has got problems. Both have implications for peer support in the classroom. Cross-age helping has also proved to be a positive innovation in some schools where some children who are struggling in their own age group are given the opportunity to support younger children. Also, more is being discovered about the influence of the peer group on motivation and achievement (Ryan, 2001). In particular, groupwork can help children learn about social skills, maintain positive behaviour and promote effective and successful learning. Groups can contribute to a satisfying working atmosphere and support the self-esteem of children, as well as create a sense of belonging and responsibility. High-level verbal interaction appears to be one of the key aspects to learning in collaborative groups and friends who are used to being together show higher levels of verbal interaction in collaborative groupwork (Littleton & Mercer, 2013).

A proliferation of literature on friendship over the last few years has recognised the advantages of friendships for children's social and academic development. How and to what extent do friends help with each other's learning? And what exactly do pupils say about friends as working partners? In general, the pattern that emerges in the research is that friendships are advantageous for pupils' cognitive and social development. However, some of my research challenges the literature's dominant claim that friendships are necessarily positive when the pupils are asked directly about the issue. Previous research had examined the influence of friendships through observation, questionnaires and interviews with teachers; the use of pupil voice had been limited. This research underscores the importance of the pupil's perspective. Significantly, it is through talking with and listening to pupils themselves that it becomes apparent that the relationship between friendships and different aspects of school is by no means a straightforward one, but instead reveals a complex pattern. The data drawn upon are from a project on transfer and transition funded by the DfES with my colleagues (Demetriou, Goalen, & Rudduck, 2000). The first phase involved researchers asking both primary and secondary school pupils about the importance of friendships in the classroom. In the second phase, schools designed their own research investigating the links between friendship and learning.

Phase 1 Friendship Study

As we have seen, the research literature displays a trend of the positive impact of friendships on learning, and in our interviews with pupils during the first phase of the project we found statements by pupils that supported this view. However, it was apparent also that pupils had a clear understanding about whom they did and didn't work well with and why, and that these classmates were not always friends. By year 3, for these children aged 7–8 years, the role of friendship in the classroom featured prominently in children's narratives. Some pupils explained their preference to work with friends because they are able to help one another on an equal basis. Such cooperative working relationships could be described as 'symmetrical':

> When I'm stuck my best friend helps me and when he's stuck I help him—in maths. (year 3 boy)

And with [X] and [X] who I work with, we've both got ideas and we mix them together and they come out really really well…because friends share ideas. (year 3 girl)

My friends work at my sort of level, work at the same speed as me, we help each other and they don't distract me. (year 10 boy)

The latter comment from an older pupil reflects the extent to which pupils are able to think analytically about the dynamics of their working relationships with their friends, and the degree of empathy they are able to express. Other pupils expressed a preference for working with friends who help them with certain aspects of their work, or who they are able to help. Such 'asymmetrical' relationships are illustrated as follows:

[X] has good ideas for writing a story…and it goes round and we get good stories in the end. (year 3 boy)

Well, my best friend is [X] and I work, get on better with him, because he's really a clever boy, and he knows hard sums that I don't know. (year 3 boy)

Even though they are my friends they are not just friends to play with or muck about. They are there to help you with something you can't do. (year 6 boy)

Other pupils, however, were aware that friends were not always the best working partners. Moreover, pupils were able to differentiate between friends who were good to work with and those who were not in relation to specific subjects or tasks:

One of my best friends gets on my nerves. When we're working he puts me off my colouring saying 'you can't get green walls'. (year 3 boy)

He's one of my friends but he messes around quite a lot. I sit next to him in science and when we do experiments I end up working with him. He's a nice person but he doesn't have much of an attention span so whenever we are using water there's a problem because he'll be squirting water everywhere. We often get strange results. (year 10 boy)

It depends what lesson. If it's history then I'd rather work with friends because we all see it from different angles—it helps me. (year 8 boy)

Children generally felt that they learnt more by working collaboratively with a partner and were also very discerning about the particular role and characteristics of friendships that enhance their work:

They must be very dedicated to what they want to do. I know I am. They've got to be vaguely intelligent about what we are doing. (year 10 girl)

Hard-working, but not completely…and cooperative as well. It's a bit annoying when you're on a table and then one person just sits there writing down, not talking. (year 10 girl)

Well I'd rather sit next to a friend cos if I sit next to someone I don't know I'm not really enjoying it and if I don't enjoy it, I don't really work as well as I do if I am happy. (year 10 girl)

If you are friends, you can argue more, you can get better results. (year 10 boy)

Pupils were also asked about their thoughts about moving to secondary school. It seems that this crucial transition time also involves issues of friendships. It was during these interviews that pupils' concerns were raised and discussed at length. A boy in year 6 for example evaluated his forthcoming move to secondary school:

I'm looking forward to making more friends—my dad told me that the main problem about me—main reason why I've been bullied in two schools running is that probably, instead of just being quiet as a doorknob and listening to what other people are interested in, I'm thinking I'm not too interested in what they're interested in… And there are some people who share my interests in this school, but I haven't used the ultimate science tactic, so they've become my enemies….I'm worried that people like [X] might find friends who have got older brothers and sisters and they might start ganging up on me.

Clearly, this boy had been thinking analytically about friendships and the Herculean task that lay ahead and raises the question of the extent to which the internalisation of his thoughts might affect his academic performance in his new school. At this point in a child's school career, parents often express concerns that their children have someone they know in the new school and the new classroom. However, setting often means that friends are separated. It may be that, for some children, sitting next to a friend or someone that the teacher knows they will get on well with, will make all the difference to the child's outlook at this important time of transition (Evangelou et al., 2008).

Phase 2 Friendship Study

The second phase of the research involved four schools conducting their own research based on aspects of friendships, with a focus on pupil voice. A summary of each school's approach is presented below.

One school focused on the degree to which teachers rather than pupils should determine seating arrangements and the role of friendship in the construction of working groups in classrooms. As a result of teachers' awareness that breakdowns in close friendships can be disruptive, and their concern that pupils need to be involved in different groupings to broaden their social confidence, it was decided that whole school 'grouping policy for learning' should be developed in which teachers controlled where and with whom pupils sat in lessons. Ten year 10 pupils interviewed 39 year 8 pupils in small groups about their experience of the seating/grouping policy. The findings revealed that whilst pupils recognised the logic of behaviour management, they did not always view enforced teacher-designated seating patterns as being the most effective for their learning. Again, pupils' comments revealed that it is not always advantageous to sit with friends. As a consequence of the research, the school employed a more flexible grouping policy which is less dependent on seating being determined by staff and which now takes account of pupils' abilities to determine which peers they work best with in particular subjects.

Another school assessed the impact of friendships on effective learning. The research grew out of the school's awareness of parents' concerns about children having a close friend in their tutor group at the start of upper school and the resulting expectation among pupils that they would always sit with friends in lessons and evidence of less time on task by some pupils as a result of working with close friends. A questionnaire was distributed to all 350 incoming year 9 pupils asking whom they worked well with in English, maths and science. Of these pupils, 10 pairs were selected, observed and interviewed: five who worked with close friends and five who were not working with friends. Data showed that for the majority of pupils, those who were close friends did not necessarily work well together. As a result of the study, the school has changed the expectations and behaviours of pupils in their working relationships with one another in the classroom so that good working relationships rather than social friendships are highlighted and valued.

With a focus on the idea of utilising friendships from primary school to help raise achievement, another school selected 30 pupils (15 single sex pairs) from its feeder primary school who were close friends and who were moving to the secondary school together. Some of these pupils worked well together and some did not. Pupils were monitored at intervals throughout year 7 for effort, attainment and behaviour, were interviewed about experiences of working with friends, and teachers were asked for their observations. The data showed that good working partnerships can be strengthened if partners are friends, but friendships in themselves do not guarantee effective working partnerships. Pupils who were friends and who worked well together could analyse what led to their effectiveness and the nature of the support they could give each other; they maintained high grades for effort with no unsatisfactory behaviour grades. Pupils who were friends but who did not work well together did not talk about supporting each other, found each other 'funny' or 'a laugh', rarely did homework and never together, had low effort grades and poor grades for behaviour. Pairs of male low achievers more often had unsuccessful partnerships, where neither boy did homework, relied on copying from one another, and generally displayed unsatisfactory behaviour. The relationship between friendship and working groups is now a major focus for new pupils in their first year of secondary school and year 6 pupils in the main feeder primary school are consulted about pupils with whom they work well rather than just pupils who are their friends.

Another school investigated pupils' perceptions of themselves as 'friend makers' or isolates. A total of 300 year 6 pupils participated in small group discussions of their experiences of friendships and also completed a questionnaire. The views of 60 year 7 pupils were also gathered. The study found that fewer pupils than expected seemed dependent on one or two close friends (17%); and over half (53%) claimed to have both close friends and a wider circle of friends. Dependence on close friends diminished during the first year at secondary school and only 60% of pupils felt they had made friends easily. Interestingly, the issue of moving up with a close friend seemed more important to the current year 7 s, looking back, than it did to the current year 6 s who were looking forward: 84% of year 7 s thought it had been crucially important compared with 64% of current year 6 s.

Where schools have investigated the potential of friendships for enhancing classroom performance, they have different reasons for doing so. The gender gap in the achievement of boys and girls is often cited as a reason for exploring the effectiveness of successful friendships in the classroom. Moreover, taking into consideration the sensitive times of transfer and transition, it may be more important than ever to consider seriously the positive and negative effects that friendships can have when moving from primary to secondary school (see Demetriou, Goalen, & Rudduck, 2000). However, the research has also revealed that friendships are not always the key to success in the classroom. Not all pupils work well with their friends; moreover, they appreciate this and would rather not sit together. It is therefore very important for teachers to be discerning about friends who do and do not work well together and seat them accordingly. The research also showed that pupils often need to talk about these issues; they sometimes feel that teachers do not listen and may not be aware of the influence that friendships have directly or indirectly, on learning.

Overall, the research suggests that peer relationships influence social, emotional and cognitive development and ultimately determine our competence as adults in these areas. With the ensuing skills from forming relationships, resolving conflicts and reaching compromise, self-esteem is developed and nurtured. But in extreme cases when children do not form stable friendships, in their search for a sense of group belonging, children may succumb to the influence of dysfunctional peer groups (Rutter & Garmezy, 1983; Schwartz, Lansford, Dodge, Pettit, & Bates, 2015). It is important to note the many and complex links between social and academic development. For example, children who are anxious or fearful about peer relations are less likely to make academic progress; and academic problems can also contribute to ineffective social behaviour, with children who cannot engage themselves with classroom work assignments often disrupting and irritating their peers.

"Teachers know intuitively that children who are suffering socially are endangered academically and emotionally" (Thompson, O'Neill Grace, & Cohen, 2001, p. 218). It is therefore vitally important to nip these potential dangers in the bud, and it seems that by listening empathically to children, such instances can be avoided, and hallmarks of successful relationships can be fostered. Moreover, it is evident that the children themselves are the authority on the subject of their social and academic well-being: they have the eloquence to talk about the relationship between their friendships and learning and even very young children can make reasoned decisions for their choice of seating partners, and are aware of gender differences and influences. They must therefore be our starting point. The next section continues the theme of pupil consultation and predominantly using interviews, but now exploring the theme of fairness. Specifically I addressed how pupils perceive what is fair and not fair in school and how this can affect their learning. Before I describe two research projects on fairness, I will bring together some of the literature on morality from psychology and education, examining its aetiology, development, educational ramifications and links with empathy.

Morality and Empathy

With the same parts of the brain implicated in both fairness and empathy, these two behaviours are at the least biologically linked. In practice, empathy is a primary source of morality as the ability to act morally is a consequence of our ability to feel empathy. Their interconnectedness was expressed by Frans de Waal (2006): "Human morality as we know it is unthinkable without empathy and reciprocity" (p. 60). Empathy and morality share a relatedness in their own right that when brought together afford an enduring and genuine concern for another (Rogers, 1975). Koseki and Berghammer (1992) for example have coined the term 'moral' empathy as being "…always long-lasting, is directed towards some goals in the future and transforms the situation by finding and executing an adequate solution to it for the people concerned" (p. 202). Such researchers have also suggested that the adaptive features of such a moral empathy override the lesser goal-directed cognitive empathy and even more so the instantaneous affective form of empathy. However such moral empathy has been disputed by some who have advocated instead that empathy is not necessarily a force for good. Such an advocate is Bloom (2017) who contends that feeling what others feel is not the best indicator for moral decision-making, thereby warning against empathy as the sole explanation for morality. Others such as Prinz (2011) and going back in time, Kant (1785) also support the case for rationality over emotionality for making moral decisions.

Perhaps a clue to the advanced nature of moral empathy lies in the development of moral understanding. We know a lot from the body of psychologically based studies about the development of moral understanding in young children; we know much less about how they think about, feel about and respond to incidents of 'unfairness' and how prominent experiences of unfairness present themselves in their everyday lives in school. It is not clear what role issues of fairness play in the ecology of the primary school pupil. What is a young pupil's idea of an incident that is unfair? When faced with an incident of unfairness, what range of response strategies is open to young people in school? How resourceful are they at managing the situation? What are the perceived constraints on the responses they might make? Do they merely accept such incidents as part of school life? And to what extent do they empathise with the one who is the source of the unfairness? These are some of the questions that my research explored. Firstly, in order to set the scene, this section will outline some theories and research that have focused on moral development.

Despite being deprived of maternal attachments, the six orphans observed by Freud and Dann (1951) revealed that very young children are able to develop a strong sense of fairness in the face of security adversities. Focusing on the middle childhood years of 6–12, Montessori observed in children a new-found sense of responsibility and social justice whereby older children would support the learning of their young peers. Hoffman (2000) looked at the structural components of morality, sense of right and wrong and associations of guilt, and specifically how we internalise and socialise moral issues and values. He visualised a person's prosocial moral structure as "a network of empathic effects, cognitive representations, and motives" (p. 134). Piaget (1932) dealt with children's conceptions of morality by presenting children with stories and asking them to describe the naughtier action. He argued that a child's thoughts about moral issues are not simply a direct mirroring of what parents and other social agents teach them, but are at least partly a reflection of the child's own level of cognitive development. In so doing, Piaget proposed two levels of moral development beginning with a *heteronomous* morality of children aged 4–8 years who tend to judge the morality of actions in terms of obvious cues, such as the amount of material damage. It is only later in development, after 8 years of age, during the subsequent *autonomous* stage, that the child can look beyond the surface cues to take into account more subtle information, such as the *intentions* behind the action. Lawrence Kohlberg (1984) developed Piaget's ideas further. Using stories that depicted moral dilemmas, Kohlberg constructed three levels of moral development: preconventional (3 to 7 years old), conventional (8 to 13 years old) and postconventional (adulthood).

However, research into the moral propensities of younger children hints at a moral sophistication earlier than both Piaget and Kohlberg gave children credit for and contradicts theories that human beings start out as amoral beings with a moral blank state. Pre-verbal babies of 3 months of age have been shown to prefer characters that display positive or prosocial behaviours, as demonstrated in the experiments by Hamlin and Wynn (2011) and Hamlin, Wynn, and Bloom (2010), thereby exhibiting moral dispositions. By 18 months, children begin to express the desire to comfort other children, and other early moral emotions such as embarrassment, pride, shame and guilt have been shown to appear around this time (Kuebli, 1994; Vaish, Carpenter, & Tomasello, 2016). Between 2 and 3 years of age, children display an even greater understanding of what may placate another child and there appears from toddlerhood a strong sense of the moral structure of 'unfairness'. For instance, between 2 and 3 years of age, children begin to use standards in evaluating their own behaviour and the behaviour of others, thereby marking the beginning of moral understanding (Buzzelli, 1992). And a study of toddlers' guilty reactions after they were led to believe they had broken a toy, were linked to their subsequent helping behaviour towards adults in distress (Drummond, Hammond, Satlof-Bedrick, Waugh, & Brownell, 2016). With increasing cognitive development, children's comprehension of the feelings and thoughts of others improves, and by 3 years of age, children can understand the links between situations and the emotional reactions they provoke (Harter, 1982). The emergence of a 'moral self' (Emde, Biringen, Clyman, & Oppenheim, 1991) around 3 years means that children are able to judge for themselves the comparative gravitas of moral and social-conventional transgressions. By 4 years children can distinguish between moral rules such as being fair to others, and social-conventional rules such as being polite, and it is this capacity that is central to the development of moral understanding. Also, children as young as 4 years have been shown to distinguish between different kinds of cultural breach (Dunn, Cutting, & Demetriou, 2000). In efforts to link moral awareness with empathy, research with cookie-stealing puppets has shown 3- and 5-year-olds as able to empathise with victims of theft and make attempts to return the item to the victim (Riedl, Jensen, Call, & Tomasello, 2015). In her classic observational study, Murphy (1937) investigated the variations in 2- to 4-year-old children's behaviour in the playground when they were confronted with their peers' distress, focusing on children's 'conventional morality or duty'. Results showed that children who displayed "…guilt and self-accusation in relation to injury to another child" (p. 191) were those who were more sensitive both to the competitive nature of their relationships with other children and to disapproval from adults.

But what factors influence the development of children's moral values? Do the previously described imitative abilities of babies hold the key for the development of conscience? Forman, Aksan, and Kochanska (2004) investigated whether differential imitation responses of toddlers aged 14 and 22 months to their mothers' actions among toddlers could predict preschool-age conscience. Preschool conscience as measured at ages 33 and 45 months revealed that imitation measures consistently predicted preschool-age conscience. Moving on from the link between early imitation and later moral leanings, can the ability to empathise with others' distress be an important factor in learning right from wrong? Aksan and Kochanska (2005) examined 33- and 45-month-old children's empathic distress and guilt as a consequence of rule-breaking. Children's empathic distress was measured in response to a stranger's simulated distress after a large box fell on her foot; and guilt was measured by children's responses to a stranger's distress caused by the child themselves. Children who displayed guilt in response to their own misconduct and empathic distress in response to another's distress were also those children who were more rule compliant. Such findings imply that a combination of empathy and guilt may play a role in children's moral development. Researchers have also demonstrated the importance of both affective and cognitive processes in the moral judgements of preschoolers (Ball, Smetana, & Sturge-Apple, 2017).

By the time children reach school age at 4 years, those who acknowledge parental standards do so, it is argued, not out of fear of being punished but out of desire to reproduce these standards that have been established within a warm and loving relationship (Kagan & Lamb, 1987). By their fifth year children are more able to take the role of the other in communication and evaluate the self from more than one point of view; this in turn can lead to an awareness of a person's shortcomings as well as a responsibility for one's own actions. By middle childhood, children have acquired a complex and rich understanding of guilt. The ages of 6 and 7 years have been thought to represent the initial and possibly critical period of moral development, at which stage children begin to comply consciously with the norms and rules of interaction and behaviour when they find themselves in situations of moral choice. Of 6- to 10-year-olds who are asked to consider a victim's feelings after wrongdoing, older children exhibit more intense guilt. By secondary school age, pupils begin to attribute adverse family circumstances and issues of fairness of teacher actions to misbehaviour at school. Other studies have shown that older pupils are able to reflect on the dynamics of their working relationships with their friends (Demetriou, 2003; Demetriou, Goalen, & Rudduck, 2000). And using the moral dilemmas of Kohlberg alongside the emotional empathic scale of empathy by Mehrabian and Epstein (1972), Kalliopuska (1983) revealed a relationship between moral judgement and empathy among 9- to 12-year-olds.

My research into fairness has focused on a variety of ages during childhood and within psychological as well as educational contexts. The first was my own PhD thesis, entitled 'Reactions of girls and boys to the distress of their peers in early and middle childhood' (Demetriou, 1998), which focused on the nature and extent of empathy and moral awareness among toddlers (18–36 months) and children in their middle childhood years (7–10 years). The toddlers were observed and filmed in pairs in the presence of their mothers in the house of one of the toddlers (the host) with a friend (the guest). Each time an incident of distress occurred among the toddlers, this was analysed for the ways in which the other toddler responded. Furthermore, incidents of distress could be either caused directly by the peer or merely witnessed (an incident where the child did not instigate their peer's distress). Incidents were analysed for the type of distress and the degree of reparation by the peer. Active prosocial interventions to alleviate the peer's distress occurred both in response to distress that the host had caused and to incidents of distress that the host had merely witnessed. However, when 35 guests became distressed, 13 children (37.1%) responded with prosocial behaviour to distress they had caused but only 5 (14.3%) to distress they merely witnessed. Such findings of prosocial responses more likely to occur in response to caused as opposed to witnessed distress, indicate that there may have been an early moral awareness of wrongdoing which impacted the non-distressed child to help to put things right. It is possible that the distress shown by children, especially after causing the distress, might represent an early precursor of guilt.

An example of this is when an 18-month-old girl guest had been playing with toys on the sofa, with her back to the host and to her tricycle nearby. Her boy host crept up furtively towards his guest and took the tricycle. Before the host reached the middle of the room, the girl noticed that her tricycle had been taken and started shrieking. The boy handed back the bicycle and the girl stopped crying. Children also reacted to distress they didn't cause themselves, so that, in another case, a 24-month-old girl guest was experiencing difficulty whilst playing with Lego-bricks. In seeming desperation she repeatedly lamented "I can't" whilst looking at her mother imploringly. Her girl host, who was playing with a doll, looked towards her guest, put her doll aside, approached her from across the room, picked up the piece of Lego with which her guest was having difficulty, and attempted to help build the model whilst the guest looked on. And there was the perhaps inevitable ambiguous reaction to distress when, for example, in one instance a 30-month-old boy guest was standing precariously on a low wall in the garden and crying because he wanted to get down. Whilst his mother, who was at the other end of the garden was encouraging him to jump off, his girl host approached and in a cavalier fashion, pushed him off the wall. The boy fell and cried and the girl host walked away. Despite appearing malicious and perfunctory, and to give the girl the benefit of the doubt, she may of course have pushed the boy in an attempt to help him off the wall, rather than intending to aggravate his distress further.

For the investigation of middle childhood, picture-stories were used to elicit reactions from the children aged from 7 to 10 years. Similar to the toddler study, results showed that these children in their middle childhood years were more evaluative of distress that had been caused by the protagonist rather than where the protagonist was an innocent bystander. An illustration of a guilty response was given by an 8-year-old girl in response to the Toy picture-story in which a toy was snatched away from a child by their peer: "I'd feel really guilty with myself and I'd give it back because I felt guilty". Also, more guilty suggestions were given when children viewed pictures in which the protagonists were girls. A 9-year-old girl claimed in response to the Sports-day picture-story in which a child was upset having lost a race at sports day having practised for a long time: "I'd feel quite guilty and upset. I'd feel very pleased that I won, but I'd still feel a bit guilty. Someone who's been practising ages to do this, and someone who has just come along and pushed you out of the scene".

My research then took me to investigate the relationship between children's views on the permissibility of transgressions between friends, and their justifications concerning such views. This research with colleagues at the Institute of Psychiatry in London (Dunn, Cutting, & Demetriou, 2000) investigated the relation of children's behavioural adjustment, pro-social behaviour and temperamental characteristics as reported by teachers, with differences in their moral understanding. There were 128 4-year-old children organised as 64 pairs of friends from a range of social backgrounds. They were interviewed about the level of acceptable behaviour between friends as depicted in a series of transgressions, they were also given theory of mind, emotion understanding and language assessments, and filmed whilst playing with a friend. Children's justifications that reflected interpersonal issues were compared with their comprehension of mental states and emotions, with their behavioural and temperamental characteristics and with the nature of their interactions with friends. Children's views about acceptable behaviour were related to their understanding of others' inner states, but in addition were related to family differences in expectations about and discussion of moral matters, such as what is acceptable behaviour, or the management of discipline and control issues.

Implications for Studying Unfairness for Education

With a shift from studies within psychology looking at developmental trajectories and individual differences in fairness, the following studies describe more of my research about fairness, but this time in the realm of education. The research relates directly to aspects of learning and school, and using the facility of pupil voice, the information comes directly from the pupils themselves. Why is it important to examine pupils' accounts of, and responses to incidents of unfairness? First, at a very general level that reflects national and international concern about interpersonal violation, it is important to ensure that children have a sound sense of what constitutes unfair behaviour and what responses are appropriate. The national curriculum guidelines for Personal, Social and Health Education (PSHE) in our schools in England include a number of recommendations relevant to our agenda. For example, they suggest that pupils should learn to recognise: what they like and dislike, what is fair and unfair, and what is right and wrong; share their opinions on things that matter to them and explain their views; and recognise, name and deal with their feelings in a positive way. Second, and related to the first point, we need to support pupils in making appropriate responses to unfair acts and to do this we must learn more about how they think about responding, what sense of agency they feel they have and how they balance managing situations themselves and seeking the intervention of the teacher. Third, what pupils have to say about how teachers can be 'unfair', or about how teachers might offer better support in pupil-pupil incidents, can offer practical guidance to teachers. Fourth, where 'unfair' is a term used by pupils of repeated behaviours that verge on bullying or harassment, the experience can affect pupils' sense of security in school and their commitment to learning, and even attending school.

Interviews with older mainly secondary school pupils during the ESRC project on pupil consultation indicated the strength of their feelings about fairness and how ready they were to recall and recount stories of incidents that they felt uneasy about, especially those that seemed to them to contradict basic principles of fairness and respect for others. In particular, boys express their belief that teachers do not trust them, especially compared with girls whom they believed teachers favour in class. Moreover, these pupils believed that the failure to get enough positive attention was a critical aspect of their ability to learn in the classroom (Rudduck et al., 2005). A 13-year-old girl's comments reflect her astute and critical observations of the teacher and empathic feelings towards her male peers:

> One of my teachers, she is completely biased to girls. She doesn't like boys and it's not really very good because the boys never get asked for questions… And she does comment on them if they do something really well, but if they say a joke…instead of saying 'oh, well done, that was quite funny' cos the whole class laughs, she tells them off. So she's just a bit biased.

Some boys expressed their belief that teachers did not trust them, especially in comparison with girls whom they thought teachers favoured in class. For instance, teachers were seen as trusting girls more in that they allowed them to sit together; whereas boys were often separated from their friends without, in their eyes, due cause. One boy's observations of the differential treatment between girls and boys led to his explanation:

> In my English class, it will be like a table full of girls that are always talking… We talk quite a lot but they will move people from my table, but when the girls are talking they won't move them. If a boy like X is late (because he has to get his brothers ready for school in the morning) then they would be in quite a lot of trouble. If you're late they think you've been walking and mucking around. But one girl in class was always late and always left her bag on the table: if a boy did that he gets in trouble straight away.

The project also revealed that consultations with pupils reflect the complex ways in which different groups of pupils in the same classroom understand notions of fairness in terms of gaining teachers' attention (see Arnot, McIntyre, Pedder, & Reay, 2004). The less able pupils found it harder to fit comfortably within the official agenda of the school (Reay, 2006; Reay & Arnot, 2002) and conveyed a distanced and hierarchical relationship with teachers through expressions of alienation and unfairness. One boy stated:

> …yeah, our English teacher, he likes the three clever girls a lot because they are always answering questions. He never gives the other people a chance to talk…

This sense of unfairness in relation to teacher attention was evident among most pupils who thought that groups other than themselves received disproportionate time and attention from the teacher. Moreover, these pupils believed that the failure to get enough positive attention was a critical aspect of their ability to learn in the classroom. Other studies have shown that older pupils are able to reflect on the dynamics of their working relationships with their friends, and expressed notions of empathy and morality in their responses thus:

> I much prefer it if we're at the same level. If I'm better than them it is really annoying that I always have to help them or if they are better than me they must find it annoying always having to help me. So if we're even then we can help each other and it is more balanced. (year 10 girl) (Demetriou, 2003, p. 13)

Awareness of Fairness

> Some things are fair, some things are not fair—and some things are not
> NOT fair. (year 2 boy)

Despite the wealth of research into issues of morality, little investigation has taken place into the kinds of incident that primary school pupils see as unfair and how they respond. In order to investigate the role played by issues of fairness in the ecology of the primary school pupil, I conducted two separate small-scale research projects, one in each of two primary schools. In one of the schools, which was small and semi-rural, 14 pupils aged between 6 and 8 years were involved; in the other school, slightly larger and inner city, 12 pupils aged between 6 and 10 years were involved and this latter study was in collaboration with a colleague (Demetriou & Hopper, 2007). The data suggest how emotionally charged many incidents of unfairness can be. Indeed, children recall some incidents, still with strong feeling, that happened some months—even years—back, and we may need to be more aware of the potentially destabilising effects of incidents that remain unsatisfactorily resolved in the eyes of the pupils who are the 'victims'.

'It's unfair' is a common refrain by children, and we were interested in whether pupils used the label for anything that they were unhappy about or whether the examples they gave suggested that they were recognising a departure from an expected standard of behaviour. In Piagetian terms the children of 6–10 years of age were experiencing the stage of concrete operations, which extends until about 11 or 12 years of age. It is during this stage of development that children acquire an awareness of emotions, as well as being able to solve a variety of logical and physical-world problems. The intention was that the study would explore young children's concept of fairness, and in general, pupils spoke freely and confidently about issues of fairness in school. Boys voiced their thoughts and concerns as vociferously as girls and thereby challenged the expected pattern of girls having a propensity to talk more openly about issues of unfairness; in our data, boys were just as ready to talk about such issues. The overarching theme in the pupils' responses is the importance of social relationships and how issues of fairness and unfairness affect them and often their learning. Moreover, pupils' responses highlight the broad range of emotions that are experienced and the numerous ways in which situations are resolved.

The research focused on the range and type of incidents of fairness and unfairness identified by the children in the sample and also examined the ways in which pupils dealt with these incidents. There was a range of examples of unfairness, including incidents in the playground, as well as in lessons and at lunchtime, and ranged from being excluded or misrepresented. Most examples identified other pupils as the source of the unfairness but there were also examples of teachers' behaviours deemed to be fair and unfair. For example, the diplomacy of teachers was noted and appreciated by pupils:

> Some teachers are fair because they explain things really, really clearly. And if we get into an argument, they sort it out fairly. (year 5 boy)

And pupils also appreciated teachers' sympathetic responses to current world issues and events, this was fairness on a global scale:

> I think the head teacher is really fair mostly and he did in assembly think about the people in the Tsunami, which we all thought was very fair. (year 3 girl)

A few incidents were recounted in which there was no attribution—such as the custard running out at lunchtime before the custard lover arrived at the serving area! The examples included unfairness experienced directly by the pupil him- or herself and unfairness that he or she observed affecting other pupils—the latter indicating pupils' sensitivity to the feelings of others and their capacity to look at situations from the perspective of another. There were also interesting insights into the emotional charge of unfairness and the ways of responding to unfair situations. The pupils talked more often about unfairness than fairness and often with a strong emotional charge. We analysed the data in terms of the kinds of behaviour that were labelled as 'unfair' and we explored the following questions: When faced with an incident of unfairness what range of response strategies is open to young people in school; what are the perceived constraints on the responses pupils might make; how resourceful are pupils at managing the situation; to what extent do pupils empathise with the one who is the source of the unfairness?

Incidents That Pupils Talked About as 'Unfair'

Pupils talked readily about unfairness and the stories they told were about incidents that occurred in the classroom as well as in the playground. Rather more examples identified other pupils as the source of the unfairness, but pupils had a lot to say about incidents where teachers' actions were also deemed to be unfair. The majority of the incidents were ones in which the pupil him or herself was directly involved but there were some accounts of incidents which happened to others and which the interviewee saw as unfair, evidence of a capacity for empathy even though the observers were not clear what action they might take.

Unfairness Experienced

Whereas concerns about social justice are mostly expressed in terms of others who have been disadvantaged in some way, children's stories of unfairness were mostly about themselves, they were self-centred. The incidents were mainly characterised by feelings of being pushed around and 'made' to do things they didn't want to do; of being left out, or missing their turn; of being misinterpreted or misrepresented.

Being Pushed Around by Others and Made To Do Things You Do Not Want To Do

Incidents involving other pupils occurred mainly outside the classroom. One pupil in year 2 recalled being told to stand, in a military-style game. He explained:

> …he was telling me to stand, not where I was wanting to stand, and telling me what to do in the game, and all I did was stand there, and at the end he pushed me backwards and then he said 'charge'. It made me feel angry.

However, this particular boy learned from the incident, "Next time I won't do what he says". A year 3 girl commented on people pushing into the front of the queue at lunch time; it was unfair because she had to wait even longer. A year 2 boy spoke about X who "is usually the boss of us" and Y who becomes boss when X is away:

> She tells us what to do—'be quiet, be quiet, be quiet' and she doesn't let us do what *we* want...she's annoying.

Some incidents in this category bordered on harassment and the principle at stake was one of respect for people and personal security: the interviewees are implicitly questioning the habit or assumed right of the socially or physically stronger children to dominate the weaker children. In some cases children who were stronger by virtue of their being among the majority in terms of physical appearance, dress or language used their secure majority status to ridicule the minority of children who were different. A year 3 girl had suffered in this way: "I used to get bullied a bit because I've got very big curly hair and people used to make fun of me because of my hair. Made me feel really upset".

There were some stories of incidents involving teachers—most were to do with being made to sit where the teacher said: "It's unfair when the teacher stops you sitting with your 'bestest' friend". But there was a reason beyond the mere thwarting of personal preference: this is 'unfair' because "I can learn things from (him) like writing smaller and running faster"; this pupil, who was a boy in year 2, weighed up the advantages and disadvantages of sitting with his friends and acknowledged that his friend does talk to him and with a big sigh said "he destructs me" so that he loses his concentration—but he does not seem to see that this might explain the teacher's caution. A year 3 boy said, simply, "I should be able to sit next to my friend in the classroom because we work well together". Pupils' expressions of annoyance and anger were prevalent when referring to peers who disturb their work, play or general thought processes. A year 3 girl protested "it's not fair that I sit with people who aren't my friends—I don't work well on the boys' table because I don't really get on with them and X is always tugging me to say what's the answer to something". A year 2 boy had a similar problem but with some complex repercussions:

> It's not fair if the teacher says I can't sit next to my friend because I can't get anyone to help me and some people are mean to me and stop me getting on with my work. If I can't get on with my work it makes me feel embarrassed because everyone keeps looking at me.

Several pupils said that it was unfair when they had to stop doing work they had enjoyed and hadn't completed just because the bell went to mark the end of the lesson.

Missing Out, Being Left Out, Not Getting Your Turn

Incidents that carried a very high emotional charge were to do with being left out, mainly by friends but sometimes by teachers. Pupils recalled occasions when their usual social group rejected them—for instance: it's unfair in assembly "when my friends talk to each other and don't talk to me" (year 3 girl). Then there is the predictable set of examples of not getting your turn, where a principle of equity is being violated or a promise broken. In a year 2 class where being allowed to collect the work sheets at the end of the lesson was a coveted privilege a boy related how other pupils push in when it is his turn:

> It was unfair when I was the last person to get out and I should have picked up the spellings when X did. The last person on the table has to pick them up and X used to pick them up even if I was the last person. I should be picking them up when he is. It made me feel sad. I tried to pick them up when X was the last person but then Y picked them up.

This pupil ends rather philosophically: "I hope I get a chance to pick them up—I might, but I can't tell the future, so…" A year 3 girl explained: "It was unfair when my friends wouldn't let me have a turn with the skipping rope"; and a year 2 boy recalls not being chosen by his friend to be in the football team which had all the best players in it. He commented, "Happens often. Makes me feel sad and annoyed". In this case, the source of the unfairness could be one of two reasons: that the incident is 'unfair' if the pupil concerned was actually as good as the other chosen players and was rejected on grounds other than competence; or the pupil is genuinely not as talented as his peers at football and is reacting to this inequity.

Emotions of frustration, annoyance and embarrassment were also expressed when pupils referred to teachers who didn't help them with their work and, with echoes of my previous research about friendships, who didn't understand the importance of pupils being able to sit with their peers:

> My best friend is X and I work well with her but she's just moved off my table. She helps me with my work and I help her. It's not fair if the teacher says I can't sit next to my friend because I can't get anyone to help me and some people are mean to me and stop me getting on with my work. If I can't get on with my work it makes me feel embarrassed because everyone keeps looking at me. (year 2 boy)

Pupils also recalled incidents where they were not chosen by teachers: "It's unfair sometimes in assembly when I want to do something and somebody else gets chosen" (year 3 girl) or were not given the attention they felt they needed or deserved. Another girl in year 3 commented:

> Sometimes when the teacher doesn't help me, I frustrate over my work and cry a couple of times. Makes me feel annoyed that she's not helping me. I don't ask my friends to help me because they're not on my table and I wouldn't ask because she normally just tells us off or makes us stand in the doorway if we talk.

Several comments were about teachers 'not listening to you' and not responding to pupils' immediate needs. The pupil complainants were sometimes aware that other children were getting more attention, especially if they were causing havoc, and this was deemed to be unfair, especially if the rest of the class was prevented in some way from getting on with its work. But what some pupils described as 'unfair' was simply not being able to command the teacher's attention when they wanted it, without reflecting on the difficulties that such expectations presented to the teacher. And then there were complaints about work that the child judged to be good, not being selected by the teacher to be put on display.

It was evident that the children were not reflecting on possible reasons why work might be selected, which might not be about always displaying 'the best' but rather about ensuring that every child had something on display. So, the unfairness of not having your work recognised on display boards provoked a strong reaction:

> I really like literacy because I like writing—stories. Sometimes the teacher puts stories up that I have written. I like that because it makes me feel impressed. If the teacher doesn't put something up on the wall, I think that's unfair and I feel annoyed. (year 2 boy)

Conversely, a year 2 boy who enjoyed art and spoke about his love of drawing and learning about art from his grandfather who was himself a sculptor, described persuasively the unfairness and his subsequent anger and embarrassment when the teacher displayed a picture he was not pleased with:

> Sometimes if I do something wrong—a picture and I don't like it—the teacher sometimes lets me draw another picture that's better; sometimes she doesn't let me do it and just puts it up on the wall with everybody else's. That makes me feel angry because I don't like having pictures I don't like being put up on the wall. When people look at the picture it makes me feel a bit embarrassed.

Some pupils however were able to appreciate that teachers do not always have time to check out how individual pupils feel about particular pieces of work, or hear the points of view of all those involved in a fracas.

Misrepresentation or Misinterpretation, and Not Being Properly Listened To

Here the incidents mainly involved teachers rather than other pupils. Many stories were about being wrongly reprimanded, for instance, the familiar situation when the teacher punished the interviewee who claimed not to be the one at fault, or when the whole class is punished because the teacher does not, or cannot, find out which pupils were in fact the wrong-doers. The following story is quoted in full because it shows the strength of feeling that can accompany what pupils see as 'teacher error' in interpreting intention:

> One time...I kicked a chalky stone by accident that hit a step and left a white mark. The teacher came and took me to the entrance and I had to sit there because they thought I had been naughty and I had drawn it with pieces of chalk. But it was an accident. Made me feel scared because the head teacher gets really strict when someone is naughty...That was when I was in class 1 and I get bad thoughts about it still—bad dreams. (year 2 boy)

A year on and this boy kept revisiting and analysing this incident. He went on to say: "She could have said, 'It's okay, X. It's just an accident'". Another pupil recalled a time when he kicked a ball at someone. He insisted that it was an accident but "instead of asking me to explain what had happened, I was told to go to stand by the office, and I missed my playtime. The teacher could have sorted it out and asked me about it" (year 5 boy). Several pupils, such as a girl in year 3, argued that:

> ...teachers should talk to people first and tell them—not just punish them, ...they should give them a warning. They should say that if they do it again, they should, say stay in at break time.

Some pupils' astute observations led them to speak passionately about the need for teachers to pay more attention to them when they were confronted with arrogant and hostile behaviour:

> I think teachers should pay attention to you more. Because I was telling one of our teachers—I won't name any names—about someone bullying me—pulling my hair. But she wasn't actually listening to me. She just said 'oh run along and play now then'. They should listen to kids a bit more. They should keep an eye out for you. There is one teacher who listens to you more than anyone—she always comes and sorts it out straight away. ... when the bully is making sure that you can't get your way to the teacher, the teachers should spot that. (year 3 girl)

Punishment for misbehaviours that placed pupils in an invidious position was another arena for the identification of unfairness. Pupils described a sense of injustice when for example, although more than one pupil had been naughty, only one pupil was reprimanded. Moreover, pupils would deem the punishment to be unfair and feel guilty when their peers and not themselves were punished, as they were also to blame. A pupil in year 2 recalled that he and his friend were shouting out and that only his friend got told off and this was unfair; and a year 3 girl, in a similar situation recalled:

> In the dinner hall X was being a bit silly. I was as well but I was the one who got the blame when she was the one who was doing it the most. She was being the silliest. We should both have been told off.

Despite being annoyed at his peer, one boy was also able to relate to the peer, especially when he himself had shouted out but escaped punishment:

> Nearly every day X keeps shouting out and he is actually only meant to put his hand up, and I actually did that sometimes and Miss X told X off but she didn't told me off because she must have not heard me. Makes me feel a bit cross that he keeps shouting out. Feel sad that he gets told off… (year 2 boy)

Pupils as young as those in year 2 also had very insightful ideas about the degree of punishment a pupil should receive depending on how naughty they had been. There were vivid stories about disproportionate punishments that the pupils thought were unfair because they did not fit the crime. A year 2 boy recounted a long story about the dreaded purple spot on the carpet which pupils who have misbehaved are made to sit on. Pupils clearly considered this as a form of public humiliation and the boy commented that it is justified if someone has done something *really* naughty, citing an example:

> X keeps trying to sit next to Y when he's not supposed to, and Y keeps trying to move away and so X now has to sit on the purple spot…The teacher should shout at him and tell him to sit on the spot for about a

year...or maybe half a year. If he's only a tiny bit naughty he'll only be there for a little bit. If someone's been *really* bad like X I do feel a bit cross and a bit sad.

However, this same pupil went on to imply that the punishment must fit the crime: "But if someone doesn't ask the teacher if can blow his nose and he has to sit on the spot, then I feel quite sorry". It was also seen as unfair if pupils were punished rather than being cautioned for a first or minor offence. A year 5 girl explained how she would handle such situations if she were the teacher, giving the pupil the benefit of the doubt:

Instead of just telling someone off (for not queuing in the playground when the whistle blows), if I was the teacher I would probably say, 'Have you heard the whistle? Because if you haven't I think you should listen more and here's the line so stand here.

Advocating a fair justice system of innocent before proven guilty, and making sure that teachers allow pupils space to give their account of what has happened was seen by pupils as very important in specific situations. For example, a year 3 boy commented: "Teachers should let pupils explain their way first and then decide which one is most truthful". But listening more to pupils was also mentioned as a general principle. However, from the teacher's perspective it is difficult to find time to sort out all the incidents that occur, and difficult too, in judging who is 'to blame' in an incident, not to be swayed by a pupil's reputation rather than to be open to the evidence of the situation. Some pupils could see this:

It's tricky to know what teachers should do when something goes wrong, because some people tell the truth and others don't...Sometimes the teacher persuades them to tell the truth. When somebody bullied me once, they lied about it and kept lying until the teacher ended up persuading them to tell the truth. (year 5 girl)

In many of the 'self-referenced' stories 'unfair' seems to mean 'things not happening the way I want them to happen' but some possibly reflected, without it being articulated, violations of the principles of equity, security and respect for people—principles which teachers are likely to talk about in assemblies and in relation to the school's mission statement. The incidents involved both fellow pupils and teachers as 'perpetrators', but there was the occasional act of God, like the unfairness described at school dinner of the custard running out before the custard lover arrived at the serving counter. This particular loquacious and charismatic pupil described how he dealt with the emotion generated by this unfair incident, explaining that he wasn't pedantic about his food, and managed the outcome by putting on a brave face:

> Once I was really looking forward to some custard waiting to be served and when I got to the pudding, there was absolutely no custard. I felt okay because I'm not fussy about my food. (year 2 boy)

The stories reveal the complex social dynamics of the pupils' world within the social conditions of learning in the classroom. A parallel account of the social dynamics of the high school classroom is described by Arnot, McIntyre, Pedder, and Reay (2004) in which they investigated how different groups of learners, male and female, pupils from different social classes, different ethnic groups and at different achievement levels, experienced their learning. Particularly interesting in our research were accounts of incidents that were 'unfair' because they contravened children's right to learn in school, impeded their learning, and presented them with social and educational dilemmas. This pupil held strong views about aspects of the classroom that helped him work well. Recalling pensively, he bemoaned the idiosyncrasies of peers that interfered with his concentration; but also expressed empathy for the class and the teacher as a result of the pernicious shenanigans of certain disruptive pupils:

> Once X was actually putting his hands on my back and making noises. ... it puts me off my *listening*. ...It was annoying. I was trying to listen to the teacher. I didn't know what to do because he was destructing me! ... X and Y actually talk when the teacher is talking. It's not very good because she has to stop and shout at them. The class probably feel a bit annoyed, because they spoil everybody's lesson and then the teacher has to shout—that's why they don't sit together. (year 2 boy)

More injustice was described during instances of reprimanding the whole class when only a minority are messing about. This was seen as unfair because it "wastes the good people's learning time" (year 5 girl). Moreover, pupils felt an empathy and concern for the teachers' welfare when others were seen as a liability through fighting or silliness. Such behaviour was described as distracting the teacher so that "she can't concentrate", and if she shouts at the miscreants too much "she loses her voice" and then they miss out because she can't teach them properly—as one boy replied vehemently "it stops my learning".

Unfairness Observed

Also apparent in pupils' dialogues were a small but interesting group of stories in which the unfair incident was observed—it happened to others and not to the child telling the story. Included also is a section about pupils' observations of the fairness that they witness among their teachers; this highlights the pupil's ability to empathise with and appreciate the role of the teacher.

A boy in year 3 talked about a new boy who got expelled on his first day: "I felt sorry for the boy but he pushed a pencil in someone's eye—but he could have been given one more chance". In his next comment the pupil revealed a sensitive understanding of the expelled boy's possible motivation: "Some people who are naughty, like this boy, he probably feels a bit strange inside but he doesn't want to show it". Another boy in year 2 described his despair on seeing a friend being rejected by another classmate and he managed to resolve the situation using effective negotiation skills:

That made me feel sad about what happened and I went over to tell X 'please let Y sit next to—he wants to sit next to Z because he's Z best friend'. That made me feel happy because everyone was happy and that was fair.

Another boy saw a girl snatch his friend's pencil after he had been doing all the writing in the group project, and she wouldn't give it back; this was judged to be unfair but at the same time the observing child from year 3 saw the benefit of the situation: "Thing is he was quite jolly because he didn't have to do any more work". Another pupil thought it unfair when some pupils hit others in the playground, and expressed the malevolent behaviour as unfair "because people get hurt" (year 2 boy). These accounts are evidence of a concern for the well-being of others and a readiness to see things from their perspective. Pupils conveyed their concerns about unfairness in relation to incidents of copying a peer's work. However, as is recounted in the following response, the empathic concern is rather for the child who is copying the work!

> It's not fair when someone's copying me because I might have got everything wrong and then they might have got everything wrong as well. Make me feel not very happy and angry.

How Do Pupils Respond to Incidents of Unfairness?

We found little in the literature about how children respond to incidents of unfairness involving themselves and others. Our data suggested that there were four kinds of response: retaliation, avoidance (i.e. withdrawing from the situation), telling the teacher and seeking comfort from friends without retaliation.

The Impulse to Retaliate

When you are treated unfairly the impulse to respond aggressively can be strong, especially if pupils have not been helped to try out alternative strategies. After sustained annoyance by another interfering pupil who didn't seem to get the message, a year 3 girl was exasperated:

> He made me feel annoyed, so I want to smack him. He doesn't want to play—he just wants to annoy us. He won't go away—he's stuck to our hips.

The year 3 girl who was ridiculed for her fuzzy hair also felt the urge to retaliate when faced with the juvenile behaviour of her supercilious peers: "It makes me feel that I have the power to say something back—they can do it to me so I can do it to them".

A pupil in year 5 talked at length about the inconsistencies she perceived in teachers' responses and actions. She moreover tried to explain why teachers behaved in such ways and went on to describe the possible consequences for pupils when they are older:

> In the corridors they don't tell you the rules and sometimes you get told off and you don't even know anything about the rule. And other times when you say 'sorry', they say 'no, sorry isn't right'—they mean don't do it anyway. It makes me feel a bit strange because sometimes they say forgive each other when someone says 'sorry', and in real life, when you're saying sorry to them, it's different. I think they should say 'I'll forgive you this time, but next time please don't do it'. I think they do that so we learn the difference between little children and grown ups. But you shouldn't tell children to do a different thing because when they're older they'll do another thing—totally different.

Withdrawing from the Situation

For some pupils, discretion is the better part of valour and they defuse the situation in whatever way is available to them. A year 3 girl became annoyed when the teacher didn't listen to her, but since direct retaliation was not within her repertoire, she let it be, "I just walk away and read a book". Annoyance at the teachers who were seemingly ignoring them, led other pupils to exclaim:

> When the teacher doesn't listen to me it makes me feel that I want to get out and play with a couple of my friends. (year 3 girl)

> Sometimes I think that the teacher should be listening to me more—that makes me feel a bit annoyed. (year 3 girl)

Another girl in year 3 became angry when others spoke during the lesson, "But I have to remember, 'just keep calm'—if you're not calm it can go terribly wrong". Another seemingly mature coping strategy was recounted by a year 3 girl who was sitting innocently with her friend in the playground when a peer accused them of staring and called them names:

> One time X and me were sitting in the playground and she was watching this person and they said 'what are you staring at?' and they started calling them names. I felt I really want to sort that out but couldn't do that. I sort of sorted it out and sort of didn't. I took X away and said 'come on let's ignore them'. She felt very relieved but was upset still.

Another pupil also saw the value of such a strategy:

> Sometimes, when some people are mean to me, my friends come along and take me away…sometimes it's better to just walk away instead of having a fight. (year 3 boy)

A year 5 girl suffered badly from unfair incidents that involved her being picked on by unrepentant peers: "Sometimes they call me names, sometimes they just physically bully me, sometimes I tell the teacher and sometimes I just ignore them". She had learned that on balance it was probably best to ignore the bullies and her resolve was strengthened by thinking analytically and taking the perspective of the bullies: "Maybe the school could talk to the bullies because it may be that they have problems at home".

Other pupils decided that the best strategy was just to put up with the unfairness: one pupil in year 3 described the hurt and rejection she felt when her friends were occasionally spiteful to her: "They said mean things and hurt my feelings. That made me feel unhappy and I thought that they'd let me down. …. But because I like them so much I didn't want to tell, I just kept it to myself". And another girl in year 5 remembered from several years back the humiliation of being reprimanded, unfairly she felt, by the head teacher for running down the corridor. She felt aggrieved because she was new to the school and didn't know the rules: "I was little—in reception. I was only four and he acted as though I was ten. I was about to cry but I went home crying instead". She sensed perhaps that crying publicly could have made things worse for her.

Telling the Teacher

While some pupils, as we have just seen, will go home and tell their parents about the unfair treatment, others will go straight to the teacher. But it is clear from some comments that pupils do not always know when, and even whether, it is acceptable to 'tell the teacher' what has happened. Several of the pupils we talked with said that their parents told them to 'tell their teacher' and this response is understandable. But on the other hand, schools are concerned that pupils learn, wherever possible to deal with incidents themselves, and in a reasonable, non-aggressive manner. At the same time, we know that the peer group culture often castigates those who 'run to teacher', 'tell tales' or 'snitch'. One year 3 girl decided not to tell a teacher about her best friend reneging on her promise because she knew what the consequences could be:

> Sometimes I really want to work with my friends. My best friend X promised me that she'd partner me and my worst enemy—who likes X but X doesn't really like her—she said who are you going with? And she said 'I'm going with X but X promised to go with me. I don't tell the teacher because if they know you've told the teacher, they try and get revenge on you by being *more* horrible.

Some pupils choose not to report unfair experiences to the teacher because they know that the teacher will reprimand them for telling tales. There are some complex interpersonal and moral issues here for young people to understand and come to terms with. 'The teacher's word helped', said one boy in year 5 who recalled an incident involving another pupil: 'It got quite annoying, following me when me and my friend were playing a game'. The teacher "told me to tell her to leave me alone" and it worked. In another case, where a fellow pupil refused to share, the boy warned him that if he told the teacher, the teacher could make him share. However this boy in year 3 went on to observe that it's not always up to the teacher to do something about unfair incidents—others could sometimes sort it out: "I could, my friends could, everyone else in my group could—the rest of the class could".

When the teacher intervened, pupils were appreciative of their fairness. One year 5 girl described an observed incident in which a boy impetuously pulled a chair away when her friend was sitting on it:

> Once when a boy pulled a chair away when my friend was sitting on it, my friend got upset. The teacher dealt with it really well. She asked both children what had happened and the boy ended up telling the truth and said 'sorry'. He probably thought that if he'd pretend he hadn't done it he would have got into deeper trouble.

And another pupil who was quick to confess what he had done to the head teacher and expecting curmudgeonly reproaches, instead to his surprise received an innocuous response as a result of his candid confession, and escaped punishment:

> Well, sometimes teachers are fair…I shouldn't have done this—I flooded the boys' toilets in year 2 last year, and – this was very nice of the head teacher—I just said 'yes, it was me' and he didn't give me any punishment at all, he just said 'good for being honest'. (year 3 boy)

Seeking the Support of Friends or Working Through It On Your Own

When the teacher seemed not to be doing anything to resolve a situation that pupils saw as unfair, then pupils might rely on the solidarity of a small and trusted peer group. In one case a year 3 pupil discussed the matter with her toys:

> Once I was on this table with a girl who always used to do better maths than me and I always used to get told off cos it was actually her who was cheating at work and she blamed it on me. That made me feel annoyed, angry and a bit upset, I told the teacher but it didn't really work. I talk to my toys when things like that happen.

One interviewee talked about a schoolmate who was being bullied. In the absence of teacher intervention they "all helped each other because we are best friends" (year 3 girl). She went on adamantly: "I think teachers should do more; teachers don't normally do much so me and my friends try and work it out". Another pupil spoke about a friend who became silly and disruptive when they played together: "I think it's unfair that he should do it to me when I'm not doing it to him" (year 5 boy). This particular pupil was able to appreciate what would happen if he retaliated and explained how it is often possible to resolve a situation among themselves: "It would probably make it worse if I do it back to him. I tried it once and it got really, really out of hand—an argument, nasty things were said. But we got over it, we sorted it out ourselves".

And some pupils were unequivocally clear about their solutions to violence that they perceived as being unfair to others to the degree that one pupil's observations of the difference in behaviour between girls and boys, and the unfairness in the playground that sometimes stemmed from these differences, led him to extend his diplomacy skills to advocate separate playtimes for them:

> I think we should have separate playtimes, the morning break is for the girls, when they play, and then they come in and the boys have a good play. It should be separate because the boys annoy the girls, so I think it might be better for the boys to have a bit of private playtime. (year 2 boy)

In a no-win situation, one girl recalled being stuck between a rock and a hard place:

> I don't really tell teachers because then the other person will carry on to get her revenge. I don't tell my mum because she just says 'oh they're just jealous' and I say 'yes I know that mum but it's annoying', and my friends just take me away and tell me to forget about it. My friends help me the most when things like that happen.

Pupils also described the companionship of their friends during unfair situations that affected their learning:

> It was unfair when I was halfway through my work and it was the end of work, cos I think we should have a little bit longer to do work. I feel annoyed. I spoke to my friends and they agreed with me. (year 3 boy)

The resourcefulness of pupils was also apparent when they felt rejected by some friends and their petulant behaviour in the playground. This pupil from year 3 didn't allow the incident to deter him and decided instead to play with his other friends:

> It's unfair when people don't share when they say they are going to. My friend said he'd let me play with a ball and at lunch play he actually didn't—he took it and went to play. But it didn't really make me feel annoyed because at least I had all the rest of my friends to play with.

Frustrated when he couldn't grasp a concept being taught him in maths, a boy in year 3 sought help from others, including his friends. However, this pupil was also able to appreciate the situation from the teacher's perspective and even offered some practical advice:

> In maths the teacher didn't explain something well. So I put up my hand and he explained it again in exactly the same words, so I still didn't understand—until I asked my friends and they explained it a bit better. At home my dad would go through it step by step. The teacher doesn't have long to explain it, so that might be part of it. He could use different words—use different terms—especially if it's something we haven't done before.

This study extended the previous work by listening now to younger children and focusing more closely on the *nature* of the incidents that they identified as unfair. The children that took part in this study displayed a host of emotions about issues of fairness and unfairness that ranged from incidents in the classroom and in the playground involving kindness and unkindness, work, exclusion from play, teasing, rule-breaking or failure to share, and in which teachers, other pupils and themselves were involved. The study demonstrates that children of 6–10 years of age feel able to understand the concept of fairness and unfairness, to give examples of these and moreover to suggest ways in which situations may be resolved. For the most part, pupils talked lucidly about incidents of unfairness, suggesting that the emotions they elicit are strongly etched in their minds.

The younger pupils were as able as their older counterparts to identify and discuss incidents of fairness and unfairness; however, and in accordance with Piaget's more mature autonomous stage of morality, whereas younger children viewed emotions in terms of external situations accompanied by behavioural reactions, older children possessed a rather more mature understanding of emotion and used internal mental states to define their feelings. It was also apparent from this study that boys were as capable as girls of communicating their feelings and emotions when talking about fairness. This may be something that is lost at a later stage among boys and makes us wonder whether we should harness boys' willingness to discuss emotional issues so that later they do not see it as taboo.

What is the nature of 'unfairness' in these pupils' eyes? And is what they call 'unfair' actually unfair? Pupils' accounts of incidents of unfairness centred predominantly on teachers and friends or peers. Instances of unfairness were also characterised by an imbalance in the relationship, which put the victim of the unfair incident at a disadvantage and often feeling sad, annoyed, embarrassed and/or frustrated. The unfairness felt by these children resulted mainly from incidents in which they were excluded, hurt or bullied, or misunderstood. The 'moral code' that these children have developed suggests that these are not ways to behave and have led them to label such incidents as 'unfair'.

As well as talking about experiences of unfairness that directly affected themselves, pupils also referred to incidents that they witnessed among their peers and teachers, and their comments reflected an ability to empathise with others and also a sensitive concern for their feelings. Some were able to view the situation from the perspective of the wrongdoer, even when the wrongdoer transgressed against the interviewee. We were particularly struck by the extent to which some interviewees were able to reflect on incidents in an attempt to understand what the motive of the perpetrator might be or to suggest, particularly in the case of teacher behaviours, alternative ways of dealing with the situation that would, in their eyes, have been better, i.e. fairer. The pupils in the research were able to convey the concept of 'caring', a term which encompasses a number of personal qualities such as altruism, empathy, responsibility and concern for others.

Our study indicated that pupils had no difficulty in identifying and talking about unfair incidents that they had experienced in school. The incidents were mainly about situations where pupils were being obliged, whether by a teacher or by bossy peers, to do things they didn't want to do, or where they felt 'left out' or neglected when others were involved or being given attention. There were also vivid stories about reprimands or punishments that, in the pupils' eyes, were not justified. One very striking finding was that pupils were very aware of teachers who didn't seem to be listening to them, those who jumped to conclusions (and often the wrong ones) too readily, and who didn't take the pupils seriously. Pupils also spoke candidly about issues of bullying, friendships and their relationships with their teachers, and how these affected their work. Moreover, even the youngest of these pupils were often very insightful about why an incident was unfair and they demonstrated an ability to view a situation on a number of levels. Many were able to view the situation not only from their own point of view, but also from that of the victim and the wrongdoer, even when the wrongdoer transgressed against the interviewee, as well as appreciating the viewpoints of both pupils and teachers.

We were intrigued by the criteria pupils were using in labelling an incident as 'unfair'. In some cases what seems to count as unfair is the thwarting of the child's immediate inclination to do something, whether to join in a game, to have their work displayed or to finish a task that they are enjoying. In some cases, however, behind the 'complaints' is a sense of their right to be included, a right that was being denied them, whilst in others it seems that the right to get on with your learning in school is being violated. In any follow-up research we would want to spend more time probing the reasons why pupils judged an incident to be unfair. Particularly surprising was how often the young pupils we interviewed used the word 'unfair' to communicate their annoyance at having their concentration and their work interrupted by others. Many pupils in this study revealed their skill at being able to differentiate between different kinds of incidents according to the severity of the situation and its impact, and they were critical of school responses that seemed to be too severe. But not all pupils were able to distinguish which incidents merited 'telling the teacher' and which ones they should try to sort out independently of the teacher. As a year 2 boy put it "…some things are fair, some things are not fair, and some things are not NOT fair". It can be said that this is true of adults also, who themselves cannot always make such distinctions. However, pupils commented very insightfully into the role that teachers have and the importance of respecting the teacher's position so that there can be an uninterrupted flow of teaching and continuity of learning. Despite this, criticism of teacher practices was also voiced by pupils; they became frustrated when teachers didn't seem to be listening to them or jumped too quickly to conclusions without fully examining the evidence from all those involved, and yet some could also see that the teacher was busy and time constraints prevented a resolution in a way that was fair to everyone.

In terms of the action that pupils felt that they could take, the interviews indicated a number of strategies that they could use to help them cope with everyday experiences of unfairness; we classified these into four patterns of response. Some pupils felt so strongly that, in the heat of the moment, their immediate response was to retaliate, but some also commented that retaliation was a negative strategy because it generally made things worse and the situation could quickly spiral out of control. Others were able to act more reflectively and several spoke about the importance of withdrawing from the situation. In some cases friends encouraged the 'victimised' child to move away and were an acknowledged source of comfort and strength. Other pupils, sometimes following the general advice of parents, responded by telling the teacher. However this strategy was a tricky one because teachers understandably could become impatient when pupils repeatedly reported trivial incidents to them and they could rebuke the child for 'telling tales' or for 'bothering' them. In this situation pupils were thrown back on their own resources, a direction that teachers were often keen to promote, not so much to protect their own time but so that pupils might learn to be resourceful and to act autonomously in situations beyond school when no approachable adult might be around to help sort things out. Another cautionary dimension of 'telling the teacher', as the pupils were often aware, is that 'tale-telling' is not a way of responding that easily finds acceptance within the peer culture.

Educationalists emphasise the importance of the school's contribution to moral development in young people (Weissbourd, Bouffard, & Jones,

2013). Pupils of primary school age are often encouraged in curriculum statements to recognise what is fair and unfair and what is right and wrong, to share their opinions on things that matter to them and explain their views, and to recognise, name and deal with their feelings in a positive way. And we know from other research how important it is to establish a climate in which young people feel able to talk through things that are troubling them with their peers and teachers (Rudduck & Flutter, 2004). Particularly interesting were accounts of incidents that were 'unfair' because they contravened the child's right to learn in school. The incidents involved both fellow pupils and teachers as 'perpetrators'. The stories reveal the complex social dynamics of the pupils' world (for a parallel account of the social dynamics of the secondary school classroom see Arnot et al., 2004). Situations like 'Circle Time' provide a secure and regular space where pupils can learn to talk about things that trouble them in school but in the case of incidents of unfairness there is the additional dilemma of knowing how to talk about incidents that others—who may be sitting in the same circle—are implicated in.

For Gilligan, Ward, and Taylor (1988), the morality of caring is based on a 'network of relationships', which develops both a feeling of connectedness and a sense of responsibility to one another. Noddings (1992) argues that it is the task of the school to "encourage the growth of competent, caring, loving and lovable people" (p. xiv). Indeed, PSHE (2013) and citizenship non-statutory guidelines list a series of recommendations under 'knowledge, skills and understanding', first and foremost of which regards the development of confidence and responsibility. Despite being highlighted as important, these issues of morality in school are non-statutory and it is often difficult for teachers to find the time and space to discuss such issues. Other documents that focus on moral issues in schools, such as the review of research for NFER (Halstead & Taylor, 2000), show little, if any, mention of issues of fairness. It is surely important to foster a sense of morality within the realm of school life and we should not underestimate the importance of studying children's views of fairness and unfairness in relation to the development of a code of moral values. The implications for this research are of both national and international significance; reflect a sense of agency and management on the part of the pupil; offer guidance for teachers; and have a direct impact on pupils' perceptions of school. Emotions contribute to children's moral development because they grow out of relationships and shared experience with parents and because they are a reflection of awareness of standards and dilemmas. Moreover, research about the emotional development of young children suggests that conversations with parents about feelings are an important context for learning about emotions and how to handle them (Kuebli, 1994). Merely the habit of talking about such issues must surely stimulate thoughts and emotions. And if this is the case, we should aim to encourage such discussion both in and outside of school. Knowing that moral sensitivity is multifaceted and that moral awareness does not occur in isolation, but as part of an individual's general approach to the social world, increasing research is examining children's moral orientation in relation to other aspects of their social functioning (Decety, Michalska, & Kinzler, 2012).

The studies of children's perceptions of friendship and fairness have illustrated the effectiveness of pupil voice through consultation. The interviews speak for themselves, listening to pupils talk with insight and imagination about issues that affect their teaching and learning is a learning process for us as researchers and teachers. Ironically, as reflected in some of the comments, harnessing pupil voice reveals just how little their voice is listened to when it matters to them. Pupil consultation of this nature has also revealed the very perceptive and precocious nature of the pupils, their predilection regarding issues of teaching and learning, and their capacity for unjudgemental empathy and justice when analysing and balancing their own, their peers' and their teachers' points of view. We now turn to the role of pupils in the lives of teachers who are starting out in the profession. In a similar way that pupils had been previously listened to in order to involve them in school life and enhance their learning, this research now looks at the ways in which new teachers can listen to pupils in order to help not only the pupils but also the new teachers themselves. The research highlighted the importance of tuning in to pupils' thoughts and feelings in order to help teachers see them through what can be particularly challenging early months and years of their teaching careers—and indeed sustain them for the long term.

References

Aksan, N., & Kochanska, G. (2005). Conscience in childhood: Old questions, new answers. *Developmental Psychology, 41*, 506–516.

Arnot, M., McIntyre, D., Pedder, D., & Reay, D. (2004). *Consultation in the classroom: Developing dialogue about teaching and learning.* Cambridge, UK: Pearson.

Ball, C. L., Smetana, J. G., & Sturge-Apple, M. L. (2017). Following my head and my heart: Integrating preschoolers' empathy, theory of mind, and moral judgments. *Child Development, 88*, 597–611.

Blatchford, P. (1998). *Social life in school: Pupils' experience of breaktime and recess from 7 to 16 years.* London: Falmer Press. (Chapter 6).

Blatchford, P., Pellegrini, A. D., & Baines, E. (2016). *The child at school: Interactions with peers and teachers.* New York: Routledge.

Bloom, P. (2017). *Against empathy.* London: Bodley Head.

Bukowski, W. M., & Sippola, L. K. (2005). Friendship and development: Putting the most human relationship in its place. *New Directions for Child and Adolescent Development, 109*, 91–98.

Buzzelli, C. A. (1992). Young children's moral understanding: Learning about right and wrong. *Young Children, 47*, 47–53.

Chauvet, M. J., & Blatchford, P. (1993). Group composition and national curriculum assessment at 7 years. *Educational Research, 35*, 189–196.

Day, J. (1996). School friendship groups and their impact on learning. *Education 3-13, 24*, 51–58.

de Waal, F. B. M. (2006). The animal roots of human morality. *New Scientist, 192*, 60–61.

Decety, J., Michalska, K. J., & Kinzler, K. D. (2012). The contribution of emotion and cognition to moral sensitivity: A neurodevelopmental study. *Cerebral Cortex, 22*, 209–220.

Demetriou, H. (1998). *Reactions of girls and boys to the distress of their peers in early and middle childhood.* PhD dissertation. King's College, University of London, London.

Demetriou, H. (2003). Pupils' views about friendships and schoolwork. *Improving Schools, 6*, 10–19.

Demetriou, H., Goalen, P., & Rudduck, J. (2000). Academic performance, transfer, transition and friendship: Listening to the student voice. *International Journal of Educational Research, 33*, 425–441.

Demetriou, H., & Hopper, B. (2007). 'Some things are fair, some things are not fair and some things are not, NOT fair': Young children's experiences of 'unfairness' in school. In D. Thiessen & A. Cook-Sather (Eds.), *International handbook of student experience of elementary and secondary school* (pp. 167–192). Dordrecht, The Netherlands: Springer Science.

Drummond, J. D. K., Hammond, S. I., Satlof-Bedrick, E., Waugh, W., & Brownell, C. (2016). Helping the one you hurt: Toddlers' rudimentary guilt, shame, and prosocial behaviour after harming another. *Child Development, 88,* 1382–1397.

Dunn, J., Cutting, A. L., & Demetriou, H. (2000). Moral sensibility, understanding others, and children's friendship interactions in the preschool period. *British Journal of Developmental Psychology, 18,* 159–177.

Dunn, J., & McGuire, S. (1992). Sibling and peer relationships in childhood. *Journal of Child Psychology and Psychiatry, 33,* 67–105.

Emde, R. N., Biringen, Z., Clyman, R. B., & Oppenheim, D. (1991). The moral self of infancy: Affective core and procedural knowledge. *Developmental Review, 11,* 251–270.

Evangelou, M., Taggart, B., Sylva, K., Melhuish, E., Sammons, P., & Siraj-Blatchford, I. (2008). *Effective pre-school, primary and secondary education 3–14 Project (EPPSE 3–14): What makes a successful transition from primary to secondary school?* Research Report No. DCSF-RR019. Nottingham, UK: DfES Publications.

Forman, D., Aksan, N., & Kochanska, G. (2004). Toddlers' responsive imitation predicts preschool-age conscience. *Psychological Science, 15,* 699–704.

Freud, A., & Dann, S. (1951). An experiment in group upbringing. *Psychoanalytic Study of the Child, 6,* 127–168.

Gilligan, C., Ward, J., & Taylor, J. (Eds.). (1988). *Mapping the moral domain: A contribution of women's thinking to psychological theory and education.* Cambridge, MA: Harvard University Press.

Halstead, M., & Taylor, M. (2000). *The development of values. Attitudes and personal qualities.* Slough, UK: NFER.

Hamlin, J. K., & Wynn, K. (2011). Young infants prefer prosocial to antisocial others. *Cognitive Development, 26,* 30–39.

Hamlin, J. K., Wynn, K., & Bloom, P. (2010). Three-month-olds show a negativity bias in their social evaluations. *Developmental Science, 13,* 923–929.

Harter, S. (1982). The perceived competence scale for children. *Child Development, 53,* 87–97.

Hartup, W. W. (1996). The company they keep: Friendships and their developmental significance. *Child Development, 67*, 1–13.

Hoffman, M. L. (2000). *Empathy and moral development: Implications for caring and justice*. New York: Cambridge University Press.

Howe, C. (2010). *Peer groups and Children's development*. Oxford, UK: Blackwell.

Howes, C. (2009). Friendship in early childhood. In K. H. Rubin, W. M. Bukowski, & B. Laursen (Eds.), *Handbook of peer interactions, relationships and groups* (pp. 180–194). New York: Guilford.

Kagan, J., & Lamb, S. (Eds.). (1987). *The emergence of morality in young children*. Chicago: University of Chicago Press.

Kalliopuska, M. (1983). *Empathy in school students*. Helsinki, Finland: Department of Psychology, University of Helsinki.

Kant, I. (1785). *The groundwork of the metaphysics of morals*. Cambridge, UK: Cambridge University Press. 1998.

Kohlberg, L. (1984). *The psychology of moral development: The nature and validity of moral stages, Essays on moral development* (Vol. 2). San Francisco/Cambridge, UK: Harper & Row.

Koseki, B., & Berghammer, R. (1992). The role of empathy in the motivational structure of school children. *Personality and Individual Difference, 13*, 191–203.

Kuebli, J. (1994). Young children's understanding of everyday emotions. *Young Children, 49*, 36–47.

Ladd, G. W. (1996). Friendship quality as a predictor of young children's early school adjustment. *Child Development, 67*, 1103–1118.

Littleton, K., & Mercer, N. (2013). *Interthinking: Putting talk to work*. Abingdon, UK: Routledge.

Mehrabian, A., & Epstein, N. A. (1972). A measure of emotional empathy. *Journal of Personality, 40*, 523–543.

Murphy, L. B. (1937). *Social behaviour and child personality: An exploratory study of some roots of sympathy*. New York: Columbia University Press.

Newcomb, A. F., & Brady, J. E. (1982). Mutuality in boys' friendship relations. *Child Development, 53*, 392–395.

Noddings, N. (1992). *The challenge to care in schools: An alternative approach to education*. New York: Teachers College Press.

Piaget, J. (1932). *The moral judgement of the child*. London: Routledge & Kegan Paul.

Pollard, A. (1985). *The social world of the primary school*. London: Holt, Rinehart and Winston.

Prinz, J. (2011). Against empathy. *Southern Journal of Philosophy, 49*, 214–233.

PSHE. (2013). Personal, social, health and economic education, UK.

Reay, D. (2006). "I'm not seen as one of the clever children": Consulting primary pupils about the social conditions of learning. *Educational Review, 58*, 171–181.

Reay, D., & Arnot, M. (2002). *Social inclusion, gender, class and community in secondary schooling.* Paper given at the BERA annual conference, University of Exeter, Exeter, UK.

Riedl, K., Jensen, K., Call, J., & Tomasello, M. (2015). Restorative justice in children. *Current Biology, 25*, 1731–1735.

Rogers, C. R. (1975). Empathic: An unappreciated way of being. *The Counselling Psychologist, 5*, 2–10.

Rosenblum, L. A. (1971). Infant attachment in monkeys. In R. Schoffer (Ed.), *The origin of human social relations* (pp. 85–113). New York: Academic.

Rudduck, J., Arnot, M., Bragg, S., Demetriou, H., Fielding, M., Flutter, J., et al. (2005). *Consulting pupils about teaching and learning: TLRP research briefing 5.* London: TLRP.

Rudduck, J., & Flutter, J. (2004). *How to improve your school: Giving pupils a voice.* London: Continuum.

Rutter, M., & Garmezy, N. (1983). Developmental psychopathology. In P. Mussen (Ed.), *Handbook of child psychology* (Vol. 4, pp. 775–911). New York: Wiley.

Ryan, A. M. (2001). The peer group as a context for the development of young adolescent motivation and achievement. *Child Development, 72*, 1135–1150.

Schwartz, D., Lansford, J. E., Dodge, K. A., Pettit, G. S., & Bates, J. E. (2015). Peer victimisation during middle childhood as a lead indicator of internalising problems and diagnostic outcomes in late adolescence. *Journal of Clinical Child and Adolescent Psychology, 44*, 393–404.

Thompson, M., O'Neill Grace, C., & Cohen, L. (2001). *Best friends, worst enemies: Understanding the social lives of children.* London: Michael Joseph/Penguin.

Vaish, A., Carpenter, M., & Tomasello, M. (2016). The early emergence of guilt-motivated prosocial behaviour. *Child Development, 87*, 1772–1782.

Weissbourd, R., Bouffard, S. M., & Jones, S. M. (2013). *School climate and moral and social development.* New York: National School Climate Centre (NSCC).

8

The New Teacher: Pupil Voice, Empathy and Emotion

It is clear from the research that pupil consultation and listening to the 'voice' of learners can make a difference to teaching and learning, to teachers and learners alike. As the proverb goes: In teaching others we teach ourselves. Within our research, experienced teachers and head teachers told us of the myriad merits of listening to the pupil voice, using empathy in affective and cognitive guises and enabling them to learn through their teaching. But can and how does it help the new teacher? Sometimes, new teachers encounter challenges when they first start teaching. So now we ask, as well as helping pupils and their teachers, can pupil voice help teachers who are new to the profession? As well as helping to support pupils in their educational endeavours, new teachers themselves often need support. The novelty of the school environment often brings with it new challenges for them. Arguably such challenges need not be negative; indeed, they may make the new teacher all the more robust and resilient. But what are the factors that help and indeed hinder teachers in their efforts to progress? Are some hurdles more easily overcome than others? And what motivates teachers to persevere? This section focuses on my research and the factors that motivate teachers: on the one hand, those that propel them to strive and improve and, on the other hand, those that

© The Author(s) 2018
H. Demetriou, *Empathy, Emotion and Education*,
https://doi.org/10.1057/978-1-137-54844-3_8

stop them in their tracks and, in the worst cases, cause teachers to leave the profession entirely and irreversibly, and often prematurely.

Within this research focusing on new teachers, despite not being on the agenda, pupil voice remerged as an important issue. Having identified a dramatic departure of newly qualified teachers in the early stages of their careers, we were funded by the Gatsby Foundation whose grants support science, engineering and maths education research, to investigate the reasons for this exodus (Wilson & Demetriou, 2008). The research was entitled: 'Supporting Opportunities for New Teachers' Professional Growth'. We investigated the much-debated issues surrounding attrition rates during the early years of teaching when teachers are newly qualified teachers (NQTs) in their first year of teaching, and recently qualified teachers (RQTs) in the subsequent early years of a teaching career. The aim was to discover the reasons for a significant number of novice teachers leaving the profession so early on and what measures we could take to curb this effect and support and sustain opportunities for them. Rather than starting with hypotheses, and we could well have assumed after initial investigation that the reasons for abandoning teaching were due to frustration with disruptive pupils, we took an open-ended approach. In so doing, our research did uncover such issues, but also a lot more besides. Using an exploratory, inductive approach to the research therefore, we discovered a number of reasons for teachers leaving or planning to leave the profession. Moreover, we were able to identify the characteristics and attitudes of those teachers who were successful in staying on during very challenging times. The teachers involved in the study were 305 secondary school science teachers who had obtained their Post Graduate Certificate in Education (PGCE) from 1997 to 2003 from the Faculty of Education at the University of Cambridge. They ranged from relatively newly qualified to being in the profession for 8 years. First of all, I will look at our findings of what the new teachers told us about what supported and motivated them. The section develops through aspects of the profession that can help as well as hinder new teachers, and then things that new teachers can do to help themselves. As you will see, it is the teachers, who when faced with adversity in their new environment and those able to help themselves using effective strategies, who were the teachers most able to persevere through the early years. Suffice to say that pupil voice again featured highly. Specifically, teachers who listened to pupil voice and appreciated, accessed and employed the emotional side of teaching, were also typically those teachers who were able to retain and thrive within their teaching posts.

What Helps and Hinders New Teachers

Acclimatising to their first school can be challenging for new teachers, and in their first few months, teachers may experience uphill struggles of anxiety, anticipation, survival, disillusionment, fulfilment and reflection. When new teachers' introductory experience is positive and encompasses moral and technical support, then they are more able to "preserve their sense of mission and develop resilience to obstacles and difficulties" (Hargreaves, 2005, p. 971). However, first experiences are not always guaranteed to be positive. Exacerbating the situation can be the frustratingly contentious and disruptive behaviour of some students, which, in extreme cases, can drive teachers away from the profession they strove so hard to attain. Despite being adults, new teachers are adults experiencing a new start in life, i.e. that of being a new teacher. Previously we have looked at the importance of attachment security at young ages, from monkeys to babies, and extended it to the pupil-teacher relationship. We will see that the concept of attachment goes beyond childhood and to any new life events where the context is unfamiliar and the novice seeks security and reassurance. Similar to parenting and the home, a new school for the new teacher represents an environment in which it is important that they feel welcomed, accepted and are nurtured. Where these conditions are lacking, new teachers may struggle through the early days and months of teaching, which may have consequences for their perceptions of the career and their motivation to continue. Similar to the attachment relationships in young children, when conditions of privation or deprivation are less than optimal, a teacher's confidence can be affected, and sometimes to the point of no return. It is important that new teachers recognise that teaching is an evolving process that requires patience, persistence and empathy. Rather than perceiving teaching as a deductive and convergent process; for it to be a pleasurable, progressive and creative experience, it should be inductive and divergent, where new ideas are exchanged, moulded and fine-tuned. Such an environment incubates an ethos of enquiry in which the teacher facilitates discussion and respects individual differences (McGuinness, 2005). Synthesising mind and spirit, John Steinbeck spoke of teaching as a creative endeavour: "You can only understand people if you feel them in yourself; and I have come to believe that a great teacher is a great artist…It might even be the greatest of the arts since the medium is the human mind and spirit".

How the School Can Help

In order to ease the transition from trainee teacher to NQT, the school can help their new teachers in a number of obvious ways, including providing support and mentoring. Unfortunately, some schools are unable to help their new teachers, either because they don't have the time or the teachers appear to them to be coping well—and often new teachers will not seek the help—when unbeknown, they are in fact struggling. We examined the contextual elements in teaching that have the ability in the extreme case to crush one's deep-seated motivation to the extent of driving teachers away from the profession. Despite the potentially powerful internal drive of one's intrinsic motivation, we showed the detrimental effects that a lack of support can have on work motivation. Specifically, looking at the importance of factors in the workplace that might inhibit a teacher's motivation, such as lack of support, direction and feedback: such conditions can result in a teacher feeling alienated and rejected, making them cynical, frustrated and critical (Wilson & Demetriou, 2007; Wilson, Demetriou, & Winterbottom, 2010).

Reading through questionnaires completed by the teachers revealed some poignant accounts, some of whom had found their early experiences of teaching to be difficult and challenging, to the point that some had decided to leave the career completely. These findings prompted us to select a small sample of teachers to interview. Of these 11 teachers, some were NQTs and some were RQTs. Many of the questions were directed at their relationships in school, communication with students, the ideal lesson, and reflection. The teachers whom we interviewed spoke fully and frankly about their experiences of teaching, and the findings corroborated the quantitative data and reflected the importance of an empathic and supportive work climate. However, some teachers reported what they believed were instances of undeserved hostility against them. And such hostility would sometimes emanate from pupils, fellow teachers and even parents:

> I think I am a good teacher but I operate in a 'system' that is unable to recognise that. (male)

> I was surprised at the hostility and lack of respect and basic manners and standards of behaviour from students and parents and STAFF! (male)

Many of our teachers accentuated the importance of establishing and maintaining a good rapport within a school and especially in the first year. But some negative feedback was relayed by teachers whose relationships with others broke down, either through pugnacious and uncooperative superiors or through feeling that they were not in control of their emotions:

> I left Cambridge full of enthusiasm and ideas that a fantastic PGCE had given me. In my NQT year that was knocked out of me by a bullying head of lower school science. (male)

For some teachers, the support provided by senior members of the school was vital and reflected the capacity for the more experienced teachers to empathise with the NQTs and help in times of need. In this example, the help provided was well-timed and tailor-made:

> My Head of Department might step in last minute if I'm looking too tired or stressed—a couple of times two weeks ago, I was tired and ill and he stepped in and got someone to cover my lessons, and things like that. So noticing things really. (male)

Some teachers who had particularly good experiences of support could not speak highly enough of the importance of support and being prepared to seek it:

You should never underestimate the importance of 'the team' and the importance of supporting and supportive colleagues in a common endeavour. (female)

However, some teachers spoke wearily of patronising or non-receptive behaviour from colleagues and were concerned that the support they receive should be finely balanced; both too much and too little support were viewed equally as being unhelpful and, in extreme cases, inadequate support proved to be damaging:

Sometimes I got too much support—too many people looking after me (NQT trainer, line manager, Fast Track mentor, mentor in school), but needed less from some and more from others, which I didn't get. (female)

I was shocked by the level of defiance from some pupils and…the complete lack of support from senior staff…I left that school quickly! (female)

My self-confidence dropped due to lack of and inappropriate support and I was made to feel very small. (male)

The work climate proved important in motivating and sustaining new teachers, specifically through providing supportive and empathic workplace conditions, by colleagues who recognise that the new teacher, however talented, is in a novel situation to which it takes time to acclimatise. Failing to understand and neglecting the needs of novice teachers can have a knock-on effect for self-esteem, self-efficacy and intrinsic motivation, all leading to significant repercussions on their development as teachers. The power of intrinsic motivation is such that it can potentially override other extrinsic-related aspects that make work rewarding, such as financial benefits, physical conditions, the amount of work and the facilities available for conducting the work. However, when work climate-related factors, such as colleague support and feedback, are limited or negative, this can have a significantly detrimental effect on what was a deep-rooted intrinsic motivation, chipping away at it, until its foundations are no longer solid enough to sustain the person.

It is easy to forget, as an experienced teacher, the degree to which new teachers can feel vulnerable, especially when the new teacher has been successful academically, encountered positive placement experiences and appears to be coping well in their first formal post. It is important for experienced colleagues, therefore, to realise that, however impressive and effective the new teacher seems, constant support is nevertheless crucial. So how do we motivate new teachers and thereby, importantly, retain them? Our research has substantiated the importance of a healthy work climate, of empathic and responsive colleagues, who appreciate the needs and requirements of new teachers. No matter how intensely a teacher is motivated intrinsically, it seems that the lack of an effective work climate can damage a teacher's self-concept, self-esteem and motivation in a relatively short space of time. It is therefore vital that new teachers are supported constructively by their mentors, colleagues and peers, in order that they flourish and respond positively and constructively to the challenges of school life. But as well as help from such external sources, it is also essential, especially when these sources are not forthcoming, that teachers are equipped to help themselves.

How Teachers Can Help Themselves

During the process of the research, it became clear that the new teachers we spoke to fell into two quite different categories: those who felt there was little they could do to remedy adverse situations and those who proactively sought to resolve conflicts and negative scenarios. Teachers who took the latter approach were able to persevere through the challenging early years. In particular, these teachers used a number of effective approaches. Turning their attention to the pupils, and particularly those who were disengaged in their learning, those new teachers who made time for the pupils were those who were able to engage with them. Such strategies took time, and for some it was a long and convoluted road to their end goal of effective teaching and learning. But teachers who battled through the early days and months of teaching used a number of strategies such as engaging with the child and listening to pupil voice, thereby incorporating an emotional side to teaching alongside learning.

Engaging with the Child and Listening to Pupil Voice

At secondary school, I was told by the head of French and in no uncertain terms that I would never do well in my French O Level; and it felt that she practically relished telling my parents and me that this would be the outcome. Luckily she didn't teach me and I was fortunate that the attitude of my actual French teacher was quite different. When I made an error in my homework one time, she commented that she made a similar mistake when she herself was learning French. The enjoyable, engaging and empathic approach that this teacher took made French pleasurable and do-able. Together with my teacher's encouragement, but also determined to show the head of French that I could do well, I went on to achieve an A grade. Speaking also of the motivation that is necessary to succeed, one of my recent undergraduate students chose to research pupil motivation across the secondary school years for her final year dissertation. Her results led her to write: "Students continually cited the passion and enthusiasm of their teachers as being key to their own excitement and enjoyment… the result is infectious" (Gooch, 2017). What is apparent once more is that the attitude of the teacher has a direct effect on pupils' attitudes towards their work. Connecting with pupils and exhibiting enthusiasm for their subject helps teachers and pupils to succeed. Going one step further and actively listening to the voice of the pupil can often be the icing on the cake. Pupil voice research has found that listening to students can often overcome hurdles in the classroom and help them to become re-engaged in their learning. In the wise words of the Greek philosopher Epictetus in approximately 50 AD: "We have two ears and one mouth so that we can listen twice as much as we speak". Could therefore pupil consultation and listening to the pupil voice in turn help teachers to re-engage in their teaching? The new teachers in our research who succeeded in relating to students, both socially and academically, were those who took time to listen to the students, to hear what they had to say not only about the teaching and learning but other issues that arose during the course of the school day (Demetriou & Wilson, 2010a, 2010b, 2010c). In particular, the consequences of encouraging students through affirming what they do well was thought to be important. As new teachers told us:

Good relations with the students are crucial. If they don't think you like/believe in them, they won't bother.

It is important to find a common denominator on which to establish communication and relationships with difficult or unmotivated students.

However, some teachers admitted that there was a fine balance between befriending students and maintaining discipline, and indeed, new teachers in particular sometimes find it difficult to strike the balance with their students (Dannels, 2015). When faced with challenging behaviour, the challenge for the teacher who listens to student voice within the framework of pupil consultation is to get the balance right. One teacher put much of her success with her students down to the rapport she had established with them, although she was keen to emphasise that it was important for her not to lose grasp of authority:

Getting to know the students generally helps with motivation, but can make discipline harder.

And they say 'what, you go home and do stuff, what did you do at the weekend Miss?' Saying that, I *am* very strict … But on the back of my door I have equipment things and if they don't have them, I put them in detention and they are quite scared. And with uniform, I just don't take any nonsense. They say 'why do you stick to the rules every time?' and I say that that is my job and they say 'okay!' It's a bit like you're performing when you're in the classroom.

For some teachers, patience proved to be a virtue, as relationships often took time to develop:

A good relationship with the students took time to develop. It took me a while to find my way with them and to be happy with my own role.

Many of the teachers we spoke to emphasised the importance of effective and affective communication with their students, and especially when students were disengaged and disinterested in learning. Indeed these teachers worked hard in order to establish a good rapport with their students, and often witnessed positive outcomes:

> They all know how much I want them to learn … I had a very good year 11 group, and the year 10 group, I feel I've cracked them, and really enjoying the rapport there.

One teacher talked at length about the boundaries that she felt were permissible between herself and her students. She realised that, in doing so, she was able to engage the students more effectively. In addition, she valued her own experiences as a pupil and comparing them with those of her friends, she understood that every child is different where their learning is concerned:

> When I was at school, I had good relationships with my teachers and I realise that I needed that—to be friendly with them. But my best friend did not need that—she felt awkward. So I leave it up to the students to see what they need from me. So you have the kids who are loud and when they come to you I really enjoy it. It's difficult to know where to draw the line—especially as I'm quite young… Or they will notice if I'm tired and ask how I am. I feel that I can trust them and tell them things and build a relationship that way. Being more social with them helps establish a rapport and helps with teaching. One girl really didn't want to do a task but when I asked her again, she said: 'because it's you miss, I will do it'. It's significant that if a class likes you and they need to do something that is boring they will do it because it is you. That felt nice.

The tailor-made relationships she experienced as a pupil made an impression on her as a teacher. Respect for individual needs of the learner by the teacher, as for the individual needs of the child by the parent, contribute hugely to motivation and attitudes to learning. Another teacher for whom effective communication with students featured prominently and spontaneously explained his teaching with the student in mind:

> I make a point of getting to know individual students in all the groups I teach. I will motivate some differently to others as they all have different attitudes to learning. This teaching style comes naturally. I didn't set out and say 'I'm going to be the nice teacher'—it just happened. I stand at the door and get to know them all. And cos I'm walking round I do listen in on their conversations

and join in for five minutes, rather than say 'shut up and get on with your work'. I join in, get to know them and ask them about themselves.

One teacher spoke about some of her unmotivated pupils and her methodical approach of luring them into learning:

> I have a bottom set year 11 group, who I've only just taken on this year…and I do find them difficult because their motivation is not there. They are not interested in science. I have a girl who wants to dance and I show an interest. I am a build-a-relationship person… As I've been building up a relationship, one girl has been showing me a baby outfit she's been designing in textiles. She wanted to show it to me so she can show something that is good. And you start the relationship by showing an interest. I ask: 'how is that coming along/what colour will that be/is it finished yet…?' So you have an inlet… And I don't know how I've done it, but just by being interested in things like that, they can talk to me. I go over the top sometimes. The girl has fluffy pens or wearing glitter: 'that's beautiful, that's gorgeous—wow!!' Just be really energetic and positive about things and that makes you more approachable, you're not going to be cross and you're there to help. It's saying 'come to me and ask me, that's what I'm here for'. I don't think I've got that with all of them yet. But hopefully once one or two are on board the rest of their group will realise it also.

Teachers commented on the importance of acknowledging that it is not always possible to get through to all students with the subject knowledge, but that other aspects of learning, such as developing confidence, social skills and personalities were equally important and should be taught as a package.

> I love my subject (biology), and want to share my passion… I've got a responsibility for that. As an experienced adult I do not underestimate my role as pastoral tutor though.

Another teacher felt immensely proud that in her two short years of teaching, she had transformed the previously intransigent perceptions of her pupils for science:

> I've got one year 7 group that is weak and at parents' evening recently the parents were absolutely lovely. They said 'thank you so much, they really hated science and they really enjoy it this year'. And I've had some year 10s whose parents said that I changed their perception of science and they love it now.

Teachers commented on the importance of acknowledging that it is not always possible to get through to all students with the subject knowledge, but that other aspects of learning, such as developing confidence and social skills were equally important and should be taught as a package. A teacher spoke of his changing perception of teaching:

> I've become less interested in science and more interested in learning and people... As [my PGCE tutor] says 'we teach children, not chemistry' and I suppose I'm fitting more and more into that...science is a vehicle...it is a means to the same end, which is developing children.

This research has shown that pupil voice can play a crucial role in the context of new teachers who encounter obstacles such as disengaged students and disruptive classrooms. Many of our teachers communicated their despondency of not fitting in to school life as a result of a breakdown in communication between themselves and their students. Lack of interest in learning by students could result in teachers' loss of self-confidence. Such teachers became discouraged at not being able to convey the subject matter in the way they had intended and this resulted in self-blame and in extreme cases, leaving the profession altogether. But the teachers in our research who took the time to listen and establish a rapport with their students, and often taking a convoluted route to learning, were the teachers for whom it was all systems go—who ultimately saved time, through curbing disruptive behaviour, instilling discipline and reaping the rewards of effective and genuine interest in learning. The merits of listening to the student voice for new teachers were apparent in this research and through reflecting on these teachers' experiences, the hope, as expressed previously by McIntyre, Pedder, and Rudduck (2005) is that new practitioners will "consider how they might use pupil consultation to develop their teaching and their pupils' self-awareness and confidence in their learning" (p. 149).

Pupil consultation takes place for a variety of reasons and can take a variety of forms. Here we discovered the power of the pupil voice for teachers in their early years who may find aspects of teaching difficult if they are confronted with disengaged students. The research and literature on pupil consultation has reinforced the potency of consulting pupils and students (Arnot, McIntyre, Pedder, & Reay, 2004; Fielding, 2004; Flutter

& Rudduck, 2004; MacBeath, Myers, & Demetriou, 2001; Rudduck & McIntyre, 2007). After all:

> Being consulted can help pupils feel that they are respected as individuals and as a body within the school. It can encourage them to feel that they belong, and that they are being treated in an adult way. Pupils who are at risk of disengaging may come back on board if they think that they matter to the school. Schools where pupils are consulted are likely to be places which have built a strong sense of inclusive membership, where differences among pupils are accepted, and where opportunities for dialogue and support are made available to those who find learning a struggle (MacBeath, Demetriou, Rudduck, & Myers, 2003, p. 1).

Such involvement and empowerment have the potential to boost pupils' self-esteem, which in turn can help foster an ethos of belonging to the school and thereby foster learning. Research provides evidence that teacher interaction with pupils about principally non-academic matters can enhance the relationships and climate in the classroom. In contrast to traditional, direct student consultation about aspects of learning, the present data indicate that teachers interacted with students about predominantly personal and social matters. However, despite such an indirect approach, teachers were beginning to see the impact from engaging with their students in this way, on a greater communication and willingness to engage in their learning, as one teacher said: "It's important to be positive with your pupils, praising them encourages them to perform to their best ability for you." Such indirect forms of pupil consultation do not always lead to instant results, but improved relationships with teachers can lead to successful resolution of issues and ultimately improved learning.

Teachers who were progressing well on the other hand appreciated that it was not always possible to communicate all the information to all of their students all of the time and that they should not necessarily blame themselves for such failures. Moreover, teachers acknowledged that it was sometimes necessary to transfer 'blame' to the students if some lessons didn't go as planned. This is not to say that teachers are infallible, but that they should realise their limitations and not take things to heart when plans go by the wayside. The ramifications for teachers who do take on such responsibilities is that the burden is overwhelming and may lead to developing a low self-esteem and self-concept. Successful teachers also appreciated the need to empathise with their students, thus combining learning with an emotional component in order to entice the students in their learning (Demetriou & Wilson, 2009; Demetriou, Wilson, & Winterbottom, 2009).

Such findings are reminiscent of Anna Freud's approach to child psychoanalysis. Recognising that unlike adults who decide voluntarily to undergo psychoanalysis, children rarely did so, she introduced a preliminary stage in the therapeutic process in which she would spend time aiming to gain the child's attention and trust, and did so with their individual needs in mind. Examples were helping a young boy write down his letters and stories; and knitting and crocheting dolls clothes for a little girl. Analysis would ensue only when the child felt comfortable with the analyst on board as an ally and confidant.

Overall, the findings of our research have shown that forming a rapport with the student can instigate and accelerate learning. Although of course, we must be cautious when generalising such findings from such a small sample, this research has provided an insight, which has potential for further research with novice teachers across the UK and indeed the world, and with the use of larger samples. For the time being, we can conclude here that in times of frustration in the classroom, being able to empathise with the student can enable a teacher to restrain negative feelings such as anger and self-doubt and instead focus on positive feelings, with thoughts focused on the child rather than feeling the need to convey instantly the subject matter. As one of our teachers said: "at the end of the day, it is about children". Such a focus will surely ensure a future of effective and successful teachers and learners.

The Role of Emotion in Teaching

As well as taking time to engage with students, and not unrelated, is appreciating the importance of tapping into the emotional sides of the teacher-student relationship based on the premise that emotions are directly relevant to teaching and complement our cognitive processes (Demetriou & Wilson, 2008; Demetriou et al., 2009; Hargreaves, 2000). In the words of Daniel Pink (2008): "Leadership is about empathy. It is about having the ability to relate and to connect with people for the purpose of inspiring and empowering their lives". Of note in our research were some striking and significant gender differences in the ways that male and female newly qualified teachers approached their teaching and the challenges they encountered. The section will therefore begin by setting the context, looking at some of the literature on gender differences in emotions and including my own research in empathy, guilt and fairness; and then moving on to our research with new teachers, some of whom used more emotional content in their teaching and in so doing made greater advances.

Gender Differences in Emotions: Empathy, Guilt and Fairness

Traditionally, boys have been discouraged from being emotionally bound. An excerpt from the poem 'IF' by Rudyard Kipling written for his son John reads:

> If neither foes nor loving friends can hurt you,
> If all men count with you, but none too much;
> …you'll be a Man, my son!

Conveyed in these words and others within the poem is the concept of distancing oneself from people and emotions as a means to becoming an independently strong person. But we live in a social world with other people, and their actions and emotions do inevitably affect our actions and emotions in turn; and moreover, it is permissible to respond in whichever way—including an emotional one—which seems appropriate. In an interview (Smith, 1970), John Lennon expressed his concerns about the upbringing of boys in particular: "They tell us to stop crying about 12 or whatever it is…. Be a man… what the hell's that? Men hurt". Talking about the importance of expressing emotion, he said that "Instead of penting up emotion, or pain, feel it rather than putting it away for some rainy day" (Kasser, 2013, p. 108). An example of the hurt he was feeling lay in the loss in his life that he often felt unable to express but which he shared with his fellow Beatle Paul McCartney. Both Beatles experienced the early loss of their mothers and this loss brought them closer. In a biography about Paul McCartney, a passage reads: "But their empathy now had an extra, sad dimension. In future…they would sometimes drop their guard, discuss their common loss and allow the tears to harmonise in their eyes" (Norman, 2016, p. 80). And as they say 'the rest is history', as we know, these musicians, and very probably as a result of such shared emotions and the outlet of their joint creativity, went on to produce music that would stand the test of time. Such emotions, when allowed to express themselves, are in the interest of the individual and beyond, and resonate back to Darwin (1872) in his book *The Expression of the Emotions in Man and Animals*, in which he described the importance of human traits that we acquire by evolution and inheritance, such as moral conscience, the capacity for sympathy with others and also expressions of joy, pity, love and sorrow.

The literature typically and consistently cites girls and women as possessing and exhibiting greater empathy and emotion than boys and men and beginning from an early age. For example, Zahn-Waxler, Radke-Yarrow, Wagner, and Chapman (1992) found that at 12–30 months, girls participated to a greater degree in others' affective states, and at 14–20 months, girls have been shown to demonstrate more concern and self-distress than boys (Zahn-Waxler, Robinson, & Emde, 1992). Hoffman (1977) claimed that 2- to 3-year-old girls display more empathic responses than boys in the form of vicarious affect, during which they show greater apprehension and experiencing of another's emotional state or condition. Eisenberg, Fabes, Miller, and Fultz (1989) and Eisenberg, Fabes, Schaller, and Miller (1989) suggested that facial sadness and self-reports of emotion were increasingly related among young girls, whilst boys experienced less vicarious emotional responsiveness and made greater efforts than girls to hide or deny their emotional responsiveness. Such findings are echoed in our research (Dunn, Cutting, & Demetriou, 2000) when girls displayed more emotion and experiencing of emotion than boys. In particular, girls were more likely than boys to justify their views in terms of interpersonal issues; and our regression analyses highlighted the association between girls' justifications in the context of their understanding of emotions in close relationships, whilst boys' justifications were associated with their understanding of mental states. Within my middle childhood research using distress as depicted in picture-stories, girls gave significantly more guilty suggestions than boys did, as well as being more articulate about issues of fairness. The greater tendency for girls to respond with emotionally related phrases corroborates past research that has shown girls to place a greater emphasis on the sympathetic component of empathy than boys do, at least during the middle childhood years.

Findings tend to favour girls as possessing a more emotional empathy compared with boys' more cognitive empathy, and give rise to speculation as to the reasons heralding from differential socialisation of the genders and/or a more biological argument of hard- or even soft-wiring in the brain leading to gender disparity. The very young ages at which girls and boys have been shown to differ in their capacity to demonstrate and appreciate emotion has led some researchers to advocate the effects of socialisation as being responsible for this. Dunn, Brown, and Beardsall (1991) and Dunn, Brown, Slomkowski, and Tesla (1991) observed sibling pairs and their mothers and found that mothers tend to discuss and explain feelings and emotional states and expressions with girls rather than boys. They also suggested that the discussion of emotions between parents and children results in children at a later age being more astute in identifying others' social cues, recognising emotional states, feelings and expressions and taking the perspectives of others. Others' findings reflect the effects of gender socialisation that result in a greater empathic awareness among girls. Negative consequences of this for more susceptible girls is that their extreme involvement can lead to internalising the problems as if they are responsible for them, and they may communicate their distress in the form of depression and anxiety, resulting in greater instances of girls developing anxiety and depression (Hay, Pawlby, Waters, & Sharp, 2008).

Neurological evidence confirms such gender differences with greater activity in the female left-side amygdala compared to the male when subjects are reflecting and reporting on emotional events. Could the soft-wiring of the amygdala be especially affected in girls by the greater propensity in the early years of parents relating more emotionally towards their daughters rather than their sons (Mascaro, Rentscher, Hackett, Mehl, & Rilling, 2017)? By adulthood, women are purported to exhibit greater empathy than men (Brizendine, 2007). Using biological, physio-logical and sociological perspectives, Baron-Cohen (2003) has argued that the differences between the male and female brain are distinct and unalterable and that males, possibly as a result of cultural and societal norms, tend to internalise their emotions in contrast to women, who externalise to a greater degree. Furthermore, women are more likely to mimic other people's expressions and score more highly in assessments of empathising quotients (Manson & Winterbottom, 2012). Studies have even shown women's seemingly greater capacity for empathy through their tendency to yawn contagiously in response to others' yawns to a greater degree than men (Norscia, Demuru, & Palagi, 2016).

Such findings, whether tested socially or biologically, bring us back to Freud's (1925) views about women who "…frequently permit themselves to be guided in their decisions by their affections or enmities" (pp. 257–258). Although the crying exhibited by girls soon after birth (Sagi & Hoffman, 1976; Simner, 1971) may not be true empathy, the possibility of a constitutional precursor together with differences in socialisation, may account for the later sex differences in empathy. There are indications that girls and women generally outscore boys and men on measures of affective empathy, and the fact that boys' perspective-taking abilities are on a par with those of girls: "…boys are no less discriminating than girls in their labelling of the affective responses of others…[so that]…boys are no less empathic than girls" (Feshbach & Roe, 1968, p. 143), leads us to wonder if girls have the advantage in emotional empathy and whether this has long-term implications.

Gender Differences in Emotion and the Implications for Teaching

Can this propensity for females to be more emotionally empathic affect the ways male and female teachers address their teaching and particularly during the challenging times of teaching? The literature on teaching often emphasises the importance of teachers' feelings and their impact on teaching and learning. Our data (Demetriou & Wilson, 2009) alerted us to the seemingly different ways that newly qualified male and female teachers approached their teaching, and led us to examine the interplay of emotion and the teacher's gender, and the implications for teaching and learning. We looked at the extent to which new teachers consider and value the emotional component of teaching for the engagement and motivation of their students and themselves as teachers. Moreover, this research investigated whether differences exist between male and female teachers' approaches to their teaching, and the extent to which their emotional responses to pupils, and to the subject matter, may affect pupils' motivation and learning through the choice of teaching methods employed. Hence, in ascertaining whether men and women do approach teaching differently, and whether, for instance, female teachers do invest more time in trying to engage and motivate their students, we looked for differences in teaching approaches.

We were interested primarily in examining how graduates of our own teacher education courses continue to develop when qualified, and how the environments within which they teach may facilitate that development. Data were drawn from two survey instruments completed by two cohorts of teachers. The first instrument was a questionnaire completed by 305 early career teachers involved in the aforementioned study concerning retention of secondary school science teachers. As mentioned previously, questionnaires were sent to all the science teachers who had obtained their PGCE from 1997 to 2003 from the Faculty of Education, University of Cambridge. These 305 teachers, who ranged from relatively newly qualified to being in the profession for 8 years, completed a questionnaire about aspects of teaching.

The second instrument was completed by 512 early career teachers. Questionnaires were sent to any school that had previously employed a teacher who had obtained their PGCE from the Faculty of Education, University of Cambridge. Within this questionnaire, we assessed aspects of teachers' motivation using instruments developed within the framework of self-determination theory (Deci & Ryan, 2000). The Basic Need Satisfaction at Work scale has been used most frequently (Baard, Deci, & Ryan, 2004). Along with self-determination theory, this draws on the idea that for optimal functioning and well-being, three sets of basic needs must be met, namely, competence, autonomy and relatedness, and examines them accordingly. We also drew on the perceived autonomy support scale (Baard et al., 2004) to examine teachers' perceptions of their management and the social environment at school in facilitating autonomy rather than control. The perceived competence scale (Deci, Schwartz, Sheinman, & Ryan, 1981) addresses teachers' feelings of aptitude about teaching which are conceptualised within self-determination theory to be important to goal attainment. We also used the general causality orientation scales (Deci & Ryan, 1985) to assess the extent to which teachers themselves felt autonomous, controlled (by rewards, deadlines and directives for example), or the extent to which they felt that attaining desired outcomes was beyond their control. We employed the intrinsic motivation inventory (Deci, Eghrari, Patrick, & Leone, 1994), using two subscales from that inventory to assess: (1) effort and importance attributed to teaching, and (2) the extent to which the teachers felt pressure and tension.

Findings from the survey prompted us to select a small sample of teachers to interview. The 11 teachers that were chosen were affiliated to the Gatsby-funded project and had maintained close ties with the Faculty of Education. Some of the teachers were Newly Qualified Teachers (NQTs) and some were Recently Qualified Teachers (RQTs). Whilst some of these teachers took up posts local to the university, others had started their teaching careers in London and the surrounding counties. The interview schedule focused on participants' first 3 years of teaching. Questions were directed at their relationships in school, communication with students, the ideal lesson, reflection, quality of teaching, and the degree to which teachers felt that they were successful in communicating the subject matter to their students. We sought to gain in-depth information from the teachers, some of whom we met two or three times, in order to ascertain their progress during their early years of teaching.

Within the group of 305 teachers, 192 (63%) were female and 113 (37%) were male. Significantly more teachers remained in teaching than had left the profession. Of the teachers who continued to teach, 76 of the 134 (57%) were female and 58 (43%) were male. Overall, there was no relationship between gender and the likelihood of leaving the profession. However, a year on year analysis revealed that females were significantly more likely to continue teaching for longer than their male counterparts having graduated in 2000. Of the larger data set comprising 512 teachers, 334 (65%) were female and 178 (35%) were male.

We found no significant differences between male and female teachers on the Basic Need Satisfaction at Work scales (Baard et al., 2004): competence, autonomy and relatedness. We also found no significant differences between the perceptions of male and female teachers on the perceived autonomy support scale (Baard et al., 2004), or the perceived competence scale (Deci et al., 1981). We also used the general causality orientation scales (Deci & Ryan, 1985) to assess the extent to which teachers themselves felt autonomous, controlled (by rewards, deadlines and directives for example), or the extent to which they felt that attaining desired outcomes was beyond their control. There was a significant difference between men and women in the extent to which they felt controlled, and the extent to which they felt goal attainment was beyond their control. There was no difference in the extent to which they felt autonomous. But these results show that whereas men felt more controlled generally by the system, women emphasised that goal attainment was beyond their control. Finally, we employed the intrinsic motivation inventory (Deci et al., 1994), using two subscales from that inventory to assess (1) effort and importance attributed to teaching and (2) the extent to which the teachers felt pressure and tension. There was no significant difference in the latter between male and female teachers, but a significant finding reflected that women attributed more effort and importance to teaching than men.

Overall, these findings indicate that female teachers are somewhat more likely to stay in teaching for longer than their male counterparts. The findings from the second data set hint at a division between the emphasis that men and women teachers place on teaching: whereas male teachers are concerned about the system as a whole and the extent to which they are controlled, female teachers place a greater emphasis on the teaching itself. It could be that the way in which male and female teachers perceive teaching may explain their longevity in the profession. The teachers whom we interviewed spoke candidly about their experiences of teaching as reflected in the following sections of the findings that corroborate the quantitative data and reflect differences in the ways that male and female teachers respond to the challenges they encounter.

Female Teachers' Student Engagement

Female teachers talked about the importance of thinking about their teaching styles and analysing students' behaviour in an attempt to empathise with their students and bridge the gaps between them. In particular, being able to reflect regularly on their teaching seemed to help teachers understand and consolidate in their minds the dynamics between the students and themselves.

> I think I'm probably still learning about myself and teaching. I think I am becoming more reflective. Looking at students and asking why they think it is okay to do certain things and why have you done that brilliantly: what has made you like that? So I start thinking about me and what made me do things and motivate and encourage me. (female NQT)

Many of the teachers we spoke to were ardent supporters of effective communication with their students, especially when the students were disengaged and disinterested in learning. Indeed, these teachers worked hard in order to establish a good rapport with their students, and often witnessed positive outcomes:

> There are a couple of groups that I'd wish I'd been stricter with to start with. But then you don't know. With those classes I don't have as much control, but I try to look at ways to get round that. (female NQT)

The teacher mentioned earlier who reflected on the relationships she formed with her own teachers when she was at school emphasised the degree to which these relationships helped her with her learning. She spoke of the need to move the goal posts, appreciating that for her, it was important to have a camaraderie with her teachers; but also understanding that different pupils require different types of relationships with their teachers and therefore tailoring her teaching to their individual needs. But overall this teacher's ethos was to establish a rapport as "Being more social with them…helps with teaching". Another teacher mentioned previously put her success down to the interest she showed in her students' interests and belongings that were unrelated to her subject, as in the girls who liked dance, made baby outfits, had fluffy pens or wore glitter.

Making an effort to appreciate and empathise with her pupils' interests, transformed these quiet and disengaged pupils to gregarious and more motivated learners.

The other teacher who in a short space of time felt that she had changed her students' perceptions of science for the better, attributed much of her success with her students to the rapport between them, and she was able to balance very skillfully the importance of adhering to uniform and equipment rules, whilst also discussing her weekend with her inquisitive pupils. This teacher went on to say that she had learnt a lot in her first year, due mostly to working through it herself. She felt that a constant reflection on her practice and trying new approaches in order to improve had helped her. As a consequence, she felt that she had established firm relationships with her students and that as a result they had made good progress:

> … And I'm proud of them and I'll be sad at the end of the year to give them up because you work so hard with them and you get to know every kid individually … Because I make a massive effort to get to know all the kids in all my classes. It pays off in terms of behaviour… (female RQT)

Some teachers had learnt very early on in their careers that it was simply not enough to merely regurgitate lessons in a rote fashion. It was important for them to consider factors such as when the lesson was time-tabled and the students' level of interest in the subject, all of which could determine their motivation. In such instances, it was important for these teachers to take the perspective of their students in order to engage them. One teacher employed a diagram that she had created herself in order to facilitate the learning of the periodic table and explained:

> … this makes it more fun because it's more creative and different. And then I check their timetable and half of them have been in period 4—in dance— before my lesson. So that affects them. …They won't do serious book work or brand new work, but on the other hand you can't let that slide because they might take it for granted. But that group will appreciate that I will put the radio on or something while they are doing some questions. And they will often then get down to working harder in the next lesson, knowing that the previous lesson was lighter. (female NQT)

Patience, perspective-taking and preparing the lesson to the students' needs were often an integral part of the teaching approaches adopted by some of the female teachers we spoke to:

> … in the classroom, something happens to me and I become patient. And the lower year 7 set are KS2 level … they are weak. But as it happens they are my favourite group now: and I think that is through sheer perseverance of trying different teaching styles and through trying to approach them in different ways. (female RQT)

> I want to be a good teacher. Confident that I can go into every lesson and engage, enthuse and control them, enjoy it and that they will enjoy it too, for especially the next few years, but for all of my teaching career. (female NQT)

Male Teachers' Student Engagement

Some of the newly qualified male teachers we spoke with were very successful in finding ways round issues in learning. Those who were most successful appreciated that teaching the subject matter, at least at the outset, was not always possible, and that it was often important to focus more on the child rather than the subject. A teacher expressed his surprise at his aptitude for teaching and the affiliation he made with his students:

> I'm much better at teaching than I thought I would be. I like children more than I thought I would. The subject is not important; being memorable and exciting is. (male RQT)

In fact, empathising with and getting to know his students through effective relationships enabled this teacher to adapt his teaching to the particular class.

> With some classes you can change your teaching style and approaches, but I think you have to know your class quite well. I'll change my teaching style by the way I address my kids. (male RQT)

A successful RQT identified the need to focus on the child, despite a clear passion for his subject:

> Obviously I have a science degree and I am keen on my subject—but I am here because I like being with kids, not because I love science. (male RQT)

By the time teachers had reached the end of their second year of teaching, many had come to the realisation that teaching needed to be people-directed, with less emphasis on the subject and more on the students themselves. In so doing, teachers felt that they were able to communicate more effectively with their students and thereby enable students to learn the subject knowledge more successfully. This was apparent for the teacher who told me that despite his passion for science, his vision of teaching had turned on its head, with the science as a tool for teaching those who ultimately mattered—the children: "…we teach children, not chemistry", he said. (male RQT)

This same teacher presented this work ethic at a conference and received feedback from colleagues:

> But what I'm doing even more now is saying it is about people and not only about the subject. I did a presentation at UCL and they were really surprised that I didn't say that I became a teacher because I like chemistry. Because I was really emphasising at the end of the day that it is about children—people—and you have got to learn how to handle them and getting chemistry through to them that way. (male RQT)

For some teachers, a year of teaching brought with it the realisation that it was not always possible to assume that students would be motivated with an automatic willingness to learn. But empathising with students and tuning into their thought processes enabled teachers to overcome the disinterest and lack of motivation of students.

> My year 7 group bottom set have been tough, but I have enjoyed teaching them because I took everything I learned last year from a difficult group and applied it and that's gone really well and positive. (male RQT)

However, some of the male teachers we spoke to explained how their attitudes to teaching had changed quite dramatically. One such teacher was shocked at the way he had developed as a person in the short space of a year and he began to think very negatively of the students with a shift in his attitude towards them:

> I'm probably not as nice to the students as I was last year—I'm quite stand-offish. I thought I would always be more jovial and welcoming and it's probably because I don't have as much time. I never thought I'd be the type of teacher to say 'come back later I'm having a sandwich' and I'm not all the time, but I've found myself doing it on a few occasions. (male RQT)

When asked about effective communication with their students, some teachers described their frustration when not being able to communicate the subject matter to the degree they would have liked, focusing instead on disciplining disruptive students:

> Although with some classes I have found it more difficult to be as positive and communicate. As things get harder, you focus more on behaviour and less on quality of teaching, which is not necessarily a good thing—one should focus on both, but with the time constraints that is not going to be as easy… (male RQT)

A recently qualified male teacher, who was moving to a new school, anticipated the issues that he would encounter:

> I imagine the biggest difference unfortunately will be behaviour. Hopefully I will be able to tackle it! … Discipline: I've got to be concerned because I've not been into such a deprived school before. (male RQT)

Some teachers spoke of their regrets at not being able to discipline a class at the outset the way they felt they should have done, and the challenging repercussions of this:

> I've had a year 8 group and because I haven't been strict enough, I've had quite a tough year with them. …en mass as a class I struggle. (male RQT)

Some teachers in their second year felt that because they were no longer NQTs, the support that they had received in their first year of teaching had waned. And a male teacher became very disheartened by the lack of enthusiasm for learning:

> There are certain classes that don't go as smoothly and aren't learning as much as I would like … low-level disruptive behaviour, which has a massive knock-on effect for the quality of learning… I haven't been able to establish any kind of decent relationship with the kids. It's a mixed ability class … It's partly behaviour. It could be time of day—I see them Friday afternoon for a double and they are normally quite weary by then … There are a group of girls who have a difficult, stormy relationship with one another … So it's dragging down the whole class and even the kids who at the start were really well behaved are being silly now. It is disheartening. (male RQT)

One male teacher reached a low point in his teaching when he encountered very disruptive behaviour:

> I'm disappointed by the general level of effort by students. Not just in science, but as a tutor you see the same things repeated in many lessons. If I wasn't a tutor I would probably be quite paranoid and feeling bad about it. But because I see similar patterns across the school, that's what disappoints me, disengaged students who don't seem to have much respect for what they are doing within school. And I have not been as good at behaviour management as I thought I would be … that's probably the thing I'm most disappointed about. (male RQT)

This same teacher spoke about the slump in his confidence and his thoughts about relinquishing his post:

> I was hit hard by the year 11 behaviour issue I had. … I'm quite capable of earning more money in another career. And so why am I taking this from these kids? … you can go home being very dejected. Another teacher here left the profession in February. Just gave up and for the same reason. He said his relationships with students were okay, probably not brilliant, but he got frustrated with the amount of time that was wasted dealing with

discipline issues in the classroom. He left not because it was getting him down, but because he felt his own time was being wasted and didn't want to waste his life battling with people who couldn't be bothered. And even though that's not the reason that people give for leaving the profession, I suppose subconsciously that is the case. They are having a hard time and don't feel like they are getting enough reward and jump ship. (male RQT)

Male teachers' previously mentioned instances of underserved hostility against them led them to become contemptuous, feeling hopeless and helpless and suffer from low self-esteem:

I am cynical about teaching when: unmotivated pupils is the norm and not the exception; senior staff give teachers unnecessary work which has little effect on pupil motivation and learning; unhelpful and unpleasant parents; new initiatives every five minutes; colleagues who perhaps should not be in teaching; and finally, covering too many lessons.

I felt that the problems in my classroom were for me alone to resolve, which I couldn't, and thus I felt a failure.

I lost my self-confidence towards the end of the first year and didn't really get it back again. It became a hard act in the end.

Despite some very difficult times during the course of their first few years of teaching, times which would have driven many teachers away from the profession, some of the male teachers we spoke to persevered and were learning from their negative experiences:

I'm a bit disappointed with the year group that didn't work out. But I have acknowledged how I need to be next year with discipline … I'm looking forward to next year and hoping it will be even better. (male RQT)

When asked about the effectiveness of his communication with students, one teacher felt that he was making progress both socially and academically:

I still need to learn about communicating science with specifically scientific ideas. Developing the way I use language to explain things. … Otherwise I communicate well—socially and during the lesson and supporting them and making them feel positive. I think it comes with experience as well. There are things that I am teaching this year that I taught last year and I know I am doing a better job. (male RQT)

In so many spheres of life, emotion and cognition go hand in hand, teaching it seems is no exception. Focusing on the importance of incorporating emotional engagement in teaching, overall, the findings of our research have shown that forming a rapport with the student can instigate and accelerate learning. In times of frustration in the classroom, being able to empathise with the student can enable a teacher to restrain negative feelings such as anger and self-doubt and instead focus on positive feelings, with thoughts focused on the child rather than feeling the need to convey instantly the subject matter. Arguably, in so doing, the time invested in focusing on the child would pay off later with the child more ready and willing to engage in learning. Drawing upon interview data from newly qualified teachers, a pattern has emerged that more than hints at the importance of emotion in teaching (Dewey, 1895, 1933; Hargreaves, 1998, 2005). And rather than delaying the learning process, our data show that incorporating the affective side of teaching can engage students, accelerate their learning and keep them focused. Moreover, this has positive repercussions for the teacher who is more likely to enjoy their work, consequently remain in teaching and reach the echelons of their choice within the profession.

We looked also at the differences between male and female teachers in their approaches to teaching and in particular when they encountered more challenging classroom scenarios of disengaged students. Drawing on the literature on gender and emotion, which consistently cites females of all ages as having a greater capacity to empathise, we looked to see if female teachers are better equipped at engaging their students. The interview data showed that many of our teachers were able to communicate effectively with their students. However, where this was not the case and there were communication barriers, teachers often became frustrated and disenchanted with teaching. Talking with the teachers, we found that the male teachers in particular often felt trapped. Male and female teachers approached teaching in different ways, visualised the role of emotion in teaching differently, and when faced with challenges and adversities in the classroom such as disruptive and disengaged students, they employed different strategies to combat them, some more successfully than others. Female teachers would go to greater lengths, often employing emotion tactics, such as the teacher who spent time showing an interest in her student's predilection for fluffy pens, or who expressed an interest in the baby outfit that her student had made in another subject. Such strategies re-engaged the students with their learning. This finding is somewhat corroborated by the quantitative analysis, which revealed that men felt more controlled generally by the system, and that women attributed more effort and importance to teaching than men did. Such findings suggest that female teachers are more likely to see each child as an individual and modify their efforts accordingly, whereas male teachers are more inclined to communicate the subject knowledge and hope this will enthuse the student enough to engage them. However, our data have shown that this is not always enough, particularly when the student is disengaged. Some of the male teachers we spoke with related instances where colleagues, also male, had abandoned the profession under such challenging circumstances; and some of those who spoke with us expressed their mounting negative perceptions of teaching. Such pessimistic perceptions echoed the quantitative findings and the danger for many of these teachers is that the negativity overrides the means by which they can pull through.

However, realising that they were not the only ones who encountered such issues and instead, that it was a school-wide issue, with such classes being cause for concern for many teachers, reassured many. In many cases, teachers accepted that they could not tackle such issues alone, and recruited help from parents and teachers. Several teachers were able to reflect on the reasons why they were not successful in conveying their teaching. Shifting the blame from themselves and realising that they were not directly responsible for student disinterest often alleviated the situation.

The teachers who were most successful in distancing themselves, whilst at the same time trying to resolve the issues, were women. This takes us back to the developmental literature and the origins of emotional expression, where boys have been shown to experience less vicarious emotional responsiveness and make greater efforts than girls to hide or deny their emotional responsiveness (Eisenberg, Fabes, Miller, Fultz, et al. 1989; Eisenberg, Fabes, Schaller, & Miller, 1989) and through to adulthood (Baron-Cohen, 2003) which suggests that whereas women externalise their emotions, men are more likely to internalise theirs. This latter 'stiff upper lip' attitude could lead to a harbouring of thoughts and emotions, which could escalate if not dealt with effectively and in a timely fashion.

When teachers sought alternative ways to communicate their subject, through focusing on the students themselves in an attempt to comprehend their behaviour, success invariably ensued. With a focus on the 'who' we are teaching, rather than the 'what' we are teaching, teachers seemed to be making a breakthrough. The most successful teachers were also those who appreciated that there was not always a quick fix and that results may take time. Listening to the child was imperative, and incorporating both the affective and cognitive strands of empathy in the classroom created a healthy balance and steadfast relationships. And allowing the student to take the lead in order to assess the best teaching method was viewed as a necessary and important starting point.

Many of these strategies were used by female teachers rather than their male counterparts. On the whole, the male teachers seemed to experience more difficulty in asking for help from their colleagues, were more self-critical and less reflective than female teachers. Male teachers also coped less well when confronted with a lack of enthusiasm for learning from their students, thinking less laterally and were less patient than the female teachers. Such negative internalisation of emotion by male teachers, such as the teacher who felt that if he wasn't a tutor: "would probably be quite paranoid and feeling bad about it", could arguably adversely affect the teacher-student relationship as well as negatively influence teachers' and students' cognitions of learning and ultimately their motivation and behaviour.

In the early years of teaching, when new teachers are still finding their feet, heavy workload and lack of skills and knowledge can hinder their

progress and may lead to low self-esteem (Day, 2007). Some newly qualified teachers are often, and unrealistically, expected to emulate their more
experienced counterparts. Where new teachers do not understand the
unreasonable nature of such requests (such as in the case of a teacher who
felt he was given a 'raw deal' in terms of the challenging class he had been
assigned), but instead take it on themselves to try to live up to these
expectations and fails, a sense of worthlessness may result. Such teachers
may blame themselves in these instances, and without support to explain
and assure them otherwise, may internalise feelings inaccurately leading
them to feel that there is something wrong with them.

Without the appropriate support and encouragement, new teachers
can find themselves going into a devastatingly downward spiral almost
before they have begun their careers. Such environments dampen the
enthusiasm that new teachers bring to the profession and the danger is
that the new teacher, along with their knowledge and innovative ideas,
becomes quashed often to a point of no return, and as the male RQT
mentioned: "…having a hard time and don't feel like they are getting
enough reward and jump ship".

Some have suggested that schools need to acquaint themselves with the
skills that new teachers bring with them, rather than assuming that they
are novices in all aspects of their work (McIntyre, 1993). Certainly our
study showed that many teachers emphasised the importance of the first
year of teaching in order to establish expectations of oneself and the students in terms of discipline and learning. It seems that a whole package of
qualities is required of the new teacher, such as patience, time for reflection, communication with others and persistence. Moore (2004) believes
that constructive and instructive dialogue between novice teachers and
their more expert colleagues is essential not least to be able to develop a
self-awareness and to have the opportunity to reflect on developing practice with more experienced teachers. Others have highlighted the importance of individuality in teaching and employing one's own original
thoughts in their teaching style. For example, Rudduck (1985) has suggested that: "…good teaching is essentially experimental, and habit, if it
is permitted to encroach too far on practice, will erode curiosity and prevent the possibility of experiment" (p. 284). Needless to say, maintaining
a friendly rapport with students whilst adhering to the remits of being a

teacher, and not least in the current results-driven environment of education, is a fine balance.

Teaching is an emotional practice as well as a cognitive and technical endeavour. Feelings and emotions have a vital role in the development of learning. The importance of being able to think and talk about such issues emerged as vital to staying in teaching. Teachers who bottled up their thoughts and did not actively seek help and advice found themselves suffering the consequences. Thinking reflectively about one's role and relationships with colleagues and students, whilst being able to put these into perspective, for example, not apportioning all the blame on oneself and shouldering unnecessary burdens, proved positive for young teachers. Such teachers were able to balance school life with home life and provide an equilibrium and quality of reflection so that they didn't over immerse themselves in thought to the detriment of their life outside school. Teachers need to be made aware of these aspects of teaching during their PGCE courses, if not before they embark on the course, so that they know exactly what they might become exposed to and whether they are suitably emotionally equipped. Often the reality is very different from the teaching course and preconceptions may be dashed. It is very important therefore to make these possibilities known as soon as possible so that student teachers are content with their choice of career. In order to prevent it becoming "… a hard act in the end", we need to ensure that adequate provision is made for our teachers when they are faced with the inevitable challenges. As well as the vital need to impart knowledge, there needs to be an awareness and incorporation of emotional engagement in the classroom breathing life into the ever-evolving process of teaching and learning.

Whilst researching the reasons for early teacher attrition, another issue arose that caught our attention. Could teachers be leaving early because they were striving for the unattainable, a pursuit that they feel should be attainable after gaining a well-recognised teaching qualification and knowing their subject inside out—that is, the pursuit of perfection? And if they were striving for perfection, was this necessarily a good thing (Demetriou & Wilson, 2012; Demetriou, Wilson, & Winterbottom, 2013; Wilson, Demetriou, & Winterbottom, 2012)? Some of the novice teachers wanted to make their mark with a good impression of themselves and memorable lessons. One teacher described his motivations to be at best 'selfish'; at the same time, this teacher very insightfully expressed the importance of seeing things from the pupils' perspective in order to enhance learning, and spoke positively about his approaches to teaching.

> In agreement with my mentor, I think my biggest strength so far is lesson planning. I am very aware to try and make my lessons fun and engaging whilst appealing to all different learners. I guess in a selfish way, I want to make my lessons memorable, the ones that vividly stand out. I believe that some teachers don't think about teaching from a pupil's perspective, particularly thinking that pupils go from one subject straight to another, which can lead to boredom and repetition. I try to plan from a pupil's perspective, trying to create a lesson that will engage all pupils and make them look forward to turning up for biology.

Enthusiasm and encouragement were seen by novice teachers as being important to engage students. The teachers emphasised the importance of striving to achieve interactive lessons that would harbour enthusiasm, minimise disruption and focus students with the end goal of enhancing learning:

> If you make yourself sound enthusiastic … they appear to respond better. This helps effective teaching as the students feel like they can relate to you, and as such will work harder for you. Also with regards to punishments, many teachers I have observed have a 'telling off tone' and a 'teaching tone' that they can switch between with no problems. This often gets instant responses from the students…

In striving to do well, some of the novice teachers realised that they had to do away with their 'tunnel vision' and in so doing gained confidence, which in turn enabled them to aim for the excellence they were seeking:

> Since last week, I am feeling a lot more confident in my delivery, especially at the start of the lesson in terms of welcoming the students at the door, asking how they are … I have definitely moved away from the apparent tunnel vision I had when I first started teaching. I am far more relaxed and I can share a joke with them and create an informal but 'wanting to learn' environment.

With a less blinkered approach, the enthusiasm expressed by teachers when a lesson went well reaped the rewards of striving. In this case the novice teacher applied an imaginative and creative approach to teaching a lesson on photosynthesis:

> Fantastic lesson today on photosynthesis and light intensity. I am so happy that I tried to get the practical to work well. …Biology is so cool when it works. I am trying different things that seem to work. I am enjoying teaching now.

Such practices of listening to the pupil voice, using emotion, involving pupils and students alike in ways that they find engaging and inspirational means that new teachers, and indeed teachers throughout their careers, can engage successfully in the classroom and infuse the knowledge that they have taken so long to acquire.

References

Arnot, M., McIntyre, D., Pedder, D., & Reay, D. (2004). *Consultation in the classroom: Developing dialogue about teaching and learning.* Cambridge, UK: Pearson.

Baard, P. P., Deci, E. L., & Ryan, R. M. (2004). Intrinsic need satisfaction: A motivational basis of performance and well-being in two work settings. *Journal of Applied Social Psychology, 34*, 2045–2068.

Baron-Cohen, S. (2003). *The essential difference.* London: Penguin.

Brizendine, L. (2007). *The female brain.* New York: Broadway Books.

Dannels, D. P. (2015). Teacher communication concerns revisited: Calling into question the gnawing pull towards equilibrium. *Communication Education, 64*, 83–106.

Darwin, C. (1872). *The expression of the emotions in man and animals.* London: John Murray.

Day, C. (2007). School reform and transitions in teacher professionalism and identity. In T. Townsend & R. Bates (Eds.), *Handbook of teacher education* (pp. 597–612). Dordrecht, The Netherlands: Springer.

Deci, E. L., Eghrari, H., Patrick, B. C., & Leone, D. (1994). Facilitating internalisation: The self-determination theory perspective. *Journal of Personality, 62*, 119–142.

Deci, E. L., & Ryan, R. M. (1985). *Intrinsic motivation and self-determination in human behaviour*. New York: Plenum.

Deci, E. L., & Ryan, R. M. (2000). The "what" and "why" of goal pursuits: Human needs and the self-determination of behaviour. *Psychological Inquiry, 11*, 227–268.

Deci, E. L., Schwartz, A. J., Sheinman, L., & Ryan, R. M. (1981). An instrument to assess adults' orientations towards control versus autonomy with children: Reflections on intrinsic motivation and perceived competence. *Journal of Educational Psychology, 73*, 642–650.

Demetriou, H., & Wilson, E. (2008). The psychology of teaching: A return to the use of emotion and reflection in the classroom. *The Psychologist, 21*(11), 938–940. The British Psychological Society. (November issue).

Demetriou, H., & Wilson, E. (2009). Synthesising affect and cognition in teaching and learning. *Social Psychology of Education: An International Journal, 12*, 213–232.

Demetriou, H., & Wilson, E. (2010a). Emotion and cognition in teaching and learning: Implications for new teachers. *Leadership in Focus* (Autumn issue).

Demetriou, H., & Wilson, E. (2010b). Student voice revisited: Its power in sustaining new teachers. *Schools Research News*. Department for Children, Schools and Families (February issue).

Demetriou, H., & Wilson, E. (2010c). Children should be seen and heard: The power of student voice in sustaining new teachers. *Improving Schools, 13*, 54–69.

Demetriou, H., & Wilson, E. (2012). It's bad to be too good: The perils of striving for perfection in teaching. *Procedia: Social and Behavioural Sciences, 46*, 1801–1805.

Demetriou, H., Wilson, E., & Winterbottom, M. (2009). The role of emotion in teaching: Are there differences between male and female newly qualified teachers' approaches to teaching? *Educational Studies, 35*, 449–473.

Demetriou, H., Wilson, E., & Winterbottom, M. (2013). Perfection in teaching…settling for excellence. In M. Evans (Ed.), *Teacher education and pedagogy: Theory, policy and practice, The Cambridge teacher series*. Cambridge, UK: Cambridge University Press.

Dewey, J. (1895). The theory of emotion: The significance of emotions. *Psychological Review, 2*, 13–32.

Dewey, J. (1933). *How we think: A restatement of the relation of reflective thinking to the educative process (1910)* (Rev. ed.). Boston: Heath.

Dunn, J., Brown, J., & Beardsall, L. (1991). Family talk about feeling states and children's later understanding of others' emotions. *Developmental Psychology, 27*, 448–455.

Dunn, J., Brown, J., Slomkowski, C., Tesla, C., et al. (1991). Young children's understanding of other people's feelings and beliefs: Individual differences and their antecedents. *Child Development, 62*, 1352–1366.

Dunn, J., Cutting, A. L., & Demetriou, H. (2000). Moral sensibility, understanding others, and children's friendship interactions in the preschool period. *British Journal of Developmental Psychology, 18*, 159–177.

Eisenberg, N., Fabes, R. A., Miller, P. A., Fultz, J., et al. (1989). Relation of sympathy and personal distress to prosocial behaviour: A multimethod study. *Journal of Personality and Social Psychology, 57*, 55–66.

Eisenberg, N., Fabes, R. A., Schaller, M., & Miller, P. A. (1989). Sympathy and personal distress: Development, gender differences and interrelations of indexes. *New Directions in Child Development, 44*, 107–126.

Feshbach, N. D., & Roe, K. (1968). Empathy in six- and seven-year-olds. *Child Development, 39*, 133–145.

Fielding, M. (2004). Transformative approaches to student voice: Theoretical underpinnings, recalcitrant realities. *British Educational Research Journal, 30*, 295–311.

Flutter, J., & Rudduck, J. (2004). *Consulting pupils: What's in it for schools?* London: Routledge Falmer.

Freud, S. (1925). Some psychical consequences of the anatomical distinction between the sexes. In J. Strachey (Ed.), *The standard edition of the complete psychological works of Sigmund Freud* (Vol. 19, pp. 241–260). London: The Hogarth Press.

Gooch, H. (2017). *An exploration of the orientations of motivation exhibited by secondary school students.* Thesis submitted for Research and Investigation, University of Cambridge, Cambridge, UK.

Hargreaves, A. (1998). The emotional practice of teaching. *Teaching and Teacher Education, 14*, 835–854.

Hargreaves, A. (2000). Mixed emotions: Teachers' perceptions of their interactions with students. *Teaching and Teacher Education, 16*, 811–826.

Hargreaves, A. (2005). Educational change takes ages: Life, career and generational factors in teachers' emotional responses to educational change. *Teaching and Teacher Education, 21*, 967–983.

Hay, D. F., Pawlby, S., Waters, C. S., & Sharp, D. (2008). Antepartum and post partum depression: Different effects on different adolescent outcomes. *Journal of Child Psychology and Psychiatry, 49*, 1079–1088.

Hoffman, M. L. (1977). Moral internalization: Current theory and research. *Advances in Experimental Social Psychology, 10*, 85–133.

Kasser, T. (2013). *Lucy in the mind of Lennon.* New York: Oxford University Press.

MacBeath, J., Demetriou, H., Rudduck, J., & Myers, K. (2003). *Consulting pupils: A toolkit for teachers*. Cambridge, UK: Pearson Publishing.

MacBeath, J., Myers, K., & Demetriou, H. (2001). Supporting teachers in consulting pupils about aspects of teaching and learning and evaluating impact. *Forum, 43*, 78–82.

Manson, C., & Winterbottom, M. (2012). Examining the association between cognitive style, gender and degree subject. *Educational Studies, 38*, 73–88.

Mascaro, J. S., Rentscher, K. E., Hackett, P. D., Mehl, M. R., & Rilling, J. K. (2017). Child gender influences paternal behaviour, language, and brain function. *Behavioural Neuroscience, 131*(3), 262.

McGuinness, C. (2005). Teaching thinking: Theory and practice. *British Journal of Educational Psychology, Monograph Series II, 3*, 107–127.

McIntyre, D., Pedder, D., & Rudduck, J. (2005). Pupil voice: Comfortable and uncomfortable learnings for teachers. *Research Papers in Education, 20*, 149–168.

McIntyre, D. H. (1993). *Mentoring: Perspectives on school-based teacher education*. London: Kogan Page.

Moore, A. (2004). *The good teacher: Dominant discourses in teaching and teacher education*. London: Routledge Falmer.

Norman, P. (2016). *Paul McCartney: The biography*. Leicester, UK: Weidenfeld & Nicolson.

Norscia, I., Demuru, E., & Palagi, E. (2016). Difference in contagious yawning between *susceptible* men and women: Why not? *Royal Society Open Science, 3*.

Pink, D. H. (2008). *A whole new mind: Why right-brainers will rule the future*. London: Marshall Cavendish.

Rudduck, J. (1985). Teacher research and research-based teacher education. *Journal of Education for Teaching, 11*, 281–289.

Rudduck, J., & McIntyre, D. (2007). *Improving learning through consulting pupils*. Harlow, UK: Pearson.

Sagi, A., & Hoffman, M. L. (1976). Empathic distress in the newborn. *Developmental Psychology, 12*, 175–176.

Simner, M. L. (1971). Newborn's response to the cry of another infant. *Developmental Psychology, 5*, 135–150.

Smith, H. (1970, December 12). John Lennon and Yoko Ono: Interview with Howard Smith.

Wilson, E., & Demetriou, H. (2007). New teacher learning: Substantive knowledge and contextual factors. *The Curriculum Journal, 18*, 213–229.

Wilson, E., & Demetriou, H. (2008). *Supporting opportunities for new teachers' professional growth*. Gatsby Technical Education Projects.

Wilson, E., Demetriou, H., & Winterbottom, M. (2010). Climate change: What needs to be done in order to motivate and sustain new science teachers. *Science Teacher Education, 57*, 22–27.

Wilson, E., Demetriou, H., & Winterbottom, M. (2012). The quest for perfection in teaching. *Science Teacher Education, 64*, 40–52.

Zahn-Waxler, C., Radke-Yarrow, M., Wagner, E., & Chapman, M. (1992). Development of concern for others. *Developmental Psychology, 28*, 126–136.

Zahn-Waxler, C., Robinson, J. L., & Emde, R. N. (1992). The development of empathy in twins. *Developmental Psychology, 28*, 1038–1047.

9

Empathy and Emotion in Education and Beyond

The literature on empathy has identified it as comprising both affective and cognitive properties, which develop at least partly as a consequence of our upbringing and the attachments we make. The examples of Benjamin Spock and Harry Harlow within the field of child psychology speak for themselves. Their works, one renowned for his enduring book and the other for his pioneering experiments, were controversial in their own way but reflected the need to discover more about the attachment process and how this relates to our capacity to form our own attachments. Despite outwardly enthusiastic discourse about the merits of attachment, ironically, both men experienced early childhoods that lacked emotional attachments, and were themselves in turn distant and critical as parents with their own children and limited in their abilities to be emotionally connected with them. It is probably no coincidence also that they delved deeply, possibly unconsciously into this area of enquiry in an attempt to understand their own emotional development and outcomes. The disparities between the knowing and the doing were evident: they were a case in point of 'do as I say, not as I do', such was their incapacity to show and discuss emotion to their own children, despite their expertise in the subject. It shows that, however much one is able to comprehend the

© The Author(s) 2018
H. Demetriou, *Empathy, Emotion and Education*,
https://doi.org/10.1057/978-1-137-54844-3_9

attachment process, if one hasn't experienced its positive effects first hand, it proves very difficult to exhibit it oneself. Whereas negative judgmental or avoidant parenting styles perpetuate insidiously down the generations and prove difficult to shake off; when parenting allows for a balance of security but within a framework that encourages exploration, the child is able to thrive and perpetuate the incarnation of empathy. Similarly within the realm of education, John Dewey and Maria Montessori saw the value in giving the child space to learn and to incorporate emotions within their learning. Between them, and despite different attachment experiences, such researchers and practitioners as Dewey, Montessori, Spock and Harlow had their finger on the pulse of emotion and its role in teaching and parenting. Harlow's claims of the need to learn how to love before one learns how to live echo within teaching, as the teacher must also learn to connect emotionally before learning how to teach. As caregivers and educators, we need to be aware of the formula of empathy as comprising both emotion and cognition. In order to relate successfully, we need to be able to draw on each other's emotions as well as taking their perspectives. Indeed the research has shown that we can and should turn to babies, children, pupils and students for the answers, just as much as they rely on us. By incorporating this empathic curiosity for knowledge and emotion, we stimulate communication and dialogue, reinforce attachments, and bolster the individual with a balanced view of life that encompasses both emotion and cognition.

My research began by identifying the emotional and cognitive aspects of empathy among very young children, from toddlers to their older counterparts in middle childhood, and then in children who were able to talk insightfully about aspects of their teaching and learning. Subsequently and still within teaching, we identified the need for teachers to employ emotion as well cognition in their teaching. What comes through clearly from the studies about friendships, fairness and newly qualified teachers is the relevance of attachment theory within the context of school and, in particular, the importance of relationships, taking time to listen to the learner and respecting their ideas and the ensuing sense of self and other. As declared by Theodore Roosevelt: "No one cares how much you know, until they know how much you care". Implications for emotional support and attentiveness towards children across the lifespan by parents and teachers and the impact on children's social and emotional competence are corroborated by studies that continue to reveal the influence of children's own emotional awareness on their motivation, engagement, self-regulation and learning outcomes. Returning to the context of distress, Spinrad and Eisenberg (2009) have linked children's responses to others' distress with school success. Specifically, empathy and prosocial behaviour have direct relevance for children's social competence and fewer problem behaviours and increased academic performance. Researchers such as Arguedas, Daradoumis, and Xhafa (2016) have found that emotionally astute students impact teachers' approaches as well as the competencies that teachers need to have in order to achieve a positive change on students' affective and cognitive states; and also that this results in increased learning performance, motivation, engagement and self-regulation. Likewise, when teachers are conscious of students' emotional state, their attitude and feedback are more effective and appropriate (Hughes, 2012). In a similar way that infants become attached to parents who are sensitive and responsive to them, the teacher-pupil relationship through consultation and the mere act of listening, is enhanced and leads to pupils feeling empowered and respected and engaged in their learning. The process of consultation works both ways and for the benefit of all concerned: teachers are helped through gaining ideas from pupils; and at the same time, engagement with pupils instills trust and respect in them. As these two primary school teachers told us:

> It only works when you have effective relationships, when there's mutual respect between staff and pupils, when pupils know that we are committed to listening, and when we treat pupils with unconditional positive regard.

> Consulting our pupils has provided a promotion of ownership and a raising of self-esteem.

Issues of self-esteem were in fact often mentioned during our discussions on the impact of pupil consultation, and are similar to attachment-related studies such as Coopersmith (1967) and Harlow's monkeys

(1961) whose early secure attachments resulted in a more confident individual. As one secondary school teacher claimed:

> We've learnt a lot…about how students rapidly improve in their learning and their self-esteem and their motivation through dialogue with staff, through feeling important, feeling care for, feeling their views matter. I think it has had a really, really significant effect.

There may be logistical concerns regarding pupil consultation such that it may take time to establish, some feedback can be idealistic, tools need to have direction and variety in order to be effective and adaptive, and it transfers into the formal curriculum. As with parent-child attachment relationships, the path of pupil consultation may not always run smooth. It has been shown to be particularly effective when some pupils develop a negative sense of themselves as learners, a feeling that they do not matter, quite early in their school careers. Being able to talk about experiences of learning in school builds on the capacity to develop the learning and autonomy of young people. They cultivate a stronger sense of membership, resilience, self-worth and self-as-learner as well as an overall healthy attachment to the establishment (Mitra, 2009; Rudduck, Demetriou, & Pedder, 2003). Giving pupils a voice through developing trust and listening to them has proved to be particularly powerful (Peacock, 2001). And a particular powerful example is of the work by Alison Peacock at The Wroxham School which was acclaimed nationally for a transformative personalised child-led approach to teaching that transcended background and ability. The results spoke for themselves, as in the wake of this approach and within the space of 3 years, the school's Ofsted inspection status metamorphosed dramatically from 'requiring special measures' to 'outstanding' (Peacock, 2010).

The concept of listening to pupils about their learning and other issues at school has the effect of bestowing value on and developing the confidence, autonomy and importantly the learning of young people. An appreciation of this approach, which resulted in pupils feeling valued was expressed by a girl in year 6, who told me:

> I think I'm very lucky to be in a school like […] where the teachers listen to your opinions and ideas. We have assemblies every week where we talk about new ideas and solutions for our school and every comment is valued.

The impetus for the original research on pupil consultation was to involve pupils in order to improve their teaching and learning. The research revealed the importance and power embedded in consulting pupils in the classroom and the potential in enhancing the quality of teaching and learning and transforming the dynamics in the classroom for the benefit of all concerned, and in particular the pupils. The advantages of consulting pupils were found often to be in favour of the pupils themselves. For example, the benefits of consultation included that pupils are respected, listened to and taken seriously; have greater control over the pace of style of teaching and learning; are able to talk about their own learning and being more confident about how to improve it; are more positive about learning and about school because they feel more involved with its purposes; and know that their views are having an impact on how things are done in school and classroom.

Cook-Sather (2002) had said: "Decades of calls for educational reform have not succeeded in making schools places where all young people want to and are able to learn. It is time to invite students to join the conversations about how we might accomplish that" (p. 9). The results have shown that being able to talk about experiences of learning in school offers pupils a greater sense of respect and self-worth so that they feel positive about themselves; and have a stronger sense of self-as-learner so that they are better able to manage their own progress in learning. Consulting young people is one way of responding to the needs of teachers as well as to the pupils themselves. And as long as teachers are on the level when considering pupils' views, provide feedback and explain the decisions as a consequence of the consultation, only then can the process of consultation be truly genuine and effective. Overwhelmingly, results have been transformative and had a powerful impact on pupils as they internalise their teachers' views of them and behave in line with teachers' expectations but also in line with an ethos to work that they themselves relish.

Similar to a secure parent-child relationship that allows for exploration but simultaneously offers security, so the learner should be allowed and encouraged to explore the limits of their learning. And just as the cognitive, perspective-taking side of empathy involves the reflection and analysis of another person's situation, critical thinking in the context of education fulfils a similar task, that of reflecting on one's own and other people's work, and analysing the whys and wherefores of teaching and learning. The Activating Children's Thinking Skills programme (ACTS: McGuinness, 2000) emphasises the importance of metacognition as utilising a variety of thinking skills and processes. Such approaches involve "… an evaluation of the quality of thought to judge or improve it" (Newton, 2014, p. 95). John Locke in his 1693 book entitled *Some Thoughts Concerning Education* stated: "…a child's mind must be educated before he is instructed, that the true purpose of education is the cultivation of the intellect rather than an accumulation of facts", thus emphasising the effectiveness of critical thinking skills as a starting point for his tabula rasa. This importance of learning *how* to learn is reiterated by Margaret Mead's (1928) conclusions: "Children must be taught how to think, not what to think". This train of thought was perpetuated by Piaget who remarked:

> When you teach a child something you take away forever his chance of discovering it for himself". Piaget also said: "We can classify education into two main categories: passive education relying primarily on memory, and active education relying on intelligent understanding and discovery. Our real problem is what is the goal of education? Are we forming children who are only capable of learning what is already known? Or should we try to develop creative and innovative minds capable of discovery from the preschool age on through life?

Such inductively oriented learning procedures have had an effect on children as young as 4 years of age in expanding their exploration and learning (Bonawitz et al., 2011), beginning with the learner who is encouraged to explore both independently and in groups, and only after which the teacher teaches, clarifies and reinforces. Others in agreement with this thinking have stated: "I never teach my pupils, I only provide the conditions in which they can learn" (Albert Einstein); and "What we want is to see the child in pursuit of knowledge, and not knowledge in pursuit of the child" (George Bernard Shaw). In order to encourage a genuine intrinsic motivation for learning, Piaget, along with others such as Skinner, Bruner, Vygotsky and Montessori, emphasised the social nature of learning and propounded the position of teachers as facilitators of learning rather than didactic knowledge-imparting agents, and stressed tailoring the teaching to the individual child in a creative and individually focused way. Indeed, as well as saying: "Never help a child with a task at which he feels he can succeed", Montessori claimed: "The greatest sign of success for a teacher… is to be able to say, 'The children are now working as if I did not exist'". Shifting the emphasis, it is not the teacher teaching anymore, but the learner learning. Such practices surely go hand in hand and encourage a growth rather than a fixed mindset (Dweck, 2012) within both child and adult, so that as well as understanding the mechanism behind one's learning, there can be a mindset that counters negative aspects of teaching and learning, learning from them and gaining confidence as a consequence.

During the course of our research, one of our teachers told us: "I have learned much from my teachers, more from my colleagues, but most from my pupils." A flurry of research continues to escalate that has advocated the merits of listening to the student voice, and teaching as a dialogic process (Kazepides, 2012), where the empathic process of perspective-taking enables critical thought among both students and teachers. Furthermore, others have advocated the importance of teachers being able to appreciate the pupil's eye-view of the lesson (Cooper, 2000). Hargreaves (2004) describes student voice as a 'gateway to change', and it is through accessing the perspectives of those who share our environment that we understand the dynamics of the classroom and effective teaching and learning. Cowie (2005) has signalled the importance of heeding the perspectives of pupils within formative assessment as essential for understanding the process and practice of assessment for learning. Cook-Sather (2006) defined student voice as instances where we envision students as having a "meaningful, acknowledged presence" and where they "have the power to influence analyses of, decisions about, and practices in schools" (p. 363). Also, Murtagh (2014) claimed that "Research with children, rather than solely about them, is vital in promoting the importance of the 'child's voice' as well as providing a means of access to it" (p. 536). Indeed, feedback has been at the heart of educational policy for many years; and the use of formative feedback or assessment for learning is considered important in helping students make progress, as is the critical thinking they use in their learning. Student voice initiatives are excellent opportunities for us to empathise with pupils, for the pupils to realise their empathic potential, and for a greater understanding of how pupils experience and explore their schools through being "…encouraged to voice their views or preferences" (Hargreaves, 2004, p. 7).

From parenting to pedagogy: in order to do the best for our young people, it is important to relate and interrelate with them effectively, and to ensure that the child comes first. Such an investment of time and energy reaps rewards. In so doing they will put themselves first—but also others too. This means making meaningful connections and to step into their shoes, so that we can see their situation from their point of view. Only then are we, as teachers and as parents, able to appreciate their perspective. Such perspective-taking also enables us to form attachments, which are valued and valuable for the developing child, generating confidence, trust and respect. Feeling valued does two things: it shows the child how they too can value others in turn, but also involves them and makes them feel that they have something of value to contribute. Dewey's contention was that the interests of the individual child should be active and central to their learning, through trusting social interactions, whilst maintaining a secure firm but fair 'base' from which the child can explore. This is in keeping with the claims of attachment theory and akin to Montessori's vision of education reflecting the rights of the child for a tailor-made, holistic education, where the child is the instigator and the teacher the facilitator as and when required. The Early Years Foundation Stage framework emphasises that "every child is a unique child, who is constantly learning and can be resilient, capable, confident and self-assured" (DfE, 2012, p. 3). And Montessori's emphasis on the rights of the child is also reflected in personal, social and emotional development now part of the curriculum. Montessori (1964) also highlighted "the union of family and school" (p. 63) which has echoes of Dewey and Bronfenbrenner's (1977) ecological standpoints of the need for education to be embedded within society as a whole, thereby harmonising and integrating home and school. Such visions are reflective of Citizenship Education within Key Stages 3 and 4 of the National Curriculum that aims to "provide pupils with the knowledge, skills and understanding to prepare them to play a full and active part in society" (DfE, 2013, p. 201).

However, there have been words of caution regarding the fine line between the teacher and pupil role. For example, Hargreaves (2004) stated that practices such as student voice and assessment for learning could potentially distort the student-teacher boundaries. While some teachers find this daunting as the thought of giving up control to students can be intimidating, the results of this blurring of roles can provide interesting insights and interpretations about student needs, learning preferences and strengths and weakness of existing systems. And perhaps a change of pupil perception is necessary in that, to use student voice effectively, teachers need to see their pupils differently, namely as responsible and capable. As Hargreaves (2004) concluded: "…inviting students to give more direct and open feedback…requires courage… However [the object] is to create a partnership between…the teacher and the student, so that teaching-and-learning are co-constructed to make the experience more rewarding and more effective for both" (p. 11). Indeed, consulting student voice can be uncomfortable for teachers because they fear losing control or hearing things they don't want to hear (MacBeath, Demetriou, Rudduck, & Myers, 2003). As well as this, some teachers are uneasy about the amount of time needed to create and sustain proper student voice initiatives (Rudduck & McIntyre, 2007). However once they get over their initial fears, many teachers are frequently surprised and delighted—even awed at what emerges from student voice. Rudduck and McIntyre (2007) echo this when they claimed: "…it's not until you invite pupils to talk about their experiences of teaching and learning that you understand how insightful their comments are" (p. 13).

The research on pupil voice has highlighted the merits of consulting children in both primary and secondary schools about their teaching and learning and has inspired Ofsted to use student voice in their judgments of schools by asking students about aspects of their schooling, including the teaching. Given the right tools, pupils can communicate effectively their learning needs. Just listening to pupils about issues in school can affect their learning and ideas about issues such as friendships and fairness. This in turn can pay dividends as they capitalise on their educational experience. Pupil voice is a tour de force that not only maximises the potential of students but also helps teachers and their newly qualified counterparts who might encounter obstacles during their early months of teaching. The findings have shown that consulting young people and creating a more inclusive and attentive learning environment is one way of responding to the needs of teachers as well as to the pupils themselves and have unveiled the potential of pupil voice in harnessing the thoughts and feelings of pupils and ultimately achieving effective teaching and learning.

The resounding voice of pupils can now be heard the world over, not least as pupil voice conferences are now being held internationally, and there is a peer-reviewed *International Journal of Student Voice* in circulation.

Further afield and learning across continents, and echoing the earlier-quoted Margaret Mead who claimed that "Children must be taught how to think, not what to think", 4000 miles away, I spoke to a Kazakh teacher who quoted Socrates to me: "I cannot teach anybody anything. I can only make them think." I have been involved in the teacher professional development programme currently taking place in Kazakhstan at the Nazarbayev University Graduate School of Education. The country is in the process of educational reform and striving for its own educational democracy. The ninth largest country in the world, Kazakhstan is keen to embrace the Western styles of teaching, and the University of Cambridge has been recruited by the Kazakh government to train and mentor its teachers with new approaches to pedagogy with more emphasis on inter-active learning, the application of knowledge, project work and critical thinking. Indeed such practices are a complete antithesis of the culture and teaching in the country's history. Some of my time in Kazakhstan was spent talking to the teachers on the training programme. I gave talks about pupil voice: the concept, the research and the applications, all of which were very positively received. But I also discussed teaching and learning with the teachers and the reasons they wanted to adopt Western styles of teaching. Despite growing up in a country with a very different education ethos, the teachers relished the thought of being able to teach with fresh, interactive and formative approaches rather than the traditional rote-oriented, didactic and summative methods.

One teacher told me of her plans to implement peer support: "I have ideas to make weak students more active and to think critically. I asked the active students to help the weak student to work together and then weak student was to present presentation and I let them speak more than the active student." A teacher took on board the merits of critical thinking: "I researched critical thinking. It is important that pupils think for themselves." And another teacher claimed that: "we should educate pupils from their perspectives, but approaches are different in Kazakhstan." The overall consensus was that, as another teacher told me: "our country is ready for transformation. This programme will truly influence teaching."

The teachers took on the role, determined that it should work: "our task is to make new teachers in a new world", said one teacher; although another realised that it would take time: "even though we all realise the necessity of the changes and we realise this intervention is timely and useful, it takes time for us to change our mentality, but we should." Another teacher corroborated this view by saying: "I think it will be challenging because our teacher training institutes have traditional programmes for their training and they do not have this experience." It has taken a lot of time and dedication from my Cambridge colleagues, as well as of course the time and dedication from the Kazakh teachers themselves. The transformation has been a gradual one and, as of October 2015, the programme had successfully trained 50,000 teachers and 750 head teachers. In 2016, colleagues at Cambridge collaborated with Nazarbayev University Graduate School of Education, using Western styles of emotional well-being and engagement to examine the impact on children and the role of teachers in order to achieve an optimal learning environment (Turner et al., 2014). Such practices across continents ultimately reflect the words of a Chinese proverb: "Give a man a fish and he will eat for a day. Teach a man to fish and he will eat for the rest of his life."

Teaching is an emotional practice. "The best teachers teach from the heart, not from the book" (author unknown); and "What the teacher is, is more important than what he teaches" (Karl Menninger). Researchers have paid much attention to teachers' emotional experiences and their impact on teachers' and students' lives (Cross & Hong, 2012; Hargreaves, 1998, 2000; Zembylas, 2005). Thinking about the potential of emotion for education is not new. John Dewey (1933) wrote of the necessity to address students' emotions in education: "… There is no education when ideas and knowledge are not translated into emotion, interest, and volition" (p. 189). More recently the field of education has begun to acknowledge the importance of emotional intelligence and encourage a focus beyond that of the acquisition of content knowledge. Coined by Salovey and Mayer (1990), they defined 'emotional intelligence' as: "the ability to monitor one's own and other's feelings and emotions, to discriminate among them, and use this information to guide one's thinking and action" (p. 189). It has been propelled to the forefront of education. In so doing, it has been recognised as being beneficial for children's professional aspirations, as the more accurate understanding of emotion is believed to lead to better problem solving and, along with cultural and social intelligence, has been associated with positive and balanced work attitudes (Crowne, 2009).

Dewey (1916) originally advocated the social conditions for learning, emphasising the importance of "…sharing in each other's activities and in each other's experiences because they have common ends and purposes" (p. 75). Others such as Noddings (1992) have regarded affect and caring teachers as crucial elements for learning in the classroom. Goleman considered students' EQ (emotional quotient) to be as important as their IQ, and especially when confronted with breakdowns in classroom communication, using programmes designed to teach students how to resolve conflict, deal with emotions, and argue effectively. Consequently, the concept of emotional intelligence can be defined based on Goleman's (2004) five basic emotional competencies: "…knowing how to express one's emotions, manage one's moods, empathise with the emotional states of others, motivate oneself and others, and exercise a wide range of social skills" (p. 814). Others have linked student motivation directly to affect and introduced the importance of the affective component within classroom interactions.

As well as providing an education, schools have a responsibility for ensuring they produce balanced mentally and physically healthy individuals. Michael Rutter (1991) said: "Schooling does matter greatly. Moreover, the benefits can be surprisingly long lasting… Schools are about social experiences as well as scholastic learning" (p. 9). The area of mental health has seen a burgeoning awareness and interest in empathy and emotion. Emotion is playing an ever-important role where the empathy of the educator encourages an empathy for and of the learner through a variety of techniques including listening to the pupil voice. Our mental health is very important and much of what has been discussed thus far reflects what we mean by mental health and why it matters. McLaughlin and Clarke (2010) have defined it as: "the ability to develop psychologically, emotionally, intellectually and spiritually; have a sense of personal well-being; sustain satisfying personal relationships; develop a sense of right and wrong; and resolve problems as well as learning from them" (p. 91). Programmes such as SEAL (Social and Emotional Aspects of Learning) in a British schooling context aim to support 3- to 16-year-old children in developing their personal and social skills of self-awareness and managing their feelings, motivation and empathy. Mindfulness programmes and mentalisation approaches ensure that a differentiated awareness of self and other is achieved for effective empathy to access the other person's inner thoughts and feelings and establishes a connection with the other person. The emotions and cognitions of which we are made play important roles, from our achievements at school to our mental health. The escalating issue of concern in education over recent decades has been the gender gap, which has seen girls outperforming boys. Some researchers believe that girls have a higher emotional intelligence than boys, and that this has led to a 'boy crisis' (Mead, 2006). With the rising number of Social Emotional Learning (SEL) programmes in schools, this points to a notion that IQ itself may not be enough to attain good grades, but instead, or at least a different intelligence—emotional intelligence—could be contributing towards success. There is currently increasing concern about children and young people's mental health, with 1 in 10 5- to 18-year-olds suffering from mental health issues, including emotional problems and conduct disorders. Reports confirm that primary school pupils are not immune from developing mental health issues (PSHE Association, 2014; The Mental Health Foundation, 2007). But studies have shown that if a teacher exhibits empathy with disruptive students, then it aids and promotes emotional well-being and academic achievement (Buyse, Verschueren, Doumen, van Damme, & Maes, 2008).

McLaughlin and Clarke (2010) reviewed over 100 published papers that investigated teacher-teacher and pupil-teacher relationships in schools and the ways in which school-based relationships impact upon mental health. Such relationships were examined in relation to academic outcomes; between social support, feelings of emotional well-being or distress, and teacher-pupil relationships; as well as the relationship between school connectedness and mental health outcomes. The overview prompted the authors to recommend greater emphasis on the interconnections between the relationships with young people and their emotional and academic well-being. But even outside the arena of mental health issues, teachers' work includes dealing with students' affective as well as cognitive responses to learning, as teachers frequently need to anticipate students' emotional responses to specific topics and tasks (Demetriou & Wilson, 2009). The claim that is made by such researchers is that taking emotions into account will provide a more comprehensive understanding of teachers' learning and thinking. Hargreaves (2000) emphasised the importance of harbouring and maintaining close relationships between new teachers and their colleagues and students, and warned that the absence of such relationships can lead to teachers experiencing emotional misunderstanding, added to which Wilson and Deaney (2010) have cautioned of the ensuing negative and potentially unchangeable self-efficacy beliefs. Moreover, Hargreaves (1998) has argued that effective teaching should be characterised by positive emotions in which teachers display their passion for learning and the subject and in turn fuel students with enthusiasm.

Regarding issues of blurring the teacher-pupil boundaries within the context of pupil voice, a study by Lasky (2005) found that teachers often struggle to remain openly vulnerable with their students, and to create trusting learning environments in a profession increasingly administrative and accountable. These teachers described being willingly vulnerable with their students because of a belief that student learning and socio-emotional development benefited from this openness. "The willingness to blur the boundaries between the personal and professional with their students was a core component of their teacher identity, reflecting their fundamental beliefs about how to teach students effectively by building rapport, being human and by grasping hold of unplanned teachable moments" (p. 908). Such findings have been repeated elsewhere as reflected in the importance of a continuity of positive teacher emotions that lead to positive and creative teaching and encourage student motivation (Frenzel, Goetz, Stephens, & Jacob, 2009). Conversely, teachers' negative emotions such as anger and frustration serve to decrease their intrinsic motivation and increase students' negative emotional experiences. Such negative instances require a critical thinking and reflection, helping teachers to gain insights into the 'big picture' and rethink their practice, learn from their experiences and help them to cope with similar situations in the future. Fullan (1999) argued that it is only through reflection at a variety of different levels, namely personal, group and organisational, that teachers will begin to analyse their practice and reform their approach to teaching and learning. Such notions of reflection originated in the writings of John Dewey as a way of thinking about a problematic situation that needs to be resolved: "…the function of reflective thought is, therefore, to transform a situation in which there is experienced obscurity, doubt, conflict, disturbance of some sort, into a situation that is clear, coherent, settled, harmonious" (Dewey, 1933, p. 100). Sixty years on reflection, as described by McIntyre (1993), became a means for teachers to sustain learning about their teaching throughout their careers. Much of the practice of experienced teachers is intuitive, and therefore learning is dependent on bringing to consciousness and constantly re-examining the assumptions and values behind their actions so that reflection enables teachers to modify their practice as and when required (Pedder, James, & MacBeath, 2005).

Above and beyond a set of cognitive competencies, teaching is an emotional endeavour permeated with passion and joy, so that the overall effect of teaching is a synthesis of emotion and cognition where teachers' emotions are central to students' learning and the relationships that they form with them (Demetriou & Wilson, 2008, 2009, 2010; Hargreaves, 1997, 2008; Vermunt & Verloop, 1999). The voice of empathy has resonated thus far, and to it has been added the emotions that are evidently instrumental for a balanced and productive education. Education is not just about the cognitive side of learning, but instead goes hand in hand with emotion, so that taken together, affect and cognition result in the most optimal conditions of teaching and learning. Such teaching approaches take us back to David Hume (1738) and his belief that passions are what spark our actions, in fact so much so that he claimed: "reason is, and ought only to be the slave of the passions" (T2.3.3, p. 415). However, the direction of causality is not a straightforward one and often, thinking is the prompt that drives people's passions. Sometimes we feel an emotion when we are made to think about it; other times our thoughts are prompted by our feelings. Regardless of the direction of the association, it is clear that for most of us, affect and cognition are inextricably interlinked. Overcome by his own emotions, C.S. Lewis (1961) attempted to escape their capture through the power of thought, and exclaimed: "Feelings, and feelings, and feelings. Let me try thinking instead" (p. 31). However, the natural synthesis of the two concepts endures and together result in a more wholesome outcome. In Aristotelian terms: "The whole is greater than the sum of its parts".

So we come full circle from the nature of childhood empathy and attachments to effective teaching: a holistic approach to life for parenting, teaching and beyond. The separate experiences and properties of affect and cognition, when brought together, are formidable. Indeed: "There can be no knowledge without emotion. We may be aware of a truth, yet until we have felt its force, it is not ours. To the cognition of the brain must be added the experience of the soul" (Bennett, 1897). Adding the emotional dimension to education, James Park (2000) stated: "…feeling and thinking are engaged in a continuous dance. Individuals who can gracefully glide between the two modes bring energy to the task of learning and thinking" (p. 11). Without emotion there is a missing link. In fact this whole endeavour is about seeing things from a holistic approach. This discourse has generated prominent pairings: emotion and cognition, psychology and education, biology and psychology, teachers and parents, teachers and pupils, teaching and learning, nature and nurture and failures and successes. Realising our failures and learning from them formed the discourse of early writers such as Michel de Montaigne (1603). Whether through a more innate propensity to learn as propounded by Montessori, or a learning as influenced by society as told by Dewey, our learning is unconsciously absorbed using those around us and from early on, thereby indicating the importance of those around us: parents, siblings, peers and teachers.

William Blake wrote: "A tear is an intellectual thing" (1908). From early on our emotional development is inextricably intertwined with our acquisition of knowledge. Psychological research has revealed similarities between human cognitive and emotional processes. Such attempts to bridge the domains of social and cognitive development have resulted in a direct behavioural link between cognition and emotion in that our thoughts affect the way we feel about stimuli and vice versa. Whereas cognition acts, affect energises, so that the understanding of another's feelings, for example, may be motivated by our own affective responses to them. Yet despite these obvious links, effective teaching and constructive learning are often regarded solely as cognitive processes. There is often little emphasis made to the feeling and emotional aspects of teaching and learning. But both affect and cognition are key to learning, and when they are brought together, they compound and strengthen it. In the field of developmental psychology, Piaget (1981) used metaphor to encapsu-late the interaction of affect and cognition: "…affectivity would play the role of an energy source on which the functioning but not the structures of intelligence would depend. It would be the gasoline, which activates the motor of an automobile but does not modify its structure" (p. 5).

Research has shown that teachers' emotional experiences and their reflection about their emotions are inextricably linked to their pedagogy and has revealed the importance of a balance between affect and cogni-tion for effective teaching and learning (Baird, Gunstone, Penna, Fensham, & White, 2007). Rather than purely trying to communicate the facts in a rote fashion, teachers who incorporate more emotion and expression in their teaching are more successful in communicating the subject matter and sustaining student engagement, interest and success. Also, the importance of listening to and heeding the student voice emerged as a crucial factor in addressing and notably curbing the decline in students' attitudes and increasing their interest in science.

A study by Gulnar (2003) examined science teachers' use of affect and cognition in their teaching. Having observed and interviewed both a physics and a chemistry teacher, the physics teacher used a greater amount and variety of instructional strategies, and was more metacognitive about his instruction than his chemistry counterpart. Realising that his students were below his expectations, the physics teacher slowed down his instruc-tion and used more repetition. This fine-tuning of his lessons reflected this teacher's dogmatic beliefs in building a strong rapport with his stu-dents and shifted the onus on the teacher to change his approach rather than become irritated with and consequently blame the students for their lack of progress. The teacher reconstructed his practice accordingly, mak-ing jokes, using humour and sometimes tolerating misbehaviours. By sharp contrast, the chemistry teacher became upset, angry, frustrated and discouraged by the students' lack of progress, which resulted in less effec-tive communication and ultimately a lack of enthusiasm for learning.

Increasingly, research is recognising the importance of the educator's empathic disposition, and the general consensus is that empathy is key in making the learner feel connected and wanting to learn. Teachers who are most successful when faced with adversities in the classroom are those who appreciate that, as well as communicating effective subject knowledge, there is also a need for affective communication with the student and thereby conceptualise teaching and learning as encompassing both emotion and cognition in order to have a balanced and healthy view of teaching, learning, the student and the school (Arghode, Yalvac, & Liew, 2013; Demetriou & Wilson, 2009; Demetriou, Wilson, & Winterbottom, 2009). As Maria Montessori said in her book *The Absorbent Mind* (1949): "The essential thing is for the task to arouse such an interest that it engages the child's whole personality" (p. 206). Such approaches to teaching result in teachers who are not only successful as teachers in their own right, but are able also to be a friend, moral support and admiring adult to the learner in the classroom. When teachers are able to achieve this balance, they are fortified with a wealth and depth of emotions that impact positively on their identity as teachers.

Of course, the practicalities of incorporating the emotional component of teaching into the classroom face a number of obstacles such as large classroom numbers, limited time, increasing curriculum demands, teacher targets and pressures to perform (Ball, 2010). Indeed, as a result of the pressure of league tables and academic results, state schools have been accused of producing blinkered children with few traditional moral values. Richard Walden (2014), chairman of the Independent Schools Association, has said controversially: "Schools are turning out too many amoral children because teachers cannot find the time to teach the difference between right and wrong…This focus on league tables and attainment levels distracts teachers and effectively disables them from providing children with a more rounded and enriching education – one that will give them the moral compass they need for life" Indeed, such narrowly directed teaching may be the cause of so many dissatisfied teachers deciding to leave the profession, with the largest number of 50,000 teachers in the UK leaving the profession in 10 years in the year from 2013 to 2014. An antidote as announced by head teachers from some of the oldest and most distinguished schools advocate practices for a rounded education through establishing good relationships. For example, the ex-head of Eton (Little, 2015) has written: "…it is through the building of good relationships with pupils…that truly effective communities are created: schools that not only can deliver the highest grades but, vitally, can enable young people to learn to stand up both for themselves and for a purpose greater than themselves" (p. 48). He goes on to talk about the often emotionally charged but effective platform for dialogue: "The default mode of adults is to talk at young people in the belief that imparting wisdom is at the heart of the educational process. We can learn much more by listening and discussing…" (p. 71). When communicating the qualities in teachers, the head teacher of Dulwich College has written: "Of course, it is not enough to love your subject – the good teacher must also be an effective communicator of his or her learning, someone who will create a passion for a subject in their pupils. He goes on to say that a teacher must have a well-developed pastoral sensibility. That means as much emotional intelligence as he or she has intellectual power. Teachers who thrive and enjoy their work empathise with all their pupils, from the strongest to the weakest, the extrovert to the introvert, the lazy and the over-committed. …The best teachers I've known have been emotionally astute, intellectually curious and great communicators…" (Spence, 2016, p. 8).

Organisations such as Ofsted remind the teaching profession that education should not only be about results but about a broad education. Speaking to the Association of School and College Leaders, the chief inspector for Ofsted presented the importance of a quality curriculum: "I suspect no one here will disagree with the vital importance of a curriculum which is broad, rich and deep. It matters so much for children, and particularly for disadvantaged children, who are less likely to have the gaps filled in at home… Childhood isn't deferrable: young people get one opportunity to learn in school and we owe it to them make sure they all get an education that is broad, rich and deep" (Spielman, 2017). And as the following quotation by Barbara Coloroso explains: "If kids come to us from strong, healthy functioning families, it makes our job easier. If they do not come to us from strong, healthy, functioning families, it makes our job more important". Over the recent years there have been increasing concerns about emotional turbulence among growing numbers of children, with adults fearing that children cannot cope with the stress of an increasing traditional subject-based curriculum. As such, subject disciplines and knowledge are arguably irrelevant and oppressive if they cannot engage with emotions (Palmer, 2006).

A recent example of good practice is a new local primary school which boasts in its values statement that: "We will create a culture in which empathy, respect, trust, courage and gratitude are explicitly and implicitly taught within a democratic community in which every voice is valued and everyone empowered to be the best that he or she can be. … Listening to children and encouraging dialogue and debate will be central to our whole school approach. …trusting that their voice will be heard" (University of Cambridge Primary School). Such a statement encompasses empathy and voice: listening carefully to others and thus enabling them to use a voice that enhances ideas. Harnessing empathy facilitates the student voice; and through listening to student voice and indeed the students listening to their own voice, they become empowered, enriched and emotionally aware individuals. Such democratic thinking and practice in schools would have been appreciated and supported by Dewey, whose book *Democracy and Education* (1916) has now celebrated its centenary. Dewey's philosophy is now part and parcel of an international way of thinking, where through pupil voice, the learner has agency and authority over their own learning, thus facilitating a greater awareness of themselves as learners. Such a learner-centred pedagogy ensures that the teacher steers the student from a passive to an active role, more integrated in a democratic school life. Through putting the learner at the heart of education, Dewey's philosophy was visionary and ahead of its time.

Such approaches are holistic in nature, taking into account the child as an emotional as well as a cognitive being. Just as we should nurture a holistic parenting strategy, there should also be a holistic teaching pedagogy. Just as Goleman (2004) felt that too much emphasis is often placed on academic achievement at the expense of emotions and social competence, Wentzel (2009) has claimed that "…emotionally supportive interactions have the potential to provide strong incentives for students to engage in valued classroom activities" (p. 307). Such claims echo of effective parenting strategies leading to secure attachment, and teachers should seek similarly to foster attachment within the classroom (Wentzel & Brophy, 2014). The result has implications for healthy social and emotional development, as well as increases in theory of mind, self-esteem, effective learning and emotional intelligence. When teachers and parents apply an open mind and treat the child as an individual, not necessarily 'going by the book', but tailoring physical and psychological needs, the result is an appreciated and appreciative individual.

Coming back to empathy—and in fact it has never been far away, weaving throughout the discourse like an invisible thread—this special power is able to transcend age, language and culture, from its origins in the young child to parents and teachers using their own empathic abilities to relate to each other. Since Rogers (1940) brought 'identification and objectivity' (p. 162) to the attention of the helping professions, teachers are increasingly recognising that personality improvement and classroom performance are associated with elements of empathy. Along with its recognition as a personality characteristic, empathy has been established as part of the diagnostic criteria for a number of psychiatric disorders such as depression in children and adults. Therefore, the question of how, when, and why children begin to show empathic concern for others is an interesting and important one for psychologists as well as for parents and teachers. In a world in constant search of effective empathy, this concept is increasingly establishing itself as a vital component in numerous contemporary disciplines such as branches of biology, sociology, education, aesthetics, and theology, as well as social, personality, clinical, and not least, developmental psychology. However, despite the contributions that have been made in empathy across these disciplines, considerable scope remains for the advancement of our knowledge into the phenomenon known as empathy. Empathy's abilities are without bounds. It has the power to gel, bond, communicate, negotiate, and can generate and germinate helpful and moral behaviour. It is of use in parenting and teaching, and should be utilised and nurtured across the lifespan in general, putting the child at centre stage and heeding the 'voice' that is present from day one. Empathy is the *mot du jour*, but for every day. It is the ultimate social skill. However, too often people make assumptions about others without really stopping to think about their situation and gathering all the facts before they speak or act. Empathy therefore can take time and require a journey to perfect, as reflected in this extract from the native American Indian proverb: "Walk a mile in my shoes, see what I see, hear what I hear, feel what I feel, then maybe you'll understand why I do what I do, 'till then don't judge me".

"…'till then don't judge me": a particularly powerful characteristic of empathy is being able to understand someone without judging them. Others who have extolled the dangers of judging others have warned: "If you judge people, you have no time to love them" (Mother Teresa); and anonymous but nevertheless wise words: "We judge what we don't understand". As parents and as teachers, we need to understand rather than judge. This book has aimed to show the effectiveness of using empathy as a tool to enhance teaching and learning unjudgementally and constructively. Research has shown that children, even at young ages, are able to display empathy and can use it insightfully and effectively. And when teachers use it too, it can enhance classroom dialogue and bodes for a winning combination. As Gandhi said: "Without this empathy there can be no genuine dialogue". Rather like Oscar Wilde's story of 'The Selfish Giant', it was through tuning in to the voices of children that enabled springtime and new beginnings, resulting in a realisation and appreciation of oneself and of others. Indeed it was Oscar Wilde too in his quintessential way who said: "I am not young enough to know everything", perhaps somewhat tongue in cheek but nevertheless also astutely, alluding to the potential of young people. And going back to Harry Harlow, it does ring true that we must learn to love before we can learn to live. Between them and within different contexts, Harlow, Spock, Dewey and Montessori, among others, have given children centre stage in their acknowledgement and appreciation of the tremendous influence of our surroundings. Speaking of the influential school years, Dewey (1923) pointed out that "no one other influence has counted for anything like as much in bringing a certain integrity, cohesion, feeling of sympathy and unity among the elements of our population as has the public school system of this country" (p. 514). Very insightfully, Ignacio Estrada said: "If a child can't learn the way we teach, maybe we should teach the way they learn". And psychiatrist and psychoanalyst Carl Jung (1943) said: "An understanding heart is everything in a teacher. One looks back with appreciation to the brilliant teachers, but with gratitude to those who touched our human feelings. The curriculum is so much necessary raw material, but warmth is the vital element for the growing plant and for the soul of the child. …an understanding heart" (para 249). This encapsulates so proficiently the emotion and cognition of empathy: to feel is to understand, and to understand is to feel.

Empathy commands a prominent and diversified role in the development of social understanding and positive social behaviours. Ranging from the behavioural interchange between mother and infant, to the intimacy and effectiveness of communication in the dyadic relationship between therapist and client, to its potential for effective learning outcomes between teacher and pupil, it is a critical determinant of social transactions. Be it partly hard-wired or soft-wired, empathy's development is affected by our experiences and in particular our early attachment relationships, and then comes to fruition in all our subsequent interactions with people. Teachers are too often faced with unpredictable classroom audiences, and alongside constant change through government agendas and changing school policy, it is sometimes difficult to make time to listen. Parents also are often too busy to stop and listen. But it is important to help children find their voice, and through listening to them with emotional knowing, we encourage confidence, autonomy, relatedness and competence and not least the dissemination of empathy. Hence the importance of the amplification of pupil voice for all concerned, as the child is equipped with a social, emotional as well as cognitive prowess which continues to thrive when aided and abetted by adults. Just when I'd finished a first draft of this book, I received an email from a teacher who had read one of my publications about the importance of emotion in teaching. He said he had attended a course and found revisiting the role of student to be an invaluable experience in identifying and empathising with his own students on his return to work, all of which culminated in the development of more effective teaching methods. Food for thought for further research!

Whenever I walk through the grounds of Homerton College, I like to pause for thought at the *Stretching Figure* sculpture of the child. Cast your mind back: we were all children once, we were all pupils once, and it wasn't so long ago that we can't remember how important it is for our emotions to be understood and our voices to be heard. From the baby to the parent to the teacher, ultimately empathy is a seismic shift, a galvanising force and the oxygen that elicits emotion and enriches education.

References

Arghode, V., Yalvac, B., & Liew, J. (2013). Teacher empathy and science education: A collective case study. *Eurasia Journal of Mathematics, Science and Technology Education, 9*, 89–98.

Arguedas, M., Daradoumis, T., & Xhafa, F. (2016). Analysing how emotion awareness influences students' motivation, engagement, self-regulation and learning outcome. *Educational Technology & Society, 19*, 87–103.

Baird, J. R., Gunstone, R. F., Penna, C., Fensham, P. J., & White, R. T. (2007). Researching balance between cognition and affect in science teaching and learning. *Research in Science Education, 20,* 11–20.

Ball, S. (2010). The teacher's soul and the terrors of performativity. *Journal of Education Policy, 18,* 215–228.

Bennett, A. (1897, March 18). *The journals of Arnold Bennett.*

Blake, W. (1908). *The poetical works.* London/New York: Oxford University Press.

Bonawitz, E., Shafto, P., Gweon, H., Goodman, N. D., Spelke, E., & Schulz, L. (2011). The double-edged sword of pedagogy: Instruction limits spontaneous exploration and discovery. *Cognition, 120,* 322–330.

Bronfenbrenner, U. (1977). Toward and experimental ecology of human development. *American Psychologist, 32,* 513–531.

Buyse, E., Verschueren, K., Doumen, S., van Damme, J., & Maes, F. (2008). Classroom problem behaviour and teacher-child relationships in kindergarten: The moderating role of classroom climate. *Journal of School Psychology, 46,* 367–391.

Cook-Sather, A. (2002). Authorising students' perspectives: Toward trust, dialogue, and change in education. *Educational Researcher, 31,* 3–14.

Cook-Sather, A. (2006). Sound, presence, and power: "Student voice" in educational research and reform. *Curriculum Inquiry, 36,* 359–390.

Cooper, B. (2000). Rediscovering the personal in education. In R. Best (Ed.), *Education for spiritual, moral, social and cultural development.* London: Continuum.

Coopersmith, S. (1967). *The antecedents of self-esteem.* San Francisco: W. H. Freeman.

Cowie, B. (2005). Pupil commentary on assessment for learning. *The Curriculum Journal, 16,* 137–151.

Cross, D. I., & Hong, J. Y. (2012). An ecological examination of teachers' emotions in the school context. *Teaching and Teacher Education, 28,* 957–967.

Crowne, K. A. (2009). The relationships among social intelligence, emotional intelligence and cultural intelligence. *Organisational Management Journal, 6,* 148–163.

de Montaigne, M. (1603). *Montaigne's essays* (J. Florio [1533–1625], Trans.).

Demetriou, H., & Wilson, E. (2008). The psychology of teaching: A return to the use of emotion and reflection in the classroom. *The Psychologist, 21*(11), 938–940. The British Psychological Society. (November issue).

Demetriou, H., & Wilson, E. (2009). Synthesising affect and cognition in teaching and learning. *Social Psychology of Education: An International Journal, 12,* 213–232.

Demetriou, H., & Wilson, E. (2010). Emotion and cognition in teaching and learning: Implications for new teachers. *Leadership in Focus* (Autumn issue).

Demetriou, H., Wilson, E., & Winterbottom, M. (2009). The role of emotion in teaching: Are there differences between male and female newly qualified teachers' approaches to teaching? *Educational Studies, 35*(4), 449–473.

Dewey, J. (1916). *Democracy and education. An introduction to the philosophy of education* (1966 ed.). New York: Free Press (Classic discussion of education for democracy).

Dewey, J. (1923). Individuality in education. *General Science Quarterly, 7*(3), 157.

Dewey, J. (1933). *How we think: A restatement of the relation of reflective thinking to the educative process (1910)* (Rev. ed.). Boston: Heath.

DfE. (2012, 2013). Department for education, UK.

Dweck, C. (2012). *Mindset: How you can fulfil your potential.* London: Robinson.

Frenzel, A. C., Goetz, T., Stephens, E. J., & Jacob, B. (2009). Antecedents and effects of teachers' emotional experiences: An integrated perspective and empirical test. In P. A. Schutz & M. S. Zembylas (Eds.), *Advances in teacher emotion research* (pp. 129–151). Dordrecht, The Netherlands: Springer.

Fullan, M. (1999). *Change forces: The sequel.* London: Falmer Press.

Goleman, D. (2004). *Emotional intelligence and working with emotional intelligence.* London: Bloomsbury.

Gulnar, N. (2003). *The relative influence of affect and cognition on changes in science teachers' practice.* Unpublished research paper, University of Wisconsin-Madison, Madison, WI.

Hargreaves, A. (Ed.). (1997). *Rethinking educational change with heart and mind, ASCD yearbook.* Alexandria, VA: Association for Supervision and Curriculum Development.

Hargreaves, A. (1998). The emotional practice of teaching. *Teaching and Teacher Education, 14*, 835–854.

Hargreaves, A. (2000). Mixed emotions: Teachers' perceptions of their interactions with students. *Teaching and Teacher Education, 16*, 811–826.

Hargreaves, A. (2008). The emotional geographies of educational leadership. In B. Davies & T. Brighouse (Eds.), *Passionate leadership in education* (pp. 129–150). London: Sage Publications.

Hargreaves, D. (2004). Personalising Learning-2 student voice and assessment for learning, international networking for educational transfer, London.

Harlow, H. F. (1961). The development of affectional patterns in infant monkeys. In B. M. Foss (Ed.), *Determinants of infant behaviour* (pp. 75–97). London: Methuen.

Hughes, J. N. (2012). Teacher-student relationships and school adjustment: Progress and remaining challenges. *Attachment & Human Development, 14,* 319–327.

Hume, D. (1738). *A treatise of human nature.* Gutenberg.

Jung, C. G. (1943/1954). The development of personality. In W. McGuire (Ed.), *Collected works of C.G. Jung* (Vol. 17). London: Routledge & Kegan Paul.

Kazepides, T. (2012). Education as dialogue. In T. Besley & M. P. Peters (Eds.), *Interculturalism, education and dialogue* (pp. 76–86). New York: Peter Lang.

Lasky, S. (2005). A sociocultural approach to understanding teacher identity, agency and professional vulnerability in a context of secondary school reform. *Teaching and Teacher Education, 21,* 899–916.

Lewis, C. S. (1961). *A grief observed.* London: Faber and Faber.

Little, T. (2015). *An intelligent Person's guide to education.* Bloomsbury: Bloomsbury Publishing PLC.

Locke, J. (1693). *Some thoughts concerning education.* London: A&J Churchill.

MacBeath, J., Demetriou, H., Rudduck, J., & Myers, K. (2003). *Consulting pupils: A toolkit for teachers.* Cambridge, UK: Pearson Publishing.

McGuinness, C. (2000). *ACTS: A methodology for enhancing thinking skills across-the-curriculum (with a focus on knowledge transformation).* Paper ESRC conference November.

McIntyre, D. H. (1993). *Mentoring: Perspectives on school-based teacher education.* London: Kogan Page.

McLaughlin, C., & Clarke, B. (2010). Relational matters: A review of the impact of school experience on mental health in early adolescence. *Educational and Child Psychology, 27*(1), 91–103.

Mead, M. (1928). *Coming of age in Samoa: A psychological study of primitive youth for western civilisation.* New York: Morrow. (Perennial).

Mead, S. (2006). *The evidence suggests otherwise: The truth about boys and girls.* Washington, DC: Education Sector.

Mental Health Foundation. (2007). *The fundamental facts* (I. Booth, Ed.). London: Mental Health Foundation.

Mitra, D. L. (2009). Collaborating with students: Building youth-adult partnerships in schools. *American Journal of Education, 15,* 407–436.

Montessori, M. (1949). *The absorbent mind* (1967 ed.). New York: Dell.

Montessori, M. (1964). *The Montessori method: Scientific pedagogy as applied to child education in 'the children's houses' with additions and revisions by the author.* New York: Frederick A Stokes Company.

Murtagh, L. (2014). The motivational paradox of feedback: Teacher and student perceptions. *The Curriculum Journal, 25*, 516–541.

Newton, D. P. (2014). *Thinking with feeling: Fostering productive thought in the classroom.* London: Routledge.

Noddings, N. (1992). *The challenge to care in schools: An alternative approach to education.* New York: Teachers College Press.

Palmer, S. (2006). *Toxic childhood.* London: Orion.

Park, J. (2000). The dance of dialogue: Thinking and feeling in education. *Pastoral Care in Education, 18*, 11–15.

Peacock, A. (2001). Listening to children. *Forum, 43*, 19–21.

Peacock, A. (2010). The Cambridge primary review: A voice for the future. *Forum, 52*, 373–380.

Pedder, D., James, M., & MacBeath, J. (2005). How teachers value and practise professional learning. *Research Papers in Education, 20*, 209–243.

Piaget, J. (1981). *Intelligence and affectivity: Their relationship during child development* (T. A. Brown & C. E. Kaegi, Trans. & Eds.). Palo Alto, CA: Annual Reviews.

PSHE Association. (2014). *Teacher guidance: Preparing to teach about mental health and emotional wellbeing.* London: PSHE.

Rogers, C. R. (1940). The processes of therapy. *Journal of Consulting and Clinical Psychology, 4*, 161–164.

Rudduck, J., Demetriou, H., & Pedder, D. (2003). Student perspectives and teacher practices: The transformative potential. *McGill Journal of Education, 38*(2), 274–288. (Spring).

Rudduck, J., & McIntyre, D. (2007). *Improving learning through consulting pupils.* Harlow, UK: Pearson.

Rutter, M. (1991). Pathways from childhood to adult life: The role of schooling. *Pastoral Care in Education, 9*, 3–10.

Salovey, P., & Mayer, J. D. (1990). Emotional intelligence. *Imagination, Cognition, and Personality, 9*, 185–211.

Spence, J. (2016). What makes a good teacher? Independent schools guide. *The Week Magazine*, 8–9.

Spielman, A. (2017, March). Ofsted's Chief Inspector, Amanda Spielman speech to the Association of School and College Leaders (ASCL).

Spinrad, T. L., & Eisenberg, N. (2009). Empathy, prosocial behavior, and positive development in schools. In R. Gilman, E. S. Huebner, & M. J. Furlong (Eds.), *Handbook of positive psychology in schools* (pp. 119–129). New York: Routledge/Taylor & Francis Group.

Turner, F., Wilson, E., Ispussinova, S., Kassymbekov, Y., Sharimova, A., Balgynbayeva, B., et al. (2014). Centres of excellence: Systemwide transformation of teaching practice. In D. Bridges (Ed.), *Education reform and internationalisation: The case of school reform in Kazakhstan* (pp. 83–105). Cambridge, UK: Cambridge University Press.

Vermunt, J. D., & Verloop, N. (1999). Congruence and friction between learning and teaching. *Learning and Instruction, 9*, 257–280.

Walden, R. (2014, May 15). UK state schools accused of turning out 'amoral' children, by Helen Warrell. *The Financial Times.*

Wentzel, K. R. (2009). Students' relationships with teachers as motivational contexts. In K. Wentzel & A. Wigfeld (Eds.), *Handbook of motivation in school* (pp. 301–322). Mahwah, NJ: Erlbaum.

Wentzel, K. R., & Brophy, J. E. (2014). *Motivating students to learn.* New York: Routledge.

Wilson, E., & Deaney, R. (2010). Changing career and changing identity: How do teacher career changers exercise agency in identity construction? *Social Psychology of Education, 13*(2), 169–183.

Zembylas, M. (2005). Discursive practices, genealogies, and emotional rules: A poststructuralist view on emotion and identity in teaching. *Teaching and Teacher Education, 21*, 935–948.

Index

© The Author(s) 2018
H. Demetriou, *Empathy, Emotion and Education*,
https://doi.org/10.1057/978-1-137-54844-3

Printed by Printforce, the Netherlands